Pro SharePoint 2010 Business Intelligence Solutions

Sahil Malik
Srini Sistla
Steve Wright

Pro SharePoint 2010 Business Intelligence Solutions

Copyright © 2010 by Sahil Malik, Srini Sistla, Steve Wright

ISBN-13 (pbk): 978-1-4302-3285-8

ISBN-13 (electronic): 978-1-4302-3286-5

Printed and bound in the United States of America (POD)

President and Publisher: Paul Manning
Lead Editor: Jonathan Hassell
Technical Reviewer: Steve Wright
Editorial Board: Steve Anglin, Mark Beckner, Ewan Buckingham, Gary Cornell, Jonathan Gennick, Jonathan Hassell, Michelle Lowman, Matthew Moodie, Duncan Parkes, Jeffrey Pepper, Frank Pohlmann, Douglas Pundick, Ben Renow-Clarke, Dominic Shakeshaft, Matt Wade, Tom Welsh
Coordinating Editor: Jennifer L. Blackwell
Copy Editor: Sharon Terdeman
Compositor: MacPS, LLC
Indexer: Potomac Indexing, LLC
Artist: April Milne
Cover Designer: Anna Ishchenko

Distributed to the book trade worldwide by Springer Science+Business Media, LLC., 233 Spring Street, 6th Floor, New York, NY 10013. Phone 1-800-SPRINGER, fax (201) 348-4505, e-mail orders-ny@springer-sbm.com, or visit www.springeronline.com.

For information on translations, please e-mail rights@apress.com, or visit www.apress.com.

Apress and friends of ED books may be purchased in bulk for academic, corporate, or promotional use. eBook versions and licenses are also available for most titles. For more information, reference our Special Bulk Sales–eBook Licensing web page at www.apress.com/info/bulksales.

The source code for this book is available to readers at www.apress.com.

Contents at a Glance

Contents

About the Authors

 **Sahil Malik**, the founder and principal of Winsmarts.com, has been a Microsoft MVP and INETA speaker for the past 9 years. He is the author and reviewer of many books and articles in both the .NET and SharePoint space, and has consulted and delivered training and talks at conferences internationally. Sahil trained with the best names in the Microsoft technology space and has architected and delivered SharePoint-based solutions for extremely high-profile clients. Sahil is deeply involved with SharePoint 2010, and he has authored a book and two DVDs, as well as licensed training for SharePoint 2010.

 **Srini Sistla** is a Microsoft Certified Technology Specialist and an INETA speaker with over 11 years of experience in designing and implementing IT solutions on a variety of platforms and domains. Srini's core skills have always involved Microsoft technologies, and he has solid experience in building both Windows- and Web-based solutions. He has worked with Windows SharePoint Services 3.0, Microsoft Office SharePoint Server 2007, and SharePoint Server 2010, and his expertise in SharePoint includes BI, ECM, the object model, and branding. As a subject matter expert, Srini is often asked to review, improve, and approve a variety of technical designs and approaches. He regularly contributes to several blogs, including his own. He has done a fair amount of speaking at various SharePoint user groups, and provides training on SharePoint 2010 and MOSS 2007. Srini is currently working as a SharePoint architect and consultant, and hails from Washington DC metro area.

 **Steve Wright** is a Senior Manager and SharePoint Solution Lead for Sogeti USA, LLC in Omaha, Nebraska. Over the last 20+ years, Steve has worked on air traffic control, financial, insurance, and a multitude of other types of systems. He enjoys speaking at user group meetings and MSDN events, and holds 43 different Microsoft certifications. Steve has contributed to and performed technical reviews for several previous titles covering Microsoft products, including Access, Windows, SQL Server, and BizTalk. For the past several years, he has focused on building highly-customized SharePoint-based Business Intelligence solutions.

Editor's Note: Steve also served as the technical reviewer for this book, in addition to contributing Chapter 6.

Acknowlegments

I didn't actually write this book. The first five chapters were written by Srini, while our technical reviewer, Steve Wright, pitched in to author Chapter 6. My role was to contribute the concept, overall outline, guidance, and code sample ideas, and to check the completeness of the content. I would therefore like to thank Srini for his tireless efforts in writing this book. I am very grateful to Steve as well. We are lucky to have such a thorough reviewer, and impromptu author. And, finally, my appreciation goes to lead editor Jonathan Hassell, whose support and guidance has made many such projects possible. Thank you all.

Sahil Malik

First, I would like to thank Sahil Malik, Jonathan Hassell, and Apress for giving me this wonderful opportunity to write, and for encouraging me. Thanks to Sahil once again, for his excellent technical skills, expertise, and guidance, which helped greatly with the chapter outlines, sample ideas, and the internal reviews on every chapter. I'd also like to thank Steve Wright for his intense technical review and very valuable comments that significantly improved the quality of the book, and also for stepping in to write Chapter 6. I want to express my appreciation to Apress for building a terrific management team, who all helped bring everything together in timely fashion. Finally, I am lucky and thankful for my family who supported me at home during the course of authoring this book.

Srini Sistla

I would like to thank Sahil, Srini, Jonathan, and Jennifer for giving me the opportunity to participate in the writing of this book. I have coauthored and reviewed many technical books over the years, but I believe this will be the most valuable among them, both for myself and (hopefully) for the reader. Finally, I would like to thank my wife, Janet, and our children, Jon, Evan and Troy, for putting up with all of the time I spent in our basement over the last few months.

Steve Wright

Introduction

In working with SharePoint and with BI, we frequently found that there was no single source of information that could address the needs of both DBAs and SharePoint administrators and developers. In fairness, given the pace of the technology we deal with, it's very difficult to find that one superhero who knows it all. But, in order to deliver solutions with these modern platforms, we sort of do need to know it all. We need to know core BI concepts as well as core SharePoint BI concepts.

SharePoint is becoming the de facto choice for delivery of BI products for Microsoft. With SharePoint 2010, Microsoft introduced Visio Services, Business Connectivity Services, Reporting Services, a much-revamped Excel Services, and to top the cake, a completely revamped PerformancePoint Services.

Even if, you are an experienced .NET developer, it is difficult to find a single book that teaches you enough of all of these technologies, and enough BI concepts, to get you on the way to being productive and effective in a project that uses these concepts and technologies.

That's why we put this book together.

We put this book together not as a bible for all BI knowledge on the Microsoft platform. There are other books that do that well enough.

We put this book together not as a bible for all SharePoint knowledge, either. There are other books that do that well enough, too.

We put this book together to address that unique and fascinating area that is the intersection of BI and SharePoint 2010.

The book is organized with that in mind. The first chapter gets you familiar with enough BI concepts to get you going, even if you have no background in BI. Expert DBAs may skip this chapter. The subsequent chapters focus on each of the core SharePoint BI concepts one by one, and give you enough examples to explore each of these topics in detail. Moreover, we made it a point not to ignore the administrative side of things. In each chapter we introduce you to the various facilities in central administration, and we also look at the PowerShell commands relevant to these features.

Writing any book is a lot of work. We hope you find it useful.

— Sahil Malik

CHAPTER 1

■■■

Business Intelligence Basics

This chapter presents the basics of business intelligence (BI). If you're an experienced data warehouse expert, you may wish to skip this chapter, except for the section that introduces SharePoint 2010 BI concepts at the end. But, since a huge part of our audience will be SharePoint experts, not data warehouse experts, we felt it necessary to include the fundamentals of data warehousing in this book. While we don't intend to cover every detail, we'll include what you need to know to get through the book, and refer you to other resources for advanced concepts.

Introduction

Effective decision-making is the key to success, and the key to making effective decisions is appropriate and accurate information. Data won't do you much good if you can't get any intelligent information from it, and to do that, you need to be able to properly analyze the data. There's a lot of information embedded in the data in various forms and views that can help organizations and individuals create better plans for the future. We'll start here with the fundamentals of drilling down into data—how to do it and how you can take advantage of it.

I couldn't resist including a picture here that highlights the benefits of BI (see Figure 1–1). This drawing was presented by Hasso Plattner of the Hasso Plattner Institute for IT Systems at the SIGMOD Keynote Talk. (SIGMOD is the Special Interest Group on Management of Data of the Association for Computing Machinery.)

Figure 1–1. Information at your fingertips!

What Will You Learn?

By the end of this chapter, you'll learn about:

1. The essentials of BI

2. The OLAP system and its components

3. SQL Server 2008 BI Tools

4. SharePoint 2010 BI Components

You'll need a basic understanding of databases and the relevant tools to get the most out of the topics in this book. You'll also need the software listed here:

- SharePoint Server 2010 Enterprise Edition

- SQL Server 2008 R2 Developer Edition and its BI tools, BIDS (Business intelligence development studio 2008)

- SQL Server 2008 R2 Update for Developers Training Kit (June 2010 Update), available for download at http://www.microsoft.com/downloads/ details.aspx?FamilyID=fffaad6a-0153-4d41-b289-a3ed1d637c0d&displaylang=en

- AdventureWorks DB for SQL Server 2008 R2, available for download at http://msftdbprodsamples.codeplex.com/releases/view/45907

- Visual Studio 2010 Professional Edition, trial version available for download at http://www.microsoft.com/visualstudio/en-us/products/2010-editions/professional

- Microsoft SharePoint Designer 2010, available for download at http://www.microsoft.com/downloads/details.aspx?FamilyID=d88a1505-849b-4587-b854-a7054ee28d66&displaylang=en

- If you'd prefer using Express editions of Visual Studio and SQL Server instead of the full versions, you can download them from http://www.microsoft.com/express/.

Why Intelligence?

Chances are you've seen the recommendations pages on sites such as Netflix, Wal-Mart, and Amazon. On Netflix, for example, you can choose your favorite genre, then the movies to order or watch online. Next time you log in, you'll see a "Movies you'll love" section with several suggestions based your previous choices. Clearly, there's some kind of intelligence-based system running behind these recommendations. Now, don't worry about what technologies the Netflix web application is built on. Let's just try to analyze what's going on behind the scenes. First, since there are recommendations, there must be some kind of tracking mechanism for your likes and dislikes based on your choices or on the ratings you provide. Second, recommendations may be based on other users' average ratings minus yours for a given genre. Each user provides enough information to let Netflix drill down, aggregate, and otherwise analyze different kinds of scenarios. This analysis can be either simple or complex depending on many other factors, including total number of users, movies watched, genre, ratings, and so on—with endless possibilities.

Now consider a related but not so similar example—your own online banking information. The account information in your profile is presented in various charts on various timelines, and so forth, and you can use different tools to add or alter information to see how your portfolio might look in the future.

Now think along the same lines, but this time about a big organization with millions of records that can be explored to give CIOs or CFOs a picture of their assets, revenues, sales, and so forth. It doesn't matter if the organization is financial, medical, technical, or whatever, or what the details of information are. There's no limit for data in how it can be drilled down and understood. In the end, it boils down to one thing—using business intelligence to enable *effective decision making*.

Let's get started on our explorations of the basics and building blocks of business intelligence.

Understanding BI

Just about any kind of business will benefit from having appropriate, accurate, and up-to-date information in order to make key decisions. The question is, how do you get this information when the data is tightly coupled with business—and is in use. In general, you need to think about questions such as:

- How can you drill down into tons of information, aggregate that information, and perform mathematical calculations to analyze it?

- How can you use such information to understand what's happened in the past as well as what's happening now, and thereby build better solutions for future?

Here are some typical and more specific business-related questions you might have to answer.

- What are the newly created accounts this month?

- Which new users joined this quarter?

- Which accounts have been removed this year?

- How many vehicles have we sold this year and what's the new inventory?

- How many issues have been addressed this week in the command center?

- What is the failure rate of products in this unit?

- What are the all-time top 10 stocks?

- Can you rank these employees in terms of monthly sales?

- Is it possible to run statistical analysis on existing data?

What kind of system could provide the means to answer these questions? A comprehensive business intelligence system is a powerful mechanism for digging into, analyzing, and reporting on your data.

■ **Note** Business intelligence is all about decisions made effectively with accurate information in timely manner.

Data always has a trend or a paradigm. When you're looking at the data, you might begin to wonder, "What if...." To answer this question, you need the business intelligence mechanism. Understanding the basics of BI or data warehouse modeling helps you achieve accurate results.

Every industry, organization, enterprise, firm, or even individual has information stored in some format in databases or files somewhere. Sometimes this data will just be read, and sometimes it needs to be modified and provide instant results. In such cases, one significant factor is the size of the data. Databases that yield instant results by adding, editing, or deleting information deal with *transactional* data. Such information needs a quick turnaround from the applications. In such cases, users seek or provide information via the UI or another source, and the result of any subsequent read, publish, edit, or even delete must happen instantly. Transaction results must also be delivered instantly, without any latency. A system that can deliver such instant results usually is based on the model called *Online Transaction Processing* or just OLTP.

OLTP vs. OLAP

Online Transaction Processing System

Data in the OLTP model is relational, and it is normalized according to database standards—such as the third or fourth normal form. An important factor in the OLTP model is that data doesn't repeat in any fashion and hence it is arranged into more than one table. In this way, transactions involve fewer tables and columns, thus increasing performance. There are fewer indexes and more joins in this model, and the tables will hold the key information.

Figure 1–2 shows a basic OLTP system.

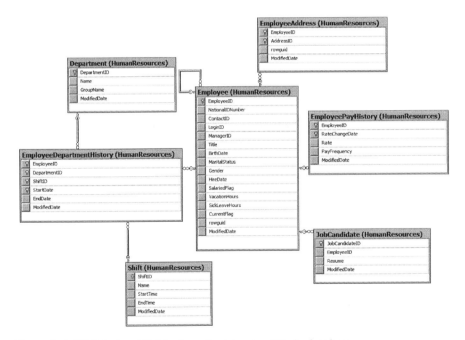

Figure 1–2. HR Relational Tables from the AdventureWorks database

---

■ **Note** We strongly recommend you download and install the AdventureWorks sample database. You'll get the most out of this chapter and the others if you can follow along.

OLTP is not meant for slicing and dicing the data, and it's definitely not meant to be used to make key decisions based on the data. OLTP is real-time and it's optimized for performance during Read/Write operations specifically for a faster response.

Now take a look at Figure 1–3. Notice how information is limited or incomplete. You wouldn't be able to tell what the numbers or codes are for various columns. To get more information on these values, you'd need to run a query that would join this table with others, and the query could become bigger and bigger as the number of relational tables increases.

	MovieID	MovieName	ReleaseDate	GenreID	ReleaseYear	AwardID	ActorID	ActressID	DirectorID	PresentorID
1	1	Defiance	2009-01-16 00:00:00.000	NULL	2009	NULL	1	2	3	6
2	2	Revolutionary Road	2009-01-23 00:00:00.000	NULL	2009	NULL	4	5	6	6
3	3	Taken	2009-01-30 00:00:00.000	NULL	2009	NULL	7	NULL	3	1
4	4	The Pink Panther 2	2009-02-06 00:00:00.000	NULL	2009	NULL	9	NULL	11	NULL
5	5	The International	2009-02-13 00:00:00.000	NULL	2009	NULL	13	NULL	14	2
6	6	Watchmen	2010-03-06 00:00:00.000	NULL	2009	NULL	15	NULL	16	4
7	7	X-Men Origins: Wolverine	2009-05-01 00:00:00.000	NULL	2009	NULL	17	NULL	18	1
8	8	Avatar	2009-12-18 00:00:00.000	NULL	2009	NULL	19	20	21	1
9	9	Sherlock Holmes	2009-12-25 00:00:00.000	NULL	2009	NULL	22	NULL	23	4

Figure 1–3. A table with incomplete information

On the other hand, it would be very easy to query the table if it were a little bit denormalized and had some data pre-populated, as shown in Figure 1–4. In this case, the number of joins would be reduced, thereby shortening the T-SQL query. This would simplify the query and improve the performance. However the performance depends on the efficiency of indexing and note that denormalizing the tables cause excessive I/O.

MovieID	MovieName	ReleaseDate	Genre	ReleaseYear	Awards	Actor	Actress	Director	PresentedBy
1	Defiance	2009-01-16 00:00:00.000	NULL	2009	NULL	Daniel Craig	Liev Schreiber	Edward Zwick	Paramount
2	Revolutionary Road	2009-01-23 00:00:00.000	NULL	2009	NULL	Leonardo DiCaprio	Kate Winslet	Sam Mendes	Paramount
3	Taken	2009-01-30 00:00:00.000	NULL	2009	NULL	Liam Nesson	NULL	Pierre Morel	20th Century Fox
4	The Pink Panther 2	2009-02-06 00:00:00.000	NULL	2009	NULL	Steve Martin	NULL	Harald Zwart	NULL
5	The International	2009-02-13 00:00:00.000	NULL	2009	NULL	Clive Owen	NULL	Tom Tykwer	Columbia Pictures
6	Watchmen	2010-03-06 00:00:00.000	NULL	2009	NULL	Patrick Wilson	NULL	Zack Snyder	Warner Bros
7	X-Men Origins: Wolverine	2009-05-01 00:00:00.000	NULL	2009	NULL	Hugh Jackman	NULL	Gavin Hood	20th Century Fox
8	Avatar	2009-12-18 00:00:00.000	NULL	2009	NULL	Sam Worthington	Zoe Saldana	James Cameron	20th Century Fox
9	Sherlock Holmes	2009-12-25 00:00:00.000	NULL	2009	NULL	Robert Downey Jr	NULL	Guy Ritchie	Warner Bros

Figure 1–4. The denormalized table

■ **Caution** As you can see in Figure 1–4, the T-SQL query would be simplified, but denormalized tables can cause excessive I/O because they contain fewer records on a page. It depends on the efficiency of the indexing. The data and indexes also consume more disk space than normalized data.

You might ask, why can't I simply run these queries on my OLTP database without worries about performance? Or create views? Simply put, OLTP databases are meant for regular transactions that happen every day in your organization. These are real-time and current at any point of time, which makes OLTP a desirable model. However, this model is not designed to run powerful analysis on these databases. It's not that you can't run formulas or aggregates, it's that the database might have been built to support most of the applications running in your organization and when you try to do the analysis, these applications take longer to run. You don't want your queries to interfere with or block the daily operations of your system.

▨ **Note** To scale operations, some organizations split an OLTP database into two separate databases (i.e., they replicate the database). One database handles only write operations while the other is used for read operations on the tables (after the transactions take place). Applications manage through code the data to write to one database and to read for presentation from another database. This way, transactions take place on one database and analysis can happen on the second. This may not be suitable for every organization.

So what can we do? Archive the database! One way that many organizations are able to run their analysis on an OLTP databases is to simply take periodic backups or archive the real-time database, and then run their queries on the disconnected-mode (non-real-time) data.

▨ **Note** A database that has been backed up and repurposed (copied) for running analysis might require a refresh as the original source database might have had data updated or values changed.

Good enough? Still, these OLTP databases are not meant for running analysis. Suppose you have a primary table consisting of information for one row in four different normalized tables, each having eight rows of information, the complexity is 1x4x8x8. But what if you're talking about a million rows? Imagine what might happen to the performance of this query!

▨ **Note** The data source for your analysis need not be OLTP. It can be an Excel file, a text file, a web service, or information stored in some other format.

We must emphasize that we are not saying that OLTP doesn't support analysis. All we are saying is that OLTP databases are not designed for complex analysis. What we need is a non-relational and non-live database where such analysis can be freely run on data to support business intelligence.

To tune your database to the way you need to run analysis on it needs some kind of cleaning and rearranging of data, which can be done via a process known as Extract, Transform, and Load (ETL). That simply means data is *extracted* from the OLTP databases (or any other data sources), *transformed* or cleaned, and *loaded* into a new structure. Then what? What comes next?

The next question to be asked is, even if we have ETL, to what system should the data be extracted, transformed, and loaded? The answer: It depends! As you'll see, the answer to lots of things database-related is "It depends!"

Online Analytical Processing System

To analyze our data, what we need is a mechanism that can make it feasible to drill down, run an analysis, and understand the data. Such results can provide tremendous benefits in making key decisions. Moreover, they give you a window that may display the data in a brand-new way. We already mentioned that the mechanism to pull the intelligence from your data is BI, but the system to facilitate and drive this mechanism is the OLAP structure, the *Online Analytical Processing* system.

The key term in the name is *analytical*. OLAP systems are read-only (though there can be exceptions) and are specifically meant for analytical purposes, which facilitates most of the needs of BI. When we say a read-only database, it's essentially a backup copy of the real-time OLTP database, or more likely a partial copy of an entire OLTP database.

In contrast with OLTP, OLAP information is considered historical, which means that though there may be batch additions to the data, it is not considered up-to-the-second data. Data is completely isolated and is meant for performing various tasks, such as drilldown and the like. Information is stored in fewer tables and so queries perform much faster since they involve fewer joins.

■ **Note** OLAP systems relax normalization rules by not following the third normal form.

Table 1–1 compares OLTP and OLAP systems.

Table 1–1. OLTP vs. OLAP

Online *Transaction* Processing System	Online *Analytical* Processing System
• Used for real-time data access.	• Used for online or historical data.
• Transaction-based.	• Used for analysis and data drilldown.
• Data may exist in more than one table.	• Data may exist in more than one table.
• Optimized for faster transactions.	• Optimized for performance and details in querying the data.
• Transactional databases include Add, Update, and Delete operations.	• Read-only database.
• Not built for running complex queries.	• Built to run complex queries.
• Line-of-business (LOB) and enterprise resource planning (ERP) databases use this model.	• Analytical databases such as Cognos, Business Objects, etc. use this model.
• Tools: SQL Server Management Studio (SSMS).	• Tools: SQL Server Analysis Services (SSAS).
• Follows database normalization rules.	• Relaxes DB normalization rules.
• Relational database.	• Relational database.
• Holds key data.	• Holds key aggregated data.
• Fewer indexes and more joins.	• Relatively more indexes and fewer joins.
• Query from multiple tables.	• Query might run on fewer tables.

You're probably already wondering how you can take your OLTP database and convert it to OLAP database so you can run some analysis on it. Before you run off to find out the solution, it's important to know a little more about OLAP and its structure.

The Unified Dimensional Model and Data Cubes

Data cubes are more sophisticated OLAP structures that will solve the above concern. Despite the name, cubes are not limited to a cube structure. The name is inherited just because it has more dimensions. Don't visualize cubes as only 3-dimensional or symmetric; cubes are used for their multidimensional value.

A simple cube can have only three dimensions, such as those shown in Figure 1–5 where X is Products, Y is Region, and Z is Time.

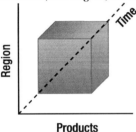

Figure 1–5. *A simple 3-dimensional cube*

With a cube like the one in Figure 1–5, you can find out product sales in a given time frame. This cube uses Product Sales as facts with the Time dimension.

Facts (also called measures) and dimensions are integral parts of cubes. Data in cubes is accumulated as facts and aggregated against a dimension. A data cube is multi-dimensional and thus can deliver information based on any fact against any dimension in its hierarchy.

Dimensions can be described by their hierarchies, which are essentially parent-child relationships. If dimensions are key factors of cubes, hierarchies are key factors of dimensions. In the hierarchy of the Time dimension, for example, you might find Yearly, Half-yearly, Quarterly, Monthly, Weekly, and Daily levels. These become the facts or members of the dimension.

In a similar vein, geography might be described like this:

- Country
  - Regions
  - East
  - West
  - North
  - South
- States
  - Counties

■ **Note** Dimensions, facts (or measures), and hierarchies together form the structure of a cube.

Figure 1–6 shows a multi-dimensional cube.

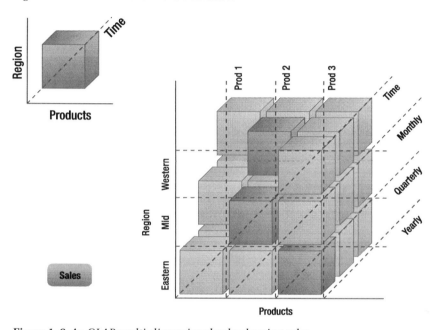

Figure 1–6. An OLAP multi-dimensional cube showing sales.

Now imagine cubes with multiple facts and dimensions, each dimension having its own hierarchies across each cube, and all these cubes connected together. The information residing inside this consolidated cube can deliver very useful, accurate, and aggregated information. You can drill down into the data of this cube to the lowest levels.

However, earlier we said that OLAP databases are denormalized. Well then, what happens to the tables? Are they not connected at all and just work independently?

Clearly, you must have the details of how your original tables are connected. If you want to convert your normalized OLTP tables into denormalized OLAP tables, you need to understand your existing tables and their normalized form in order to design the new mapping for these tables against the OLAP database tables you're planning to create.

In order to plan for migrating OLTP to OLAP, you need to understand a more about OLAP internals. OLAP structures its tables in its own style, yielding tables that are much cleaner and simpler. However, it's actually the data that makes the tables clean and simple. To enable this simplicity, the tables are formed into a structure (or pattern) that can be depicted visually as a star. Let's take a look at how this so-called *star schema* is formed and at the integral parts that make up the OLAP star schema.

Facts and Dimensions

OLAP data tables are arranged to form a star. Star schemas have two core concepts: facts and dimensions. Facts are values or calculations based on the data. They may be just numeric values. Here are some examples of facts:

- Dell US Eastern Region Sales on Dec 08, 2007 are $1.7M.

- Dell US Northern Region Sales on Dec 08, 2007 are $1.1M.

- Average daily commuters in Loudoun County Transit in Jan. 2010 are 11,500.

- Average daily commuters in Loudoun County Transit in Feb. 2010 are 12,710.

Dimensions are the axis points, or ways to view facts. For instance, using the multidimensional cube in Figure 1–6 (and assuming it relates to Wal-Mart), we can ask

- What is Wal-Mart's sales volume for *Date* mm/dd/yyyy? Date is a dimension.

- What is Wal-Mart's sales volume in the Eastern *Region*? Region is a dimension.

Values around the cube that belong to a dimension are known as members. In Figure 1–6, examples of members are Eastern (under the Region dimension), Prod 2 (under Products) and Yearly (under Time). You might want to aggregate various facts against various dimensions. Generating and obtaining a star schema is very simple using SQL Server Management Studio (SSMS). You can create a new database diagram by adding more tables from the AdventureWorks database. SSMS will link related tables and form a star schema as shown in Figure 1–7.

■ **Note** OLAP and star schemas are sometimes spoken of interchangeably.

In Figure 1–7, the block in center is the fact table and those surrounding the center block are dimensions. This layout—a fact table in the center surrounded by the dimensions—is what makes a star schema.

OLAP data is in the form of aggregations. We want to get from OLAP information such as:

- The volume of sales for Wal-Mart last month.

- The average salaries paid to employees this year.

- A statistical comparison of our own company details historically, or a comparison against other companies.

and so on.

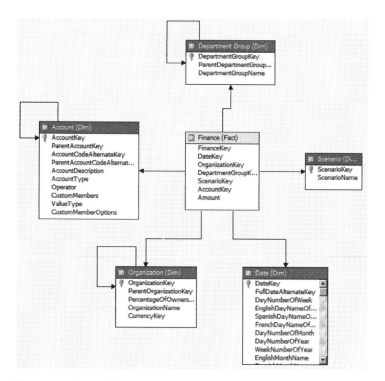

Figure 1–7. A star schema

■ **Note** Another model similar to the star schema is the snowflake schema, which is formed when one or more dimension table is joined to another dimension table(s) instead of a fact table. This results in reference relationships between dimensions, or in other words they are normalized.

So far so good! Although the OLAP system is designed with these schemas and structures, it's still a relational database. It still has all the tables and relations as an OLTP database, which means that querying from these OLAP tables might still have performance issues and thus creates a bit of concern in aggregation.

■ **Note** Aggregation is nothing but summing or adding data or information on a given dimension.

Extract, Transform, and Load

It is the structure of the cubes that solves those performance issues; cubes are very efficient and fast in providing information. The next question then is how to build these cubes and populate them with data. Needless to say, data is an essential part of your business and, as we've noted, typically exists in an OLTP database. What we need to do is retrieve this information from the OLTP database, clean it up, and transfer the data (either in its entirety or only what's required) to the OLAP cubes. Such a process is known as Extract, Transform, and Load (ETL).

▓ **Note** ETL tools can extract information not only from OLTP databases, but also from different relational databases, web services, file systems, or various other data sources.

You will learn about some of the ETL tools later in this chapter. We'll start by taking a look at data transfer from an OLTP database to an OLAP database using ETL, at a very high level. But we can't just jump right in and convert these systems. Be warned, ETL requires some preparations, so we'd better discuss those now.

Need for Staging

The ETL process pulls data from various data sources that can be in a form as simple as a flat text file or as complex as a SQL Server or Oracle database. Moreover, the data may come from different sources of unknown formats, as when an organization has merged with another. Or it could be an even worse scenario, where not only the data schemas are different but the data sources are completely be different as well. There might be different databases such as SQL, Oracle, or DB2, or, for that matter, even flat files and xml files. And these data sources may very well be real-time OLTP databases that can't be directly accessed to retrieve information. Furthermore, the data likely needs to be loaded on a periodic basis as updates happen in real time—probably every second. Now imagine that this involves terabytes of data. How much time would it take to copy the data from one system and load into another? As you can tell, this is likely to be a very difficult situation.

All of these common issues essentially demand an area where you can happily carry out all your operations—a staging or data preparation platform. How would you take advantage of a staging environment? Here are the tasks you'd perform:

1. Identify the data sources and prepare a data map for the existing (source) tables and entities.

2. Copy the data sources to the staging environment or use a similar process to achieve this. This step essentially isolates the original data source.

3. Identify the data source tables, their formats, column types, etc.

4. Prepare for common ground; that is, make sure mapping criteria is in sync with the destination database.

5. Remove unwanted columns.

6. Clean column values. You definitely don't want unwanted information; this brings in less data but enough to run the analysis.

7. Prepare, plan, and schedule for reloading the data from the source and going through the entire cycle of mapping.

8. Once you are ready, use proper ETL tools to migrate the data to destination.

Transformation

Let's begin with a simple flow diagram, shown in Figure 1–8, which shows everything put together very simply. Think about the picture in terms of rows and columns, as we have three rows—for system, language used, and purpose, and 2 columns—one for OLTP and the other for OLAP.

On OLTP databases you use the T-SQL language to perform the transactions, while for OLAP databases you use MDX queries instead to parse the OLAP data structures (which, in this case, are cubes). And, finally, you use OLAP/MDX for BI analysis purposes.

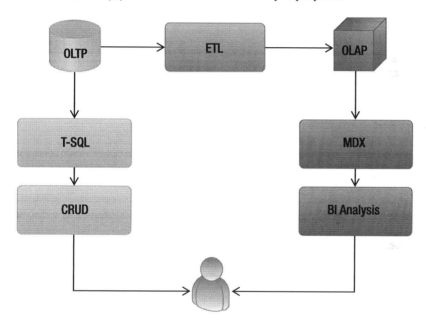

Figure 1–8. Converting from OLTP to OLAP

What is ETL doing in Figure 1–8? As we noted, ETL is the process used to migrate an OLTP database to an OLAP database. Once the OLAP database is populated with the OLTP data, we use MDX queries and run them against the OLAP cubes to get what need (the analysis).

Now that you understand the transformation, let's take a look at MDX scripting and see how you can use it to achieve your goals.

MDX Scripting

MDX stands for *Multidimensional Expressions*. It is an open standard used to query information from cubes. Here's a simple MDX query (running on the AdventureWorks database):

```
select [Measures].[Internet Total Product Cost] ON COLUMNS,
[Customer].[Country] ON ROWS
FROM [AdventureWorks]
WHERE [Sales Territory].[North America]
```

MDX can be a very simple select statement as shown above, which consists of the select query and choosing columns and rows, much like a traditional SQL select statement. In a nutshell, it's like this:

Select x, y, z from cube where dimension equals a.

Sound familiar?

Let's look at the MDX statement more closely. The query is retrieving information from the *measure* "Internet Total Product Cost" against the *dimension* "Customer Country" from the *Cube* "AdventureWorks." Furthermore, the *where* clause is on the "Sales Territory" *Dimension,* as we are intrested in finding the Sales in North America.

▧ **Note** Case sensitivity for columns and rows is not mandatory. Also, you can use 0 and 1 as ordinal positions for columns and rows respectively. If you extend the ordinal positions beyond 0 and 1, MDX will return the multidimensional cube.

MDX queries are not so different from SQL queries except that MDX used to query an analysis cube. It has all the rich features, similar syntax, functions, support for calculations, and more. The difference is that SQL retrieves information from tables that basically results in a two-dimensional view. In contrast, MDX can query from a cube and deliver mutidimensional views.

Go back and take a look at Figure 1–6, which shows sales (fact) against three dimensions: Product, Region, and Time. This means you can find the sales for a given product in a given region at a given time. This is simple. Now suppose you have regions splitting the US into North, East, West and South, and the time frame further classified as Yearly, Quarterly, Monthly, and Weekly. All of these elements serve as filters, allowing you to retrieve the finest aggregated information about the product. Thus a cube can range from a simple 3-dimensional one to a complex hierarchy where each dimension can have its own members or attributes or children. You need a very clear understanding of these fundamentals in order to write efficient MDX queries.

In a multidimensional cube, you can either call the entire cube a cell or count each cube as one cell. A cell is built with dimensions and members.

Using our example cube, if you need to retrieve the sales value for a product, you'd do it as

```
(Region.East, Time.[Quarter 4], Product.Prod1)
```

Notice that square brackets—[ ]—are used when there's a space in the dimension/member.

Looks easy, yes? But what if you need just a part of the cube value and not the whole thing? Let's say you need just prod1 sales in the Eastern region. Well that's definitely a valid constraint. To address this, you use *tuples* in a cube.

Tuples and Sets

A tuple is an address within the cube. You can define a tuple based on what you need. It can have one or more dimensions and one measure as a logical group. For instance, if we use the same example, data related to the Eastern Region during the fourth Quarter can be called one tuple. So

```
(Region.East, Time.[Quarter 4], Product.Prod1)
```

is a good example of a tuple. You can design as many as tuples you need within the limits of dimensions.

A set is a group of zero or more tuples. Remember that you can't use the terms tuples and sets interchangeably. Suppose you want two different areas in a cube or two tuples with different measures and dimensions. That's where you use a set (see Figure 1–9).

For example, if (Region.East, Time.[Quarter 4], Product.Prod1) is one of your tuples, and (Region.East, Time.[Quarter 1], Product.Prod2) is the second, then the set that comprises these two tuples looks like this:

```
{(Region.East, Time.[Quarter 4], Product.Prod1), (Region.East, Time.[Quarter 1],
Product.Prod2) }
```

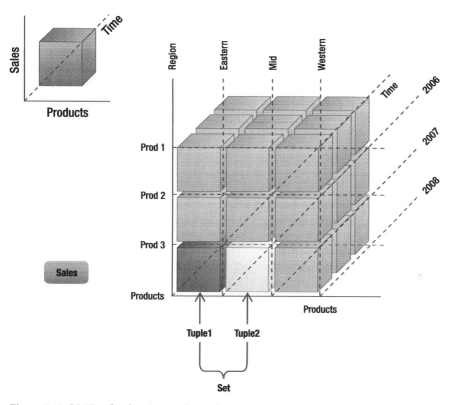

Figure 1–9. OLAP cube showing tuples and a set

■ **Best Practices:** When you create MDX queries, it's always good to include comments that provide sufficient information and make logical sense. You can write single-line comments by using either "//" or "—" or multiline comments using "/*…*/".

For more about advanced MDX queries, built-in functions and their references, please consult the book *Smart Business Intelligence Solutions with Microsoft SQL Server 2008*, available for purchase at microsoft.com/learning/en/us/book.aspx?ID=12663&locale=en-us.

Putting It All Together

Table 1–2 gives an overview of the database models and their entities, query languages, and the tools used to retrieve information from them.

Table 1–2. Database models

Nature of usage	Transactional (R/W) Add, Update, Delete	Analytics (R) Data Drilldown, Aggregation
Type of DB	OLTP	OLAP
Entities	Tables, Stored Procedures, Views etc.	Cubes, Dimensions, Measures, etc.
Query Language(s)	T-SQL/PL-SQL	MDX
Tools	SQL Server 2005 (or higher), SSMS	SQL Server 2005 (or higher), SSMS, BIDS, SSAS

Before proceeding, let's take a look at some more BI concepts.

The BI Foundation

Data Warehouses

You can now visualize how big a cube can become, with infinite dimensions and facts. A *data warehouse* is a combination of cubes. It is how you structure enterprise data. Data warehouses are typically used at huge organizations for aggregating and analyzing their information.

Since cubes are integral parts of a data warehouse, it's evident that a data warehouse comprises both relational and disconnected databases. Data warehouses are a consolidation of many other small slices (as shown in Figure 1–10) that includes data marts, tools, data sources, and ETL.

Data Marts

A *data mart* is a baby version of the data warehouse. It also has cubes embedded in it, but you can think of a data mart as a store on Main Street and a data warehouses as one of those huge, big-box shopping warehouses. Information from the data mart is consolidated and aggregated into the data warehouse database. You have to regularly merge data from OLTP databases into your data warehouse on a schedule that meets your organization's needs. This data is then extracted to the data marts, which are designed to perform specific functions.

▓ **Note** Data marts can run independently and need not be a part of a data warehouse. They can be designed to function as autonomous structures.

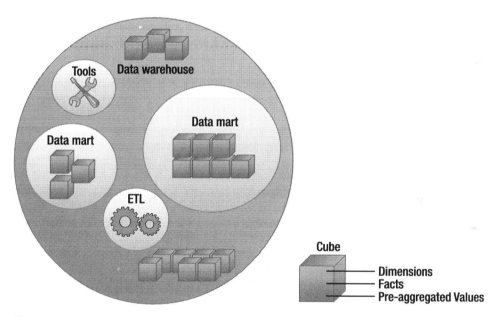

Figure 1–10. Data warehouse and data marts

Consolidating data from a data mart into a data warehouse needs to be performed with utmost care. Consider a situation where you have multiple data marts following different data schemas and you're trying to merge information into one data warehouse. It's easy to imagine how data could be improperly integrated, which would become a concern for anyone who wanted to run analysis on this data. This creates the need to use *conformed dimensions* (refer to http://data-warehouses.net/glossary/conformeddimensions.html for more details). As we mentioned earlier, areas or segments where you map the schemas and cleanse the data are sometimes known as staging environments. These are platforms where you can check consistency and perform data-type mapping, cleaning, and of course loading the data from the data sources. There could definitely be transactional information in each of the data marts. Again, you need to properly clean the data and identify only the needed information to migrate from these data marts to the data source.

Decision Support Systems and Data Mining

Both decision support systems and data mining are accomplished using OLAP. While a decision support system gives you the facts, data mining provides the information that leads to prediction. You definitely need both of these as one lets you get accurate, up-to-date information whereas the other leads to questions that can provide intelligence for making future decisions (see Figure 1–11). For example, decision support provides accurate information such as "Dell stocks rose by 25 percent last year." That's precise information. Now if you pick up Dell's sales numbers from last 4 or 5 years, you can see the growth rate of Dell's annual sales. Using these figures, you might predict what kind of sales Dell would make next year. That's data mining.

▓ **Note** Data mining leads to prediction. Prediction leads to planning. Planning leads to questions such as "What if?" These are the questions that help you avoid failure. Just as you use MDX to query data from cubes, you can use the DMX (Data Mining Extensions) language to query information from data mining models in SSAS.

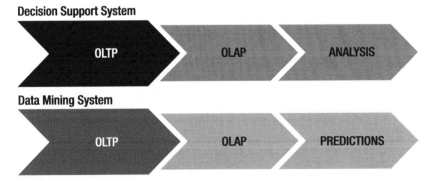

Figure 1–11. Decision support system vs. data mining system

Tools

Now let's get to some real-time tools. What you need are the following:

- SQL Server Database Engine (Installation of the SQL Server 2008 R2 will provision it)

- SQL Server Management Studio

- SQL Server Integration Services

- SQL Server Analysis Services

- Business Intelligence Development Studio

- AdventureWorks 2008 R2 DW2008 sample database.

■ **Note** Installing SQL Server 2008 R2 with all the neccessary tools is beyond the scope of this book. We recommend you go to Microsoft's SQL Server installation page at `msdn.microsoft.com/en-us/library/bb500469.aspx` for details on installation and administration.

SQL Server Management Studio

SSMS is not something new to developers. You've probably used this tool in your day-to-day activities or at least for a considerable period during any development project. Whether you're dealing with OLTP databases or OLAP, SSMS plays a significant role, and it provides a lot of the functionality to help developers connect with OLAP databases. Not only can you run T-SQL statements, you can also use SSMS to run MDX queries to extract data from the cubes.

SSMS makes it feasible to run various query models, such as the following:

1. **New Query:** executes T-SQL queries on a OLTP database.

2. **Database Engine Query:** executes T-SQL, XQuery, and sqlcmd scripts.

3. **Analysis Services MDX Query:** executes MDX queries on a OLAP database.

4. **Analysis Services DMX Query:** executes DMX queries on a OLAP database.

5. **Analysis Services XMLA Query:** executes XMLA language queries on a OLAP database.

6. **SQL Server Compact Query:** executes queries of the SQL Server Compact database.

Figure 1–12 shows that the menus for these queries can be accessed in SSMS.

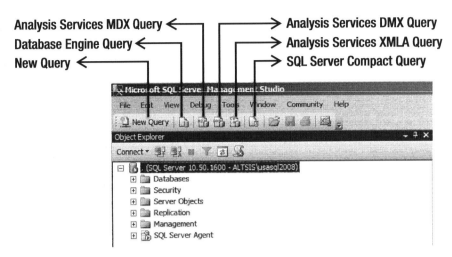

Figure 1–12. Important menu items in SQL Server Management Studio

Figure 1–13 shows an example of executing a new query against an OLTP database.

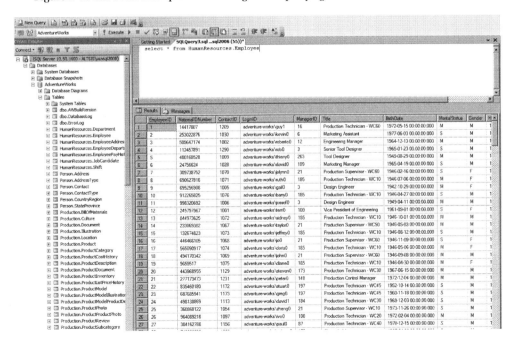

Figure 1–13. Executing a simple OLTP SQL query in SSMS

SQL Server BIDS

While Visual Studio is the developer's rapid application development tool, SQL Server Business Intelligence Development Studio (BIDS) 2008 is the equivalent development tool for the database developer (see Figure 1–14). BIDS looks like Visual Studio but it supports only a limited set of templates:

- **Analysis Services Project:** The template used to create cubes, measures, and dimensions, and other related objects.

- **Integration Services Project:** The template used to perform ETL operations.

- **Import Analysis Services Database:** The template for creating an analysis services project based on a analysis services database.

- **Integration Services Connections Project Wizard:** Wizard for creating new package with connections for various data sources.

- **Report Server Project Wizard:** Wizard that facilitates creation of reports from a data source and provides options to select various layouts, etc.

- **Report Model Project:** The template used to create report models based on a SQL Server database.

- **Report Server Project:** The template for authoring and publishing reports.

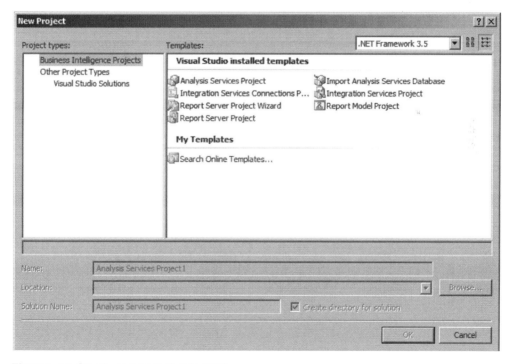

Figure 1–14. Creating a new project in BIDS

Transforming OLTP Data Using SSIS

As discussed earlier, data needs to be extracted from the OLTP databases, cleaned, and then loaded into OLAP in order to be used for business intelligence. You can use the SQL Server Integration Services (SSIS) tool to accomplish this. This section will run through various steps detailing how to use Integration Services and how it can be used as an ETL tool.

SSIS is very powerful. You can use it to extract data from any source that includes a database, a flat file, or an xml file, and you can load that data into any other destination. In general, you have a source and a destination, and they can be completely different systems. A classic example of where to use SSIS is when companies merge and they have to move their databases from one system to another, which includes the complexity of having mismatches in the columns, etc. The beauty of SSIS is that it doesn't necessarily use a SQL Server database.

▓ **Note** SSIS is considered to be the next generation of Data Transformation Service (DTS), which shipped with SQL Server versions prior to 2005.

The important elements of SSIS packages are *control flows, data flows, connection managers*, and *event handlers*. Let's look at some of the features of SSIS in detail, and we'll demonstrate how simple it is to import information from a source and export it to a destination.

Since we will be working with the AdventureWorks database here, let's pick some its tables, extract the data, and then import the data back to another database or a file system.

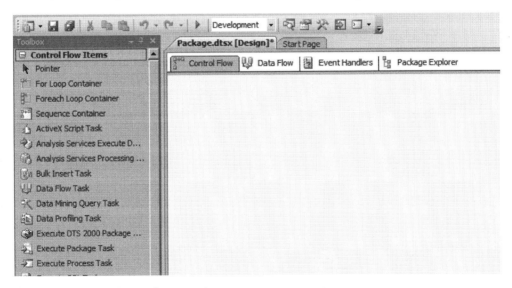

Figure 1–15. SSIS project package creation

Open SQL Server BIDS and from the File menu, choose New, then select New Project. From the available Project Types, choose Business Intelligence Projects and from the Templates, choose Integration Services Project. Provide necessary details (such as Name, Location, and Solution Name) and click OK.

Once you create the new project, you'll land on the Control Flow screen as shown in Figure 1–15. When you create an SSIS package, you get a lot of tools in the toolbox pane that is categorized by context based on selected design window or views. There are four views namely Control Flow, Data Flow, Event Handlers and Package Explorer. Here below we will discuss two main views, the Data Flow and the Control Flow:

Data Flow

- Data Flow Sources (e.g., ADO.NET Source, to extract data from a database using a .NET provider; Excel Source, to extract data from an Excel workbook; Flat File Source, to extract data from flat files, and so on).

- Data Flow Transformations (e.g., Aggregate, to aggregate values in the dataset; Data Conversion, to convert columns to different data types and add columns to the dataset; Merge, to merge two sorted datasets; Merge Join, to merge two datasets using join; Multicast, to create copies of the dataset and so on).

- Data Flow Destinations (e.g., ADO.NET destination, to write into a database using an ADO.NET provider; Excel Destination, to load data into a Excel workbook; SQL Server Destination, to load data into SQL Server database and so on).

- Based on the selected data flow tasks, event handlers can be built and executed in the Event Handlers view.

Control Flow

- Control Flow Items (e.g., Bulk Insert Task, to copy data from file to database; Data Flow Task, to move data from source to destination while performing ETL; Execute SQL Task, to execute SQL queries; Send Mail Task, to send email, and so on).

- Maintenance Plan Tasks (e.g., Back Up Database Task, to back up source database to destinations files or tapes; Execute T-SQL Statement Task, to run T-SQL scripts; Notify Operator Task, to notify SQL Server Agent operator and so on).

Let's now see how to import data from a system and export it to another system.

- Launch the Import and Export Wizard from the Solution Explorer as shown in Figure 1–16.

- Right-click on SSIS Packages and select the SSIS Import and Export Wizard option.

■ **Note** Another way to access the Import and Export Wizard is from `C:\Program Files\Microsoft SQL Server\100\DTS\Binn\DTSWizard.exe`.

Figure 1–16. Using the SSIS Import and Export Wizard

Here are the steps to import from a source to a destination:

1. Click Next on the Welcome screen.

2. From the Choose a Data Source menu item, you can select various options, including Flat File Source. Select "SQL Server Native Client 10.0" in this case.

3. Choose the available server names from the drop-down or enter the name you prefer.

4. Use Windows Authentication/SQL Server Authentication.

5. Choose the source database. In our case, select the "AdventureWorks" database.

6. Next, choose the destination options and in this case select "Flat File Destination".

7. Choose the destination file name and set the format to "Delimited".

8. Choose to "Copy data from one or more tables or views" from the "Specify Table Copy or Query" window.

9. From the Flat File Destination window, click on "Edit mappings", leave the defaults to "Create destination file", and click on OK.

10. Click Finish, then click Finish again to complete the Wizard.

11. Once execution is complete, you'll see a summary displayed. Click Close. This step would create the .dtsx file and you need to finally run the package once to get the output file.

Importing can also be done by using various data flow sources and writing custom event handlers. Let's do it step-by-step now:

PROBLEM CASE

The Sales data from the AdventureWorks database consists of more than seven tables but for simplicity let's consider the seven tables displayed in Figure 1–17. Now, you need to retrieve the information from these seven tables, extract the data, clean some of the data or drop the columns that aren't required, and then load the desired data into another data source—a flat file or database table. You might also want to extract data from two different data sources and merge it into one.

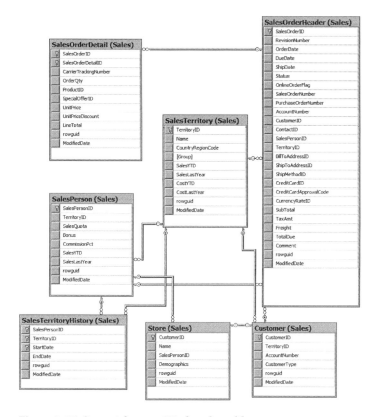

Figure 1–17. Seven AdventureWorks sales tables

Here's how to accomplish our goals:

1. Open BIDS and from the File menu choose New, then select New Project. From the available project types choose Business Intelligence Projects and from the Templates choose Integration Services Project. Provide necessary details (such as Name, Location, and Solution Name) and click OK.

2. Once the project is created, in Solution Explorer right-click on Data Sources, Add a New Data Source to the project, and choose the option "Create a data source based on an existing or new connection". The list of data connections will be empty the first time. Click the New button and connect to the server using one of the authentication models available.

3. Select or enter a database name—AdventureWorks in this example—and click the Test Connection button as shown in Figure 1–18. On success, click OK and then Finish to complete the Data Source Wizard.

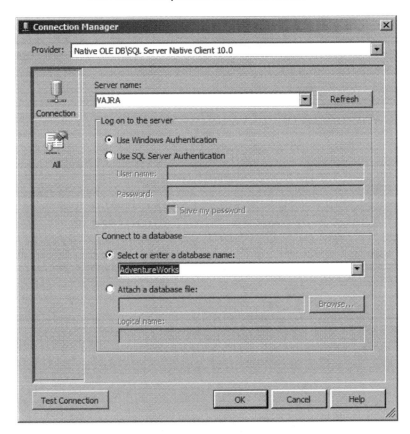

Figure 1–18. SSIS Connection Manager

4. Now double-click on Package.dtsx and open the Data Flow tab. This is where you build the data flow structures you need. You might not have the data flow ready when you run the project first time. Follow the instructions onscreen to enable the Task panel, as shown in Figure 1–19.

No Data Flow tasks have been added to this package. Click here to add a new Data Flow task.

Figure 1–19. Enabling the Data Flow Task panel

Clicking on the link 'No Data Flow tasks have been added to this package. Click here to add a new Data Flow task' (figure 1–19) would enable the data flow task pane where you can build a data flow by dragging and dropping the tool box items as shown in figure 1.-20.Add an ADO NET Source from the Toolbox to the Data Flow Task panel as shown in Figure 1–20.

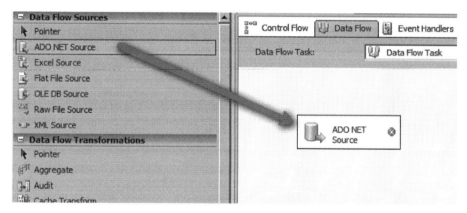

Figure 1–20. Adding a Data Flow Source in SSIS

5. Double-click on the ADO NET Source and configure the Connection Manager (see Figure 1–21). Click the New button and follow the same steps to make the connection.

6. Under Data access mode, choose SQL command, as shown in Figure 1–21.

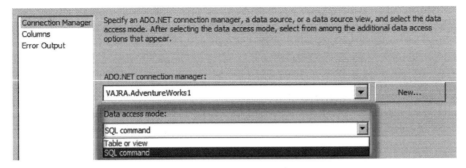

Figure 1–21. SSIS Connection Manager data access mode settings

7. Under SQL command text, enter a SQL query or use the Build Query option as shown in Figure 1–22. (Since I had already prepared a script for this, that's what I used. You'll find the SQL script 'salesquery.txt' in the resources available with this book.) Then click on the Preview button to view the data output.

Figure 1–22. ADONET Source Editor settings

8. Check the Columns section to make sure the query was successful, then click OK to close the editor window (See Figure 1–23).

Figure 1–23. ADONET Columns

9. From the Data Flow Destinations section on the Toolbox, choose a destination that meets your needs. For this demo, we'll select Flat File Destination.

10. Drag and drop the Flat File Destination onto the Data Flow Task panel as shown in Figure 1–24. If you see a red circle with a cross mark on the flow controls, hover over the cross mark to see the error.

11. Connect the green arrow from the ADO NET source to the Flat File Destination.

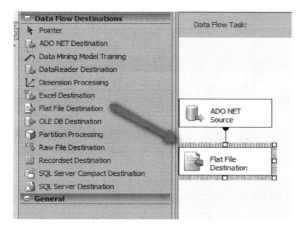

Figure 1–24. Setting an SSIS Data Flow destination

12. Double-click on the Flat File Destination, which will open the Editor (Figure 1–25).

13. Click the New button to open the Flat File Format window, where you can choose among several options. For our demo, select Delimited.

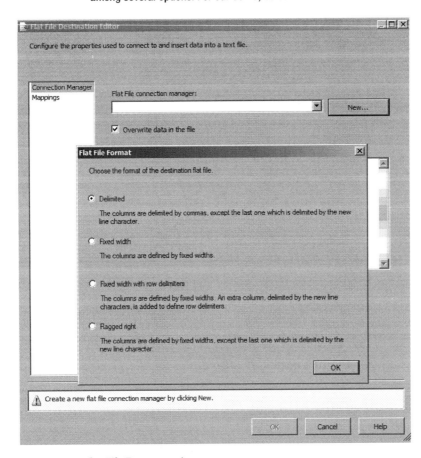

Figure 1–25. Flat File Format settings

14. The Flat File Connection Manager Editor window will open next, with options for setting connection manager name and, most importantly, the delimited format, as shown in Figure 1–26. Click OK to continue.

15. On the next screen, click on Mapping. Choose the Input Column and Destination Columns and then click OK.

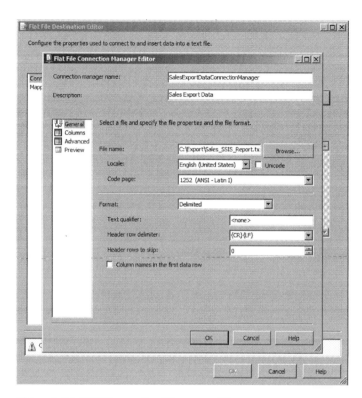

Figure 1–26. SSIS Connection Manager settings

16. The final data flow should look like what's shown in Figure 1–27.

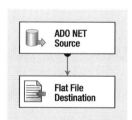

Figure 1–27. SSIS Data Flow

17. Start debugging by clicking F5, or click Ctrl+F5 to start without debugging.

18. During the process, you'll see the data flow items change color to yellow.

19. Once the process completes successfully, the data flow items change to green, as shown in Figure 1–28.

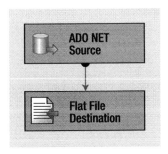

Figure 1–28. SSIS Data Flow completion

20. Click the Progress tab to view the progress of the execution of an SSIS package (see Figure 1–29).

Figure 1–29. SSIS package execution progress

21. Complete the processing of the package by clicking on Package Execution Completed at the bottom of the package window.

22. Now go to the destination folder and open the file to view the output.

23. Notice that all the records (28,866) in this case are exported to the file and are comma-separated.

24. In a more general case, you would probably be using Data Flow Transformations such as Aggregate or Data Conversion. If you did this, the output would then be the aggregation of a chosen input column. You can set the Data Flow Transformations as shown in Figure 1–30.

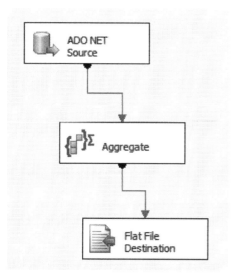

Figure 1–30. SSIS data flow using the Aggregate transformation

In many cases, you might actually get a flat file like this as input and want to extract and load it back into your new database or an existing destination database. In that scenario, you'll have to take this file as the input source, identifying the columns based on the delimiter, and load it.

As mentioned before, you may have multiple data sources (such as two sorted datasets) that you want to merge. You can use the merge module and load the sources into one file or dataset, or any other destination, as shown Figure 1–31.

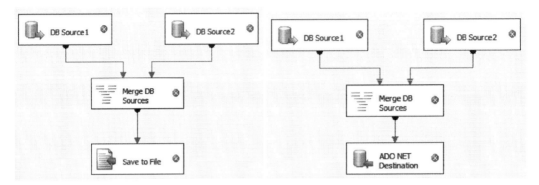

Figure 1–31. SSIS data flow merge options

■ **Tip** If you have inputs you need to distribute to multiple destinations, you might want to use Multicast Transformation, which directs every row to each of the destinations.

Now let's see how to move our OLTP tables into an OLAP star schema. As we've chosen tables in the Sales module, let's identify the key tables and data that need to be or can be analyzed. In a nutshell, we need to identify one fact table and other dimension tables first for the Sales Repository (as you see in Figure 1–32).

The idea is to extract data from the OLTP database, clean it a bit, and then load it to the model shown in Figure 1–32. The first step is to create all the tables in the star schema fashion.

Table 1–3 shows the tables you need to create in the AdventureWorksDW database. Once you've created them, move the data in the corresponding tables of the AdventureWorks database to these newly created tables. So your first step is to create these tables with the specified columns, data types, and keys.

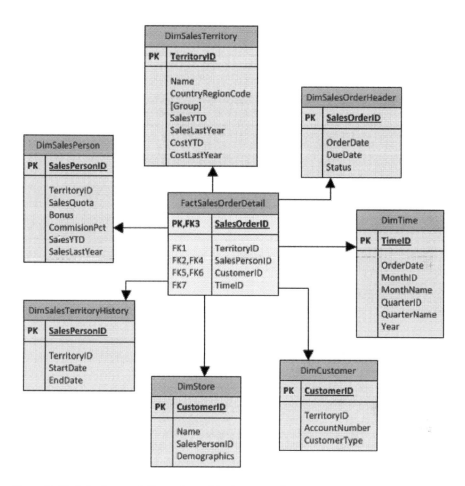

Figure 1–32. Sales fact and dimension tables in a star schema

Table 1–3. Tables to create

Table Name	Column Name	Data Type	Key
Dim_Customer	CustomerID	Int, not null	PK
	AccountNumber	Nvarchar(50), null	
	CustomerType	Nvarchar(3), null	
Dim_DateTime	DateKey	Int, not null	PK
	FullDate	Date, not null	
	DayNumberOfMonth	Tinyint, not null	
	DayNumberOfYear	Tinyint, not null	
	MonthNumberOfYear	Tinyint, not null	
	MonthName	Nvarchar(10), not null	
	Quarter	Tinyint, not null	
	Year	Smallint, not null	
Dim_SalesOrderHeader	SalesOrderHeaderID	Int, not null	PK
	OrderDate	Datetime, null	
	DueDate	Datetime, null	
	Status	Tinyint, null	
Dim_SalesPerson	SalesPersonID	Int, not null	PK, FK (to SalesPersonID in Dim_SalesTerritoryHistory, Dim_Store tables)
	SalesQuota	Money, null	
	Bonus	Money, null	
	CommisionPct	Money, null	
	SalesYTD	Money, null	
	SalesLastYear	Money, null	
	TerritoyID	Int, null	FK (to TerritoryID in Dim_SalesTerritory table)

Table Name	Column Name	Data Type	Key
Dim_SalesTerritory	TerritoryID	Int, no null	PK
	Name	Nvarchar(50), null	
	CountryRegionCode	Nvarchar(3), null	
	Group	Nvarchar(50), null	
	SalesYTD	Money, null	
	SalesLastYear	Money, null	
	CostYTD	Money, null	
	CostLastYear	Money, null	
Dim_SalesTerritoryHistory	SalesTerritoryHistoryID	Int, not null	PK
	SalesPersonID	Int, not null	FK (to SalesPersonID in Dim_SalesPerson table)
	TerritoryID	Int, not null	FK (to TerritoryID in Dim_SalesTerritory table)
	StartDate	Date, null	
	EndDate	Date, null	
Dim_Store	StoreID	Int, not null	PK
	CustomerID	Int, not null	FK (to CustomerID in Dim_Customer table)
	SalesPersonID	Int, not null	FK (to SalesPersonID in Dim_SalesPerson table)
Fact_SalesOrderDetails	SalesOrderID	Int, not null	PK
	SalesOrderHeaderID	Int, not null	FK (on SalesOrderHeaderID in Dim_SalesOrderHeader table)
	DateKey	Int, not null	FK (to DateKey in Dim_DateTime table)
	CustomerID	Int, not null	FK (to CustomerID in Dim_Customer table)
	TerritoryID	Int, not null	FK (to TerritoryID in Dim_SalesTerritory table)

After you build these tables, the final tables and their relations would look pretty much as shown in Figure 1–33.

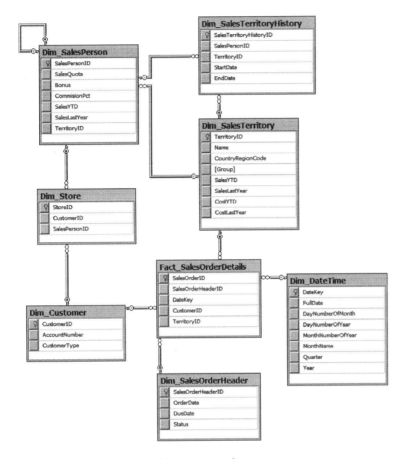

Figure 1–33. Sample OLAP tables in a star schema

Notice the Fact_SalesOrderDetails table (fact table) and how it is connected in the star. And the rest of the tables are connected in the dimension model making up the star schema. There are other supporting tables but we'll ignore for a while since they may or may not contribute to the cube.

■ **Note** Make sure the column data types are in sync or at least while extracting the data and loading, alter the data so it matches the column types.

You may be wondering how we came to the design of the tables.

Rule #1 when you create a schema targeting a cube is to identify what you would like to accomplish. In our case, we would like to know about how Sales did with stores, territory, and customers, and across various date and time factors (recollect the cube in Figure 1–6). Based on this, we identify the dimensions as Store, Territory, Date/Time, Customer, Sales Order Header. Each of these dimensions will join to the Facts Table containing sales order details as facts.

As with the SSIS example we did earlier (importing data from a database and exporting to a flat file), we can now directly move the information into these newly generated tables instead of exporting them to the flat files.

One very important and useful data flow transformation is the Script Component, which you can use to programmatically read the tables and columns values from the ADO NET Source (under AdventureWorks database) and write to the appropriate destination tables (under AdventureWorksDW database), using a script. While you do the extraction from the source, you have full control over the data and thus can filter the data, clean it up, and finally load the it into the destination tables, making it a full ETL process. You simply drag and drop the Script Component from the Data Flow Transformations into the Data Flow, as shown in Figure 1–34.

Figure 1–34. Using the SSIS Script Component

■ **Note** For more information on using the Script Component to create a destination, see the references at msdn.microsoft.com/en-us/library/ms137640.aspx and msdn.microsoft.com/en-us/library/ms135939.aspx.

■ **Tip** Many other operations, including FTP, e-mail, and connecting web services can be accomplished using SSIS. Another good real-time example of when you could use SSIS is when you need to import a text file generated from another system or to import data into a different system. You can run these imports based on schedules.

Now that we've create the tables and transformed the data, let's see how to group these tables in a cube, create dimensions, run an MDX query, and then see for the results.

Creating Cubes Using SSAS

Microsoft SQL Server Analysis Services (SSAS) is a powerful tool that lets us create and process cubes. Let's now look at how cubes are designed, what the prerequisites are, and how cubes are created, processed, and queried using the MDX query language.

▨ **Note** SQL Server 2008 R2 comes with a lot new features. Visit `msdn.microsoft.com/en-us/library/bb522628.aspx` for more information.

SSAS is used to build end-to-end analysis solutions for enterprise data. Because of its high performance and scalability, SSAS is widely used across organizations to scale their data cubes and tame their data warehouse models. Its simplicity and rich tools give developers the power to perform various drill-down options over the data.

Let's take care of the easy part first. One way to get started with cubes is by using the samples provided with the AdventureWorks database. BIDS sample projects are located at `C:\program files\microsoft sql server\100\tools\samples\AdventureWorks 2008 Analysis Services Project\`. You should have two projects for both the Enterprise and Standard versions.

1. Open one of the folders based on your server license, then open the AdventureWorks.sln file using BIDS.

2. Check the Project properties and make sure to set the Deployment Target Server and Database properties.

3. Build and deploy the solution.

This project contains lots of other resources, including data sources, views, cubes and dimensions. However, these provide information relating to the layout, structure, properties, and so forth of BIDS, and little information about cube structures, and the like.

Once the project is deployed successfully (with no errors), open SSMS. You'll find the cubes from the previous deployment available for access via MDX queries. Later in this chapter you'll learn how to create a simple cube. For now, we'll use the available AdventureWorks cubes.

Executing an Analysis Services MDX query from SSMS involves few steps, as follows:

1. Run SQL Server Management Studio and connect to the Analysis Services… instance on your server by choosing Analysis Services under Server type.

2. Click on the New Query button, which launches the MDX Query Editor window.

3. In the MDX Query Editor window, from the Cube drop-down, select one of the available cubes from the Analysis Services database you're connected to, "AdventureWorks" in this case.

4. Under the Metadata tab, you can view the various measures and dimensions available for the cube you selected.

5. Alternatively, you can click on the Analysis Services MDX Query icon at the top to open the query window.

6. Writing an MDX query is similar to writing a T-SQL query. However, instead of querying from tables, MDX queries from a cube's measures and dimensions.

7. Enter your MDX query in the query window and execute to view the output, as shown in Figure 1–35.

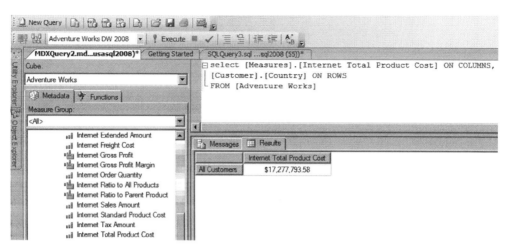

Figure 1–35. Executing a simple MDX query

Ok, so far you've seen the basic cube (using one from the AdventureWorks database) and also how to query from the cube using a simple MDX query. Let's now begin a simple exercise to build a cube from scratch.

Using data from the Sales Repository example we looked at earlier, let's configure a cube now using the Dimension and Fact tables you created manually with the AdventureWorksDW database.

1. Once you have the data from SSIS in the designated tables (structured earlier in this chapter), you can create a new project under SSAS.

2. Open BIDS and create a New Project by selecting Analysis Services Project.

3. Provide a valid project name, such as AW Sales Data Project, a Location, and a Solution Name. Click OK.

4. A basic project structure is created from the template, as you can see in Figure 1–36.

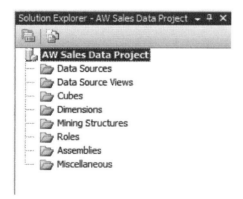

Figure 1–36. The basic AW Sales Data Project in Solution Explorer

5. Create a new data source by right-clicking on Data Sources and selecting New Data Source; this opens the New Data Source Wizard.

6. Click the New button and choose the various Connection Manager options to create the new Data Connection using the database AdventureWorksDW.

7. Click Next and choose "Use the service account" for the Impersonation option. You can also choose other options based on how your SQL Server is configured.

8. Click Next and provide a valid Data Source Name (AW Sales Data DW in our case) and click Finish, as shown in Figure 1–37.

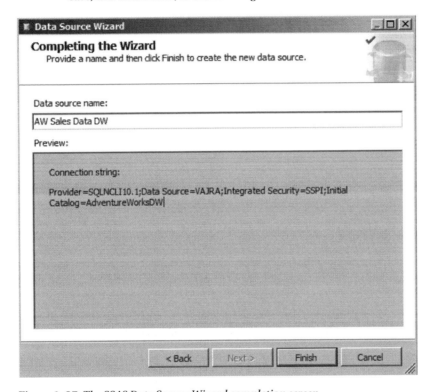

Figure 1–37. The SSAS Data Source Wizard completion screen

9. The next step is to create the data source views, which are important because they provide the necessary tables to create the dimensions. Moreover, a view is the disconnected mode of the database and hence won't have any impact on performance.

10. Right-click on Data Source Views and choose New Data Source View, which brings up the Data Source View Wizard.

11. Select an available data source. You should see the AW Sales Data DW source you just created.

12. Click Next and choose the available tables from the Select Tables and Views window (see Figure 1–38). Select the dimension and fact tables we created earlier and click Next.

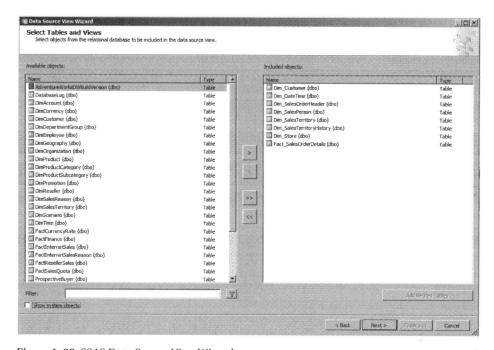

Figure 1–38. SSAS Data Source View Wizard

13. To save the data source view, provide a valid name (AW Sales Data View) and click Finish.

14. Notice that Design View now provides a database diagram showing all the tables selected and the relations between each of them.

15. Now you can create either a dimension or a cube, but it's always preferable to create dimensions first and then the cube, since the cube needs the dimensions to be ready. Right-click on Dimensions and choose New Dimension, which brings up the Dimension Wizard.

16. Click Next. On the Select Creation Method screen, choose "Use an existing table" to create the dimension source, then click Next.

17. On the next screen, choose the available Data source view. For the Main table, select Dim_DateTime and then click Next.

18. The next screen displays the available attributes and types (see Figure 1–39). Notice the attribute types that are labelled "Regular." By default, only the primary keys of the tables are selected in the attributes for each dimension. You need to manually select the other attributes. This step is important since these are the values you query in MDX along with the available measures.

19. Choose the attributes Month Name, Quarter, and Year in our sample and change the attribute types to Month, Quarter, and Year, respectively, as shown in Figure 1–39. Click Next.

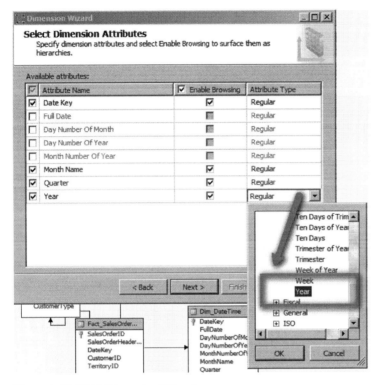

Figure 1–39. SSAS Dimension Wizard

20. Provide a logical name for the dimension (Dim_Date in our case) and click on Finish. This creates the Dim_Date.dim dimension in the Dimensions folder in your project.

21. In Solutions Explorer, right-click on the Cubes folder and choose New Cube to bring up the Cube Wizard welcome screen. Click Next.

22. On the Select Creation Method screen, choose "Use existing tables" and then click Next.

23. From the available Measure group tables, select the fact table or click the Suggest button (see Figure 1–40.

Figure 1–40. Measure group table selection in the Cube Wizard

24. If you choose Suggest, the wizard will select the available measure group tables. You can choose your own Measure Group tables in the other case. Click Next to continue.

25. The Select Measures screen displays the available measures, from which you can either select all or just what you need. Leave the default to select all and click Next to continue.

26. Now you can choose to Select Existing Dimensions from any available. For now, you can leave the default—the existing dimension. Click Next to continue.

27. The Select New Dimensions screen gives us the option to choose new dimensions that the wizard identifies from the data source selected. If you have already chosen a dimension in the previous step, ignore that dimension or just click Next to continue. If you have previously created a dimension and also selected the same one that's listed here, the wizard would create another dimension with a different name. Click Next.

28. Provide a valid cube name, AW Sales Data View, as shown in Figure 1–41. Notice that Preview displays all the measures and dimensions chosen for this cube. Click Finish to complete the step.

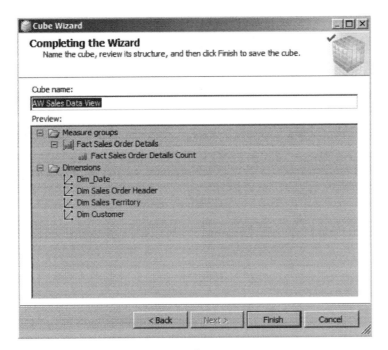

Figure 1–41. The Cube Wizard completion page

29. The cube structure will now be displayed in the form of star, with the fact table in the center (yellow header) and the dimensions around it (blue header), as shown in Figure 1–42.

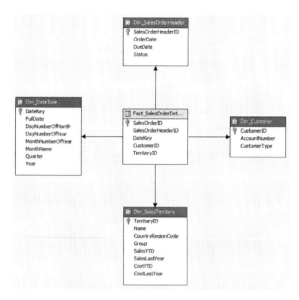

Figure 1–42. *The structure of the AW Sales Data View cube*

30. In the Dimensions window (usually found in the bottom left corner), expand each of the dimensions and notice that the attributes are just the primary key columns of the table (see Figure 1–43). You need all the attributes or at least the important columns you wish to run analysis on.

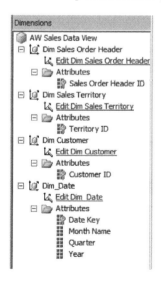

Figure 1–43. *SSAS project dimension settings*

31. From the Dimensions folder in Solution Explorer, double-click each of the dimensions to open the Dimension Structure window (Figure 1–44).

32. Choose the Dimension columns from the Data Source View pane and drop them on the Attributes pane as shown in Figure 1–44.

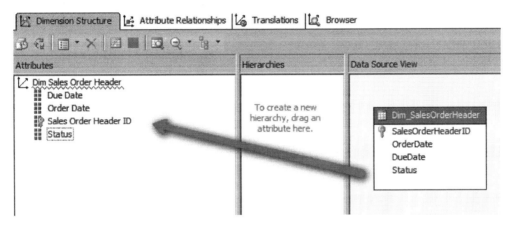

Figure 1–44. The Dimension Structure screen showing Attributes, Hierarchies, and Data Dource View

33. Repeat the same steps for the rest of the dimensions and click Save All. Refresh the window and notice that all columns now appear under attributes and have been added to the Dimensions.

34. To add hierarchies, drag and drop the attribute(s) from the Attributes pane to the Hierarchies pane. Repeat the step for all of the dimensions. When you're done, go back to the Cube Structure window.

35. On the left hand in the Measures pane, you now have only one measure—Fact Sales Order Details Count. To create more measures, simply right-click on the Measures window and choose New Measure.

36. From the New Measure dialog box, select the option "Show all columns".

37. For the Usage option, select Sum as the aggregation function. Then choose Dim_SalesTerritory as the Source Table and SalesYTD as Source Column, and click OK. What this does is provide a new measure, Sales YTD, by summing the values from a given territory against the available dimensions.

38. All is well at this time. Our final window looks something like what's shown in Figure 1–45.

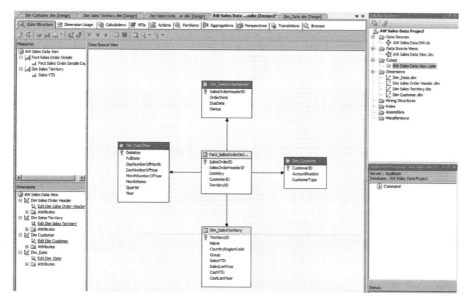

Figure 1–45. The AW Sales Data Project sample

39. Now right-click on the project properties and check the deployment options. Leaving the options as is would deploy the project to the local SQL Server. Right-click again on the project properties and select Deploy.

40. This step builds and deploys the project to the target server. You can view the deployment status and output in the deployment progress window.

41. If the deployment is successful, you'll see a "Deployment Completed Successfully" message at the bottom of the progress window, as shown in Figure 1–46.

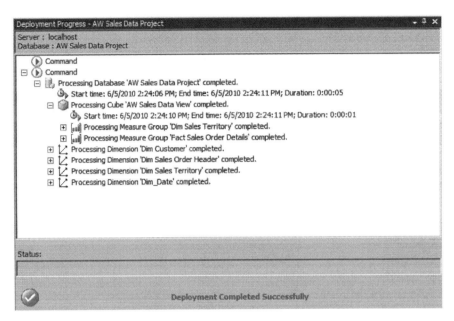

Figure 1–46. The Deployment Progress window

42. Let's now switch applications and open SSMS.

43. On the Connect to Server dialog box (Figure 1–47), choose Analysis Services as the Server type, provide a Server name and credentials if applicable, and click on Connect.

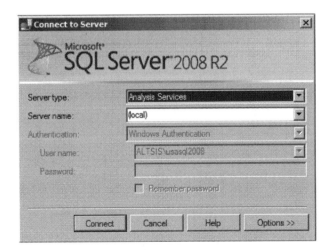

Figure 1–47. Connecting to SQL Server Analysis Services

44. Object Explorer displays the available databases. You'll find the AW Sales Data Project you created earlier in BIDS and deployed locally. Expand the options and notice various entities available under the Data Sources, Data Source Views, Cubes and Dimensions (see Figure 1–48).

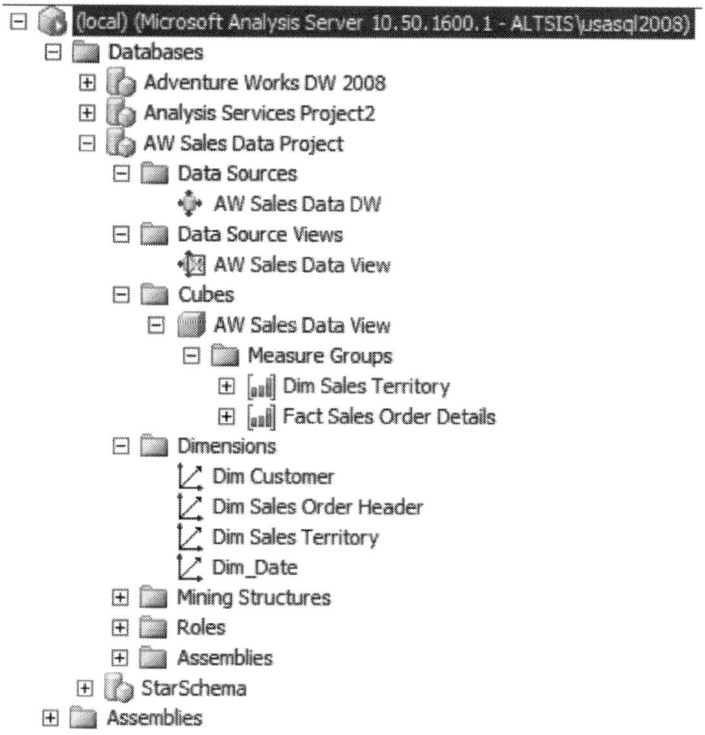

- (local) (Microsoft Analysis Server 10.50.1600.1 - ALTSIS\usasql2008)
  - Databases
    - Adventure Works DW 2008
    - Analysis Services Project2
    - AW Sales Data Project
      - Data Sources
        - AW Sales Data DW
      - Data Source Views
        - AW Sales Data View
      - Cubes
        - AW Sales Data View
          - Measure Groups
            - Dim Sales Territory
            - Fact Sales Order Details
      - Dimensions
        - Dim Customer
        - Dim Sales Order Header
        - Dim Sales Territory
        - Dim_Date
      - Mining Structures
      - Roles
      - Assemblies
    - StarSchema
  - Assemblies

Figure 1–48. BIDS Databases

45. Click on the MDX Query icon on the toolbar to open the query window and the cube window. Make sure the appropriate data source is selected at the top.

46. The cube will display the available Measures and Dimensions, as shown in Figure 1–49.

47. In the query window, type the MDX query to retrieve the values from the cube. In our case, to get the Sum of Sales YTD in the Sales Territory Measure, the query should look like the one in Figure 1–49.

48. Execute and parse the query to view the output in the results window.

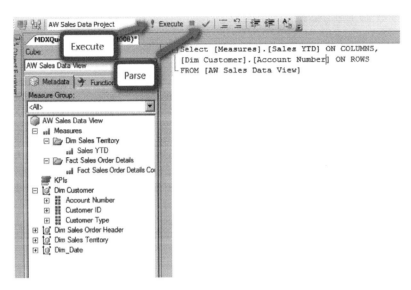

Figure 1–49. Running a simple MDX query

Final Pointers for Migrating OLTP Data to OLAP

Now that you know the concepts, let's see some of the important factors to keep in mind while planning for a migration. First, you need to be completely aware of why you need to migrate to an OLAP database from an OLTP database. If you are not clear, it's a good idea to go back to the section "Why do I need to migrate to OLAP?" and make a checklist (review as well the need for a staging section).

- Make sure that there is no mismatch in column names on both ends. Well, this is not a requirement. Most of the time, you don't have same columns. In such cases, maintain metadata for the mapping. ETL tools (in this case SSIS) support different column names.

- While mapping columns between source and destination, there is a good possibility that the data types of the columns might not match. You need to ensure type conversion is taken care during transformation.

- With OLAP, the idea is to restrict the number of columns and tables and denormalize as much as possible. So, it's a good idea to remove unwanted columns.

- You already know that data can be migrated from different data sources—such as databases, flat files, XML, Excel, and so forth—to a single OLAP system of your choice. OLAP tools provide the necessary framework to accomplish this.

- Migrating data from OLTP system to OLAP is as good as copying and pasting your enterprise database. Clean up the data either during staging or during the transformation process to avoid unwanted data.

- What you have in many tables in your OLTP database might be aggregated into a single table or even one column.

- Move to more sophisticated and structured cubes. Review decision support systems and data mining systems and choose your model accordingly.

- Use the features of ETL tools efficiently for migration.

SQL Server 2008 R2 Parallel Data Warehouse

We won't actually be using SQL Server 2008 R2 Parallel Data Warehouse in our explorations here, but it's worth mentioning as it can provide a robust foundation for business intelligence.

What is the new parallel data warehouse from SQL Server 2008 R2? It's a combination of hardware and software that uses a massively parallel architecture and industry-standard hardware to enormously increase performance and scalability when analyzing data. And it's not just for SQL Server databases but also extends the power for Oracle databases and others. Key features and capabilities include:

- Scalability supporting hundreds of terabytes of data

- Low cost

- Tight integration with existing SQL Server 2008 data warehouses using hub-and-spoke architecture

- High performance

- ROI improvements using SQL Server BI Tools.

However, as noted above, it's a software/hardware combination that requires SQL Server 2008 R2 to run on specific hardware to provide the advantages and capabilities. Business need to have the OEM hardware/software packages (provided by Bull, Dell, EMC, HP, and IBM) to get the optimized scalability and performance. For more details on SQL Parallel Data warehouse, please visit microsoft.com/sqlserver/2008/en/us/parallel-data-warehouse.aspx

SharePoint and Business Intelligence

What do you have so far?

Microsoft Office SharePoint Server (MOSS) 2007 has decent capabilities relating to BI integration. Major components include Excel Services, Reporting Services and Dashboards.

- SSIS components can extract information from various data sources, and load it into Excel and it can be published back into SharePoint. This enables possibilities for seamless end-to-end integration and collaboration using the portals.

- Business applications use powerful out of the box web parts that can display their KPIs.

- The BDC (Business Data Catalog) provides a mechanism for integrating external data sources into the system.

> ■ **Note** By now you have some familiarity with business intelligence and some of the components of OLAP. For more information, please visit `microsoft.com/casestudies/`.

What's New in SharePoint 2010?

SharePoint 2010 adds significantly more BI functionality. In the next chapters we will cover each of SharePoint 2010's BI components in depth. Here's a preview.

Secure Store Service

Remember the single sign-on (SSO) functionality in MOSS 2007? SharePoint 2010 introduces Secure Store Service (SSS) as its next-generation SSO. This claims-aware (that is, using claims-based authentication) service is part of the Foundation Server and it enables mechanisms by which you store credentials for each application by ID, and reuse the credentials to gain access to external data sources. Visio Services, PerformancePoint Services, and Excel services work in conjunction with Secure Store Services. We will examine SSS in Chapter 2.

> ■ **Note** For more information on Secure Store Service, please see Chapter 12 of *Building Solutions with SharePoint 2010* by Sahil Malik (Apress, 2010).

Visio Services

What if Visio diagrams came alive? Can they be powered by data in real time? The answer is yes! Visio Services is now available as part of SharePoint 2010 Enterprise edition, allowing you to connect real-time data and update your Visio diagrams on the fly. Share and view published Visio diagrams using the Visio Web Access Web Part, which provides the functionality to integrate Visio diagrams into the SharePoint platform. With a basic knowledge of JavaScript and the client object model, you can create compelling, rich, interactive UIs. Learn more about Visio Services in Chapter 2.

Reporting Services and Report Builder

A lot of new functionality has been added to Reporting Services in SharePoint 2010. New features include support for claims-based authentication and user tokens, deployment utilities, support for multiple languages, and connectivity with list and document libraries.

Because report-authoring tools are an integral part of SQL Server Tools, they are integrated in SharePoint so that generating and customizing reports has been easy in a SharePoint Server (as well as MOSS 2007) environment.

Out-of-the-box Reporting Services web parts take care of other needs by providing a platform to load reports designed using Report Builder. Learn more about Reporting Services in Chapter 3.

PerformancePoint Services

With SharePoint 2010, PerformancePoint Services is now available as an integrated part of the SharePoint Server Enterprise license. You can now consume context-driven data, build dashboards with the help of the built-in Dashboard Designer, and take advantage of KPIs, and scorecards. Data from various sources can be integrated using SSIS, loaded using SSAS, and finally published into SharePoint. Support for SharePoint lists and Excel Services are additional benefits. The RIA-enabled Decomposition Tree is a powerful new visualization report type that lets you drill down into to multidimensional data. Learn more about PerformancePoint Services in Chapter 4.

Excel and Power Pivot

Excel Services is also available now as part of SharePoint Server Enterprise licensing, and now support multiple data sources aggregation in a single Excel workbook. Excel Services allows these workbooks to be accessed as read-only parameterized reports via the thin web client. You can choose to expose the entire workbook or only portions of the workbook, such as a specific chart or a specific pivot table. Content in Excel can be accessed though various methods, such as REST services, Web Services, publishing to the SharePoint environment, and using JavaScript.

With the addition of PowerPivot to Excel 2010 and its in-memory data store capabilities, it's now possible to connect to the OLAP data sources that give users the flexibility to analyze their data. Learn more about Excel Services and PowerPivot in Chapter 5.

Business Connectivity Services

Business Connectivity Services (BCS) is a part of SharePoint 2010 Composites, prebuilt components you can use to create custom business solutions. BCS is the next version of Moss's well-known Business Data Catalog. BCS is now bi-directional (in that it can both display business data and, with appropriate permissions, update it), and it is much easier now to connect with various other systems. Tools such as SharePoint Designer and Visual Studio provide the functionality that lets you connect with external data sources such as SQL Server, WCF services, and .NET connector assemblies. Visual Studio and custom code make it possible to address almost any problem. While Business Data Connectivity services, External Data columns and External lists are available in the Foundation Server, data search, profile pages, and Secure Store belong to Standard version, and the rest of the external data Web Parts, and Office Client Integration reside under Enterprise Client Access License (CAL). Learn more about BCS in Chapter 6.

Summary

This chapter introduced you to

- Why you need business intelligence.
- The various elements of BI, as shown in Figure 1–50.
- Data warehouse components, OLAP, and cubes.
- Querying from OLAP using MDX.
- Understanding SQL Server tools for BI, including SSIS and SSAS.
- SharePoint 2010 BI components.

Figure 1–50. *Business intelligence components*

■ **Note** By now you have some familiarity with business intelligence and some of the components of OLAP. For more information on busines intelligence, please visit `http://www.microsoft.com/casestudies/`

What's Next?

In the next chapter you'll learn about Visio Services in SharePoint 2010. You will also find out about and implement Secure Store Services, which is an essential platform for other BI services in SharePoint 2010.

CHAPTER 2

■ ■ ■

Visio Services

You've probably heard that a picture is worth 1,000 words, and also that actions speak louder than words. If you put those two axioms together, you get the idea of Visio. It is often far easier to understand and simpler to explain a concept, a theory, or even a story by presenting actions visually in blocks and diagrams rather than words. Visio is a very powerful vector graphic tool you can use for exactly that.

Introduction

Let me walk you through a small story called "My day begins with…". I *wake up* early in the morning, get ready, and *start* from home at about 7:15AM. On my way *driving* to office, I stop by the nearest coffee shop to pick up my morning beverage. I choose hot chocolate and head for the office—yet another *decision* to make, whether or not take the freeway. I quickly look over my shoulder and as there's not a lot of traffic, I choose to drive on local streets. At 8:45AM, I *arrive* at the office.

Notice the *italicized* words in my little story. It's all about initiation, actions, decisions, and concluding. Well, of course these four elements and maybe few others are required to run our lives and, in fact, any job too. Simply put, if I want to tell my story in the form of diagram or a flow chart, it becomes a sort of storyboard—a logical sequence of boxes connected together, as shown in Figure 2–1.

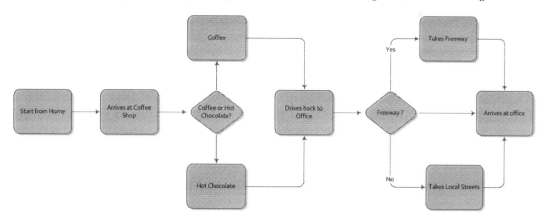

Figure 2–1. *"My day begins with…" storyboard*

This chapter introduces you to Visio Services and discusses using Visio with SharePoint 2010. If you're familiar with Visio 2007, a few concepts might be redundant. You might want to either skip them or parse them quickly.

What Will You Learn?

By the end of the chapter, you'll learn about:

- The essentials of Visio Services.

- Setting up Visio Services on SharePoint 2010.

- Publishing a basic Visio diagram to SharePoint.

- Connecting Visio diagram to

  - A SharePoint List.

  - SQL Server with and without Secure Store Services.

  - Data using a custom data provider (using Visual Studio and WCF).

  - Workflows and Visio with SharePoint Designer 2010.

- Management of Visio Services using Central Administration (CA).

- Management of Visio Services using Windows PowerShell.

To be able to use this book successfully, you'll need the following software:

- SharePoint Server 2010 Enterprise Edition

- SQL Server 2008 R2 Developer Edition x64 / SQL Server 2008 x64

- Visio 2010 x64

- SharePoint Designer 2010 x64, available for download at
  www.microsoft.com/downloads/en/details.aspx?FamilyID=566D3F55-77A5-4298-
  BB9C-F55F096B125D

- Visual Studio 2010 Professional Edition, trial version available for download at
  www.microsoft.com/visualstudio/en-us/products/2010-editions/professional

- If you'd prefer using the Express editions of Visual Studio and SQL Server, you can
  download them from www.microsoft.com/express/

Why Visio?

With Visio you can create a wide range of diagrams easily with the help of inbuilt shapes, stencils, and templates. The diagram scope can encompass the simple, like my storyboard, or the complex, like the network representation of an entire organizational infrastructure. It can target various audiences, from business analyst to a developer to a solutions architect. A construction engineer or an interior designer can create a floor plan. An electrical engineer can create a basic electrical circuit or a logic diagram. There are endless possibilities using Visio; you just need to focus your imagination on the available templates to create your own diagrams.

Now, what if your Visio diagrams could come to life? What if you could power these diagrams with data and share them with your colleagues?

Let me give you a real-time example. As an architect in the organization where I work, I'm often asked to give introductory sessions to many people on the project team, and I typically use a Visio diagram to explain the project details. Whenever there are enhancements, updates, or changes to the project, I have to redo my Visio diagram and present it to the team.

Instead of calling for another meeting, I could update and e-mail a new version of the Visio diagram and get final approval. But not everyone has Visio installed. Moreover, where does this information end up? E-mails! Or maybe in yet another set of printed documents that will just collect dust on the shelf. What's missing here?

1. Collaboration.

2. Easy viewing. For a Visio diagram you need either the Visio client and related licenses, or at least a Visio viewer (there's a free viewer available at www.microsoft.com/downloads/details.aspx?FamilyID=f9ed50b0-c7df-4fb8-89f8-db2932e624f7&displaylang=en).

3. Instant update of the diagrams.

4. Data connectivity

You've all probably thought at some point, wouldn't it be great to be able to share a Visio diagram that's connected to data, where the diagram updates automatically when the data changes. And wouldn't it be wonderful to be able to have end users view the diagram in their browsers, without having to install the actual Visio client.

Well, that solution is here. With Visio Services in SharePoint 2010, *you can* publish Visio diagrams to SharePoint, drive them with real-time data, and share them easily even when the client is not installed. All of this by using Visio Services in SharePoint 2010.

Presenting Visio Services

Visio Services is new in the SharePoint 2010 service layer. These services are available as part of the Enterprise Client Access License (CAL) and they provide a platform where users can share the Visio diagrams using the SharePoint infrastructure. Visio Services provide various data connectivity models to drive Visio diagrams with data, both real-time and historic.

Setting up Visio Services

Setting up Visio Services is quite simple, requiring just few basic steps. Before beginning, however, ensure you have Farm Administrator privileges.

There are two approaches. In the first, in SharePoint 2010, simply go to *Central Administration* ➤ *Configuration Wizards* and launch the *Farm Configuration wizard* as shown in Figure 2–2.

▓ **Tip** If you are installing SharePoint for the first time, you'll be prompted to run this step toward the end of the installation. If you prefer, you can just skip it for now and run it later.

Figure 2–2. *Launching the Farm Configuration wizard*

Now you are prompted to start the wizard, as Figure 2–3 shows.

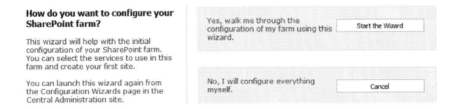

Figure 2–3. *Choosing to configure the farm using the wizard*

To set up the services, you need to have a service account and choose required services from the wizard (Figure 2–4). Be sure you have Visio Graphics Service checked. If this is a fresh installation, this option will be enabled.

Click Next. SharePoint will provision all services selected in this step, and prompts to create a new site collection with the selected services. You cannot choose a service that's already installed since it will be disabled as shown in below figure 2–4.

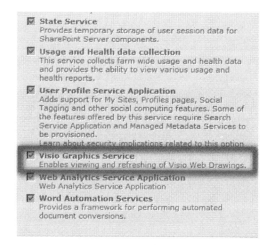

☑ **State Service**
Provides temporary storage of user session data for
SharePoint Server components.

☑ **Usage and Health data collection**
This service collects farm wide usage and health data
and provides the ability to view various usage and
health reports.

☑ **User Profile Service Application**
Adds support for My Sites, Profiles pages, Social
Tagging and other social computing features. Some of
the features offered by this service require Search
Service Application and Managed Metadata Services to
be provisioned.
Learn about security implications related to this option.

☑ **Visio Graphics Service**
Enables viewing and refreshing of Visio Web Drawings.

☑ **Web Analytics Service Application**
Web Analytics Service Application

☑ **Word Automation Services**
Provides a framework for performing automated
document conversions.

Figure 2–4. Select the desired services using the Farm Configuration wizard.

■ **Note** With this default mode and the service application already available to the default web application, you
can now create a site collection using one of the available templates.

This approach is very straightforward. Things get a little more interesting when you haven't set up
the services during installation or if you later upgrade your licensing model. In such situations, you can
set up Visio Services using the following approach.

Go to *Application Management ➤ Service Applications ➤ Manage Service Applications.* Click the
New button on the ribbon and then choose Visio Graphics Service. Provide a valid application name,
and choose or create a new application pool under which this service application will run. As you create
the application pool, you'll have the option to use any already configured service accounts or to register
a new managed account, as shown in Figure 2–5.

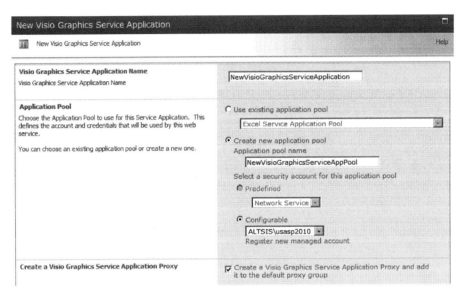

Figure 2–5. *Setting up a new Visio Graphics Service application*

Your new service application will now appear in the list of available service applications and you can configure it, as we'll discuss later in this chapter.

▓ **Note** Once you create the new service application, you have to associate it with a web application. You can associate a new service application with a new web application or existing web application.

To associate a new service application with a web application, on the Central Administration go to *Application Management ➤ Service Applications ➤ Configure service application associations* and select the Web application you want to associate the service with. For the *Configure service application association connections* option, choose Custom. Select the desired custom service application and click on OK.

Let's now look at an example and see how to perform basic operations using Visio and Visio Services in SharePoint 2010.

PROBLEM CASE

Check the status of five major airline carriers at the airport using a Visio diagram that's been published to SharePoint using Visio Services 2010.

Solution

1. Open Visio 2010 and choose *Directional Map Shapes 3D (US Units)* from the available diagrams, and add Airport to the page. Add a few images or shapes, such as Store 1, Tree, and Roof 1 from Directional Map Shapes 3D, and an Airplane from *More Shapes* ➤ *Visio Extras* ➤ *Symbols (US units)* ➤ *Airport* as shown Figure 2–6.

Your diagram doesn't need to look exactly like this. You can design a scene that uses your own images and creativity to try this example.

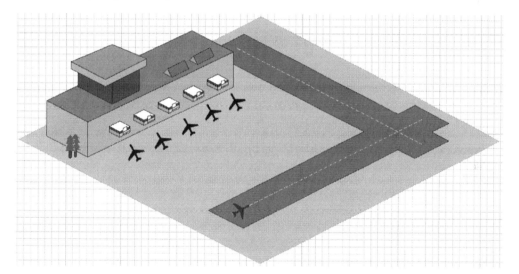

Figure 2–6. Airport stencil with various shapes

2. On the File menu, click on Save and save the drawing to a local file location as a Visio Drawing, airport.vsd in this example.

3. Click on the File menu again, and this time click on Save As and choose the type as a Web Drawing (*.vdw).

▓ **Note** .vdw is the new file format. When published to SharePoint, this is the file that is rendered in the browser. You can edit this file and republish it in the event of any modifications. In contrast, a .vsd file can't be used on the SharePoint platform and can't be rendered.

.vdw files use Extensible Application Markup Language (XAML) to represent diagrams. XAML is primarily meant for creating UI elements using the .NET framework with WPF or Silverlight. For more information on XAML, read the article at `http://msdn.microsoft.com/en-us/library/cc189036(VS.95).aspx`.

To run Visio web diagram (.vwd) files, be sure that the SharePoint Server Enterprise Site Collection Features feature is activated. You'll find this on the Site Collection Features under the Site Collection Administration of your web application.

4. Enter a valid file name and click Save.

5. Close Visio and return to the folder where you saved the <*filename*>.*vdw*

6. Open your SharePoint site and create a new document library from *Site Actions* ➤ *View All Site Content* ➤ *Create*; name it *Visio Library*.

7. Click on Add document and on the upload document window, use the Browse option and choose the .vdw file and click OK.

After the document is successfully uploaded, you'll be returned to the document library, where you'll see a new item—the document you just uploaded.

8. Click on the document *Name* column to open the Visio diagram in full screen mode in the browser, as shown in Figure 2–7.

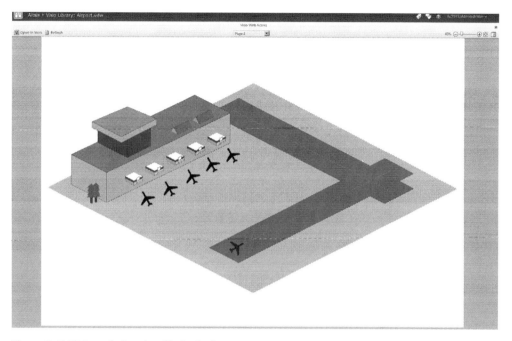

Figure 2–7. *Visio web drawing file in the browser*

As you've seen, it's very easy to create, publish, and view Visio drawings on SharePoint platform. Now let's discuss some of the features and capabilities of Visio Services.

Visio Services Features

- Visio diagrams are compatible with Internet Explorer, Mozilla Firefox, and Apple Safari.

- Diagrams are rendered using Silverlight. If Silverlight is not installed on the client machine, diagrams are rendered as PNG image files.

  - You can connect data to shapes[1] in a diagram from various supported data sources.

  - You can use a variety of data graphics[2] for a given data field, and corresponding shapes based on the conditions and data. Figure 2–8 show the idea at a very high level.

---

[1]Connecting data to shapes is explained in the "Understanding Data Tab in Visio 2010 Client" section.

[2] Data graphics are explained in the "Understanding Data Tab in Visio 2010 Client" section.

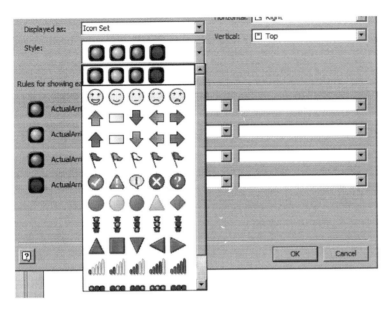

Figure 2–8. Data graphics that can be used on shapes

- You can set hyperlinks on the shapes. You can link to an Internet address or another local Visio diagram, as shown in Figures 2–9 and 2–10.

Figure 2–9. Adding a hyperlink to a shape

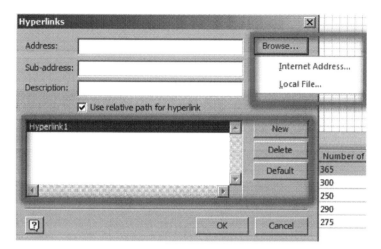

Figure 2–10. Linking a shape to an Internet address or local file

- No client-side installation is required—diagrams are fully loaded in the client browser.

- Real-time data refresh means you can connect your diagrams with real-time data using various data sources, including

  - SQL Server

  - Excel

  - SharePoint Server Lists

  - OLE DB

  - ODBC

  - Custom data providers

▓ **Caution** Note that some data sources, such as SQL Server Analysis Services, are not supported.

- Publish once, use multiple times. You can create the diagrams, connect them to data, and publish them to your SharePoint environment. The diagrams load data from the underlying data sources and you won't have to modify them unless and until the source diagrams change. When the data changes, the shapes will automatically reflect the changes.

- Various authentication models[3] are supported, including

---

[3] Explained in the "Using SQL Server Data Source" section.

- Secure Store Services (SSS)[4]

- Kerberos or Integrated Windows Authentication

- Unattended Authentication

■ **Info** In this chapter, we will discuss how to connect to a SQL Server data source, a SharePoint Server list, and a custom data provider, with examples.

In our first example, you saw how to publish a Visio drawing to SharePoint and view it. That's one of the ways to integrate Visio with SharePoint. There are a number of other methods for loading and interacting with a Visio drawing on SharePoint 2010, including

- Visio Web Access Web Part—Use a Web part that can load a .vdw file.

- JavaScript Mashup API—Communicate with a Visio Web Access Web part and change HTML content as needed *asynchronously*.

- Web Part connections—Connect and communicate with other Web parts on the page.

- SharePoint Designer with Visio—Create diagrams in Visio, import them into SharePoint Designer, and publish them to the SharePoint environment.

We'll discuss these later in this chapter, but first we'll take a look the architecture and building blocks of Visio Services.

Architecture

Figure 2–11 shows the components a Visio Services environment. Visio Services is loaded into and becomes an integral part of SharePoint Server 2010, which runs on Windows Server 2008 in conjunction with IIS, SQL Server, and Windows Identity foundation (formerly known as Geneva Framework). Visio Services can run in both hosted and non-hosted environments.

■ **Note** Hosted environments are platforms provided by external vendors on which you can run your own applications. You may have some access to the physical servers and file system, but it can be rather limited. Still, this can be a very cost-effective solution and may reduce a lot of your operating costs. Non-hosted or in-house environments, on the other hand, are fully controlled by your own organization. These are physical servers commissioned in your own network that you have full access to.

---

[4] Explained in the "Secure Store Services" section.

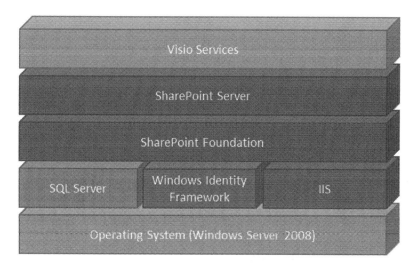

Figure 2–11. *The architecture of a Visio Services 2010 environment*

To understand the architecture, let's take a look at the life cycle of a Visio drawing, as shown in Figure 2–12. A designer or a business analyst retrieves data from one of the supported data sources and creates a Visio diagram. He saves it as a drawing file (.vsd), then uploads or publishes the diagram into the SharePoint Server document library as a web drawing file (.vdw). Visio Services then renders this document by accessing the data source and displaying the output to the end user(s) in either Silverlight or as a PNG file. Note that you don't actually need a data source.

Now here's the interesting part: the designer who creates the diagram may not be a part of the entire life cycle of the diagram. He doesn't need to have any knowledge of SharePoint. He can simply create the designs and provide them to the next level in the hierarchy who can publish them to SharePoint. End users' will access the diagrams through application servers and view them in the browser directly. However, the process of publishing a diagram to Visio Services is simple.

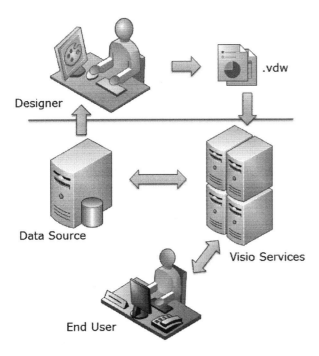

Figure 2–12. *Life cycle of a Visio diagram*

Now let's see how Visio lets you bind your web drawings to data.

The Visio 2010 Client's Data Tab

To bind data to a data source in the Visio 2010 client, you use the options accessed by clicking on the Data tab of the ribbon (Figure 2–13). To enable all the buttons that belong to this tab, you should have at least one diagram open. Let's understand what each button does.

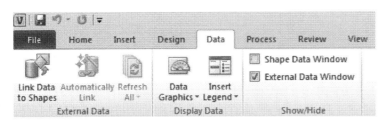

Figure 2–13. *Data tab in Vision 2010*

Link Data to Shapes

Link Data to Shapes is one of the ways you can connect a data source to a shape. You get a simple Data Selector wizard that connects to various supported data sources, as shown in Figure 2–14. You can create more than one data source using this option and use them to connect data to the shapes.

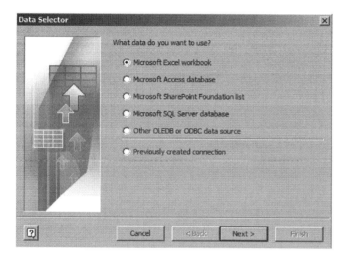

Figure 2–14. *The Data Selector window*

▓ **Note** Another way to create a data source is by using VBA code, as you'll see when we look at designing a custom data provider.

Data Graphics

Data Graphics is the mechanism that lets you can connect data to the shape and customize the appearance of the shape. It allows you to add visual information about the data to the shape on the Visio diagram. You can build your own data graphic, assign it to any data field and display the corresponding value in one of these forms: *Text, Data Bar, Icon Set, or Color by Value*. Data fields are the columns that belong to a list or data table available through the data source you selected.

Data Graphics define additional design structures for the shape, and you can create more than one. Once you set your own custom data graphics, they can be used on any other shapes on the Visio diagram using the *Automatically Link* button.

Data Graphics get data from the data source specified in *Link Data to Shapes* or *Shape Data Window*[5]. When you link to the data source, the data graphics display real-time or historical information based on the customizations you've set on the Visio Graphics Services in the Central Administration.

---

[5] Explained in the "Shape Data Window" section.

71

Here's how to create new Data Graphics:

1. Click on the Data Graphics icon on the Data tab. This pops up a settings window as shown in Figure 2–15.

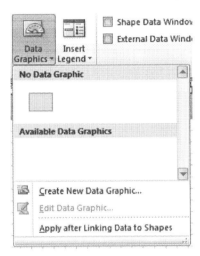

Figure 2–15. Creating a new Data Graphic

2. Click Create New Data Graphic… to open a New Data Graphic window.

3. Click New Item and a new window opens that with settings for display and position as shown in Figure 2–16.

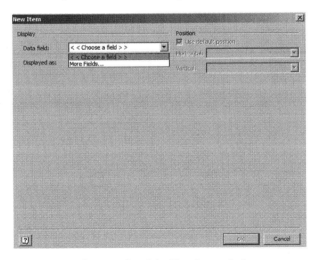

Figure 2–16. The Data Graphics New Item window

4. In the display section, the *Data field* drop-down consists of the available fields from the connected data source. When there's no data source, few fields are displayed. If you need a data field and don't have a data source, you can define a custom shape data label that can be used as a data field in this context.

5. To create a custom shape data label, right-click on the shape on your diagram and, from the Data menu, select *Define Shape Data…*. In the window that opens, enter the Label as "Text" (or your own custom label); select the Type as String (or whatever data type you need); set the Value to a specific data value, and optionally configure other settings if necessary, and click OK.

6. The label will now appear in the *Data field* drop-down in the data graphics New Item window.

7. Once you select your new *Data field* label, the *Displayed as* drop-down is enabled and has options for *Text, Data Bar, Icon Set,* and *Color by Value.*

For this example, let's go with the Text option.

1. Choosing Text in the *Displayed as* field displays the *Style* drop-down, with various options.

2. Once you've chosen the style, you can use the Position section to set the style either horizontally or vertically for the shape. For instance, if you want to display the value of the Text within a *Circle callout* and position it horizontally to the *Right* and vertically at the *Bottom* of t*he* shape, the settings would be similar to those in Figure 2–17.

3. In the Details section, you can set the data field metadata values. For instance, @ in the Value Format field represents Text format.

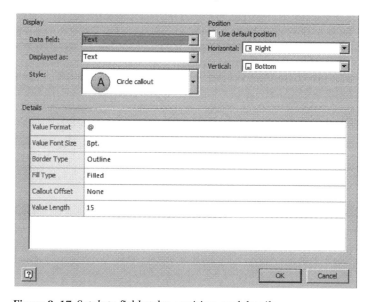

Figure 2–17. Set data field styles, position, and details

4. Clicking OK returns you to the New Data Graphic window.

5. You can edit an existing item by clicking Edit Item, and you can delete an item by clicking the Delete button. Click OK to close the wizard.

6. You can also set the value of the shape using the *Shape Data* Window that's available when you check this option in the Show/Hide section of the Data tab. You can set the Text value and view how the value is displayed for the shape. For instance, to set the *Text value* for the flight shape as "Passenger Airplane," select the shape and on the Shape Data Window, type in *Passenger Airplane*. The text will appear in the bottom right corner of the image as a call out, as per the previous position settings (Figure 2–18).

Passenger Airplane

Figure 2–18. *Adding text to the shape*

▓ **Note** You can obtain this shape from More Shapes ➤ Visio Extras ➤ > Symbols (US units) ➤ Airport.

▓ **Tip** You'll notice the same text label beneath the shape; this is the general text that comes with the shape and it's what would be used as a condition for automatically linking other shapes.

Automatically Link

To use the Data tab's *Automatically Link* functionality, first you need to set a Text value either by double-clicking on the shape or by using the Shape Data Window on all the shapes. Using the Data Graphics option, you can create items based on data fields (as shown in the previous section). First, you will have to create a complete data graphic for at least one shape. After you create the data sources, you can bind a shape to a row of data by simply dragging and dropping the row onto the shape. This process creates a link between the shape text, the data column name (for instance *Title)*, and the column values of the row. This is the final step before linking all the shapes. Click on the Automatically Link button in the External Data section of the Data tab. The wizard lets you decide whether to link *Selected shapes* or *All shapes on this page*, as shown in Figure 2–19.

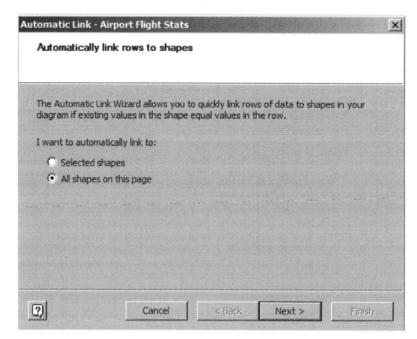

Figure 2–19. Automatically link data to shapes

Choosing one of these options takes you to the next step—mapping the Data Column to the Shape Field, as shown in Figure 2–20. Click Next to reach the Details page, or click Finish to complete the automatic linking. This step links all shapes with the text matching the Data Column name.

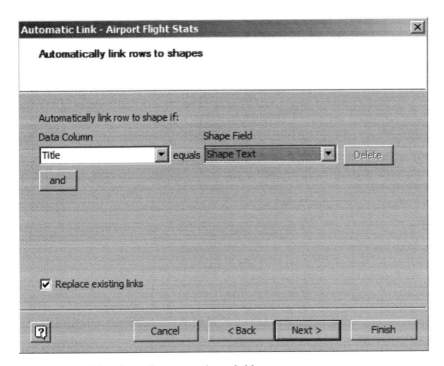

Figure 2-20. Link a data column to a shape field

Refresh All

Once you create the data sources using Link Data to Shapes, you can refresh them either individually or all at once to get the updated data. When you hover on the *Refresh All* button, it opens a context menu as shown in Figure 2–21.

Figure 2-21. Refresh All data window

▓ **Note** Using Refresh All or Refresh Data doesn't affect SharePoint in any way. These options work only with respect to the Visio diagram and the related data source.

You can choose the data source (if one is available) and click on either Refresh or Refresh All to refresh the available data sources as shown in the Figure 2–22. Either action will connect to the data source and retrieve the most recent data. Choosing the data source and clicking on Configure... opens the data source configuration wizard. If no data source was configured earlier, none would be listed in this window.

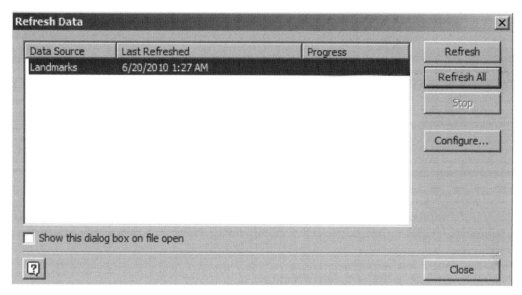

Figure 2 22. Refresh Data window

Insert Legend

Use Insert Legend to display information regarding Data Bar, Icon Set, or Color by Value display options available from the Data Graphics dialog. Legends display information related to the existing page. You can set the legend direction to be either horizontal or vertical. However, legends are not automatically updated. If you modify the diagram, legends need to be manually deleted and inserted once again to reflect the changes.

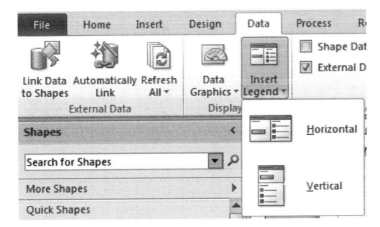

Figure 2–23. *Insert Legend wizard*

Shape Data Window

The *Shape Data Window* is available by checking the appropriate box on the Data tab. It displays data information about the shape, and you can also set the data values for the shape, as shown in the Figure 2–24.

Wood Fence Thickness	5
Wood Post Type	Round
Wood Post Size	5.5 in.
Masonry Fence Thickness	10 in.
Masonry Post Type	Round
Masonry Post Size	18 in.
Stone Fence Thickness	12 in.
Chain Link Fence Thickness	3 in.
Metal Post Type	Round
Metal Post Size	3 in.
Road Thickness	0.0625 in.

Figure 2–24. *Shape Data window*

External Data Window

You can check the External Data Window box on the Data tab to make this window accessible. It displays all the available data sources for a given page of the Visio diagram, and you can create a new data source by clicking on Link Data to Shapes… as shown in Figure 2–25.

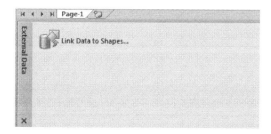

Figure 2–25. External data window

With the help of these options and settings, you can design the Visio diagrams with shapes, connect the shapes to data, and then publish the drawings to a SharePoint environment. In the next section, you'll see how to integrate all that you've learned so far with Visio and Visio Services.

Integrating Visio with SharePoint

So far you saw at a very high level how to integrate Visio diagrams with SharePoint. Now you'll learn this practically, using some examples.

Let's create a Visio diagram using a SharePoint list as a data source and see how to deploy the diagram to the SharePoint platform.

PROBLEM CASE

Take the Airport flight status example and populate information from a SharePoint list to the diagram, then publish the diagram to the SharePoint environment and view it with real-time data.

Solution

1. Open a SharePoint site and create a custom list with the name Airport Flight Stats, with columns as shown in Figure 2–26.

Columns

A column stores information about each item in the list. The following columns are currently available in this list:

Column (click to edit)	Type	Required
Title	Single line of text	✔
Number of flight run	Number	
Number of cancelled flights	Number	
Right time arrivals	Number	
Right time departures	Number	
Arrival delays	Number	
Departure delays	Number	
Missing baggage count	Number	
Number of flights crashed	Number	
Crew strikes	Number	
Created By	Person or Group	
Modified By	Person or Group	

Figure 2–26. Sample custom SharePoint list structure

2. Populate a few rows of data for various airline carriers, as in Figure 2–27.

	Title	Number of flight run	Number of cancelled flights	Right time arrivals	Right time departures	Arrival delays	Departure delays	Missing baggage count
	British Airways	365	12	300	315	65	50	11
	Air France	300	15	270	280	15	5	18
	US Airways	250	0	245	248	5	2	4
	Lufthansa	290	1	285	282	4	8	1
	Air India	275	4	261	270	10	5	5

✦ Add new item

Figure 2–27. Custom list with data used as a data source

3. When you've created the list, open Visio.

4. Open the Airport.vsd file and click on the Link Data to Shapes icon either on the Data tab or from the External Data pane at the bottom of the page (Figure 2–28).

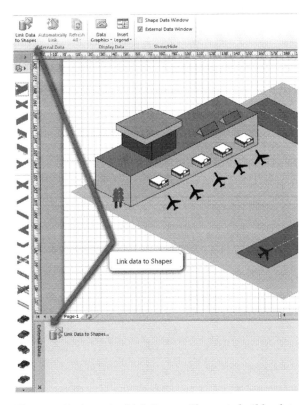

Figure 2–28. Accessing Link Data to Shapes to build a data source

5. From the Data Selector window, choose the Microsoft SharePoint Foundation list option and click Next.

6. Enter the URL for the site where you created the custom list and click Next.

7. Choose Airport Flight Stats from the List box and select the option *Link to a list*. You can also create a View on the custom list and choose *Link to a view of a list*. Click Next to continue.

8. On the final screen, click Finish to complete the Data Selector wizard.

9. If External Data Window is checked on the Data tab, you should now have the External Data window visible at the bottom of the screen with the custom list data loaded, as shown in Figure 2–29. Notice that the list name is added to the External Data Source window at the bottom.

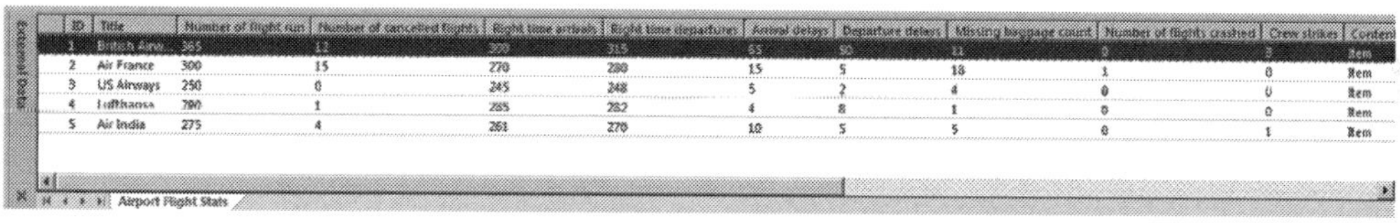

Figure 2–29. External Data window populated with selected data

10. To link data to the shape, simply drag one of the rows to a particular shape on the page. If the data is properly linked, you'll see a link icon in the External Data window next to the row (first column), as shown in Figure 2–30. Alternatively, you can select the shape first and right-click on the row you'd like to bind, then from the context menu choose the option *Link to Selected Shapes*.

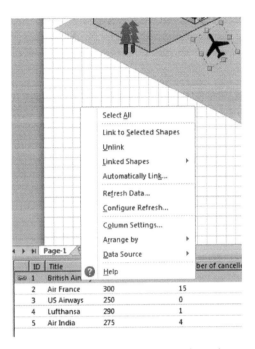

Figure 2–30. Linking data to shapes from the External Data window

11. As you can see, you can also disconnect the row data from the shape using the Unlink option from the context menu.

12. When all the rows are linked, the leftmost columns will display link icons for all the rows.

■ **Caution** If there is any mismatch between the column name and the text on the shapes, the linking will not work. Also, if you add a new row of data, you'll need to create a new shape and link the row data to the that shape.

---

13. Click on Data Graphics and choose the Create New Data Graphic option.

14. Click on New Item and from the Data field choose *Arrival delays*, and from the Displayed as options choose *Icon Set*.

15. From Style, choose the face icons as shown in Figure 2–31.

16. Under the *Rules for showing each icon*, set the conditions and values for each icon as in Figure 2–31.

17. Choose the position as Right for Horizontal and Top for Vertical and click OK.

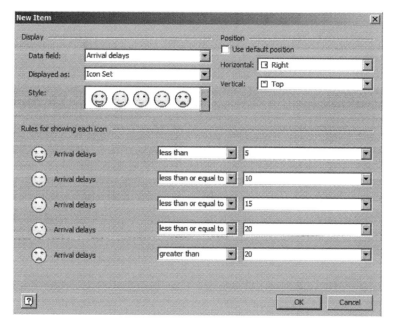

Figure 2–31. *Choosing a style for Arrival delays*

18. Once again from the New Data Graphic window, click on New Item and in the Data field, choose *Missing baggage count*.

19. Under the Displayed as option, choose Data Bar and select Star rating as the Style.

20. In the Details section, set Minimum Value to 18 and Maximum Value to 0 and leave the other options as is, as shown in Figure 2–31. Uncheck *Use default position* and set Horizontal to Center and Vertical to Top and click OK.

▨ **Note** Since the maximum baggage count by any airline carrier in this example is 18, we'll use this for easy comparison.

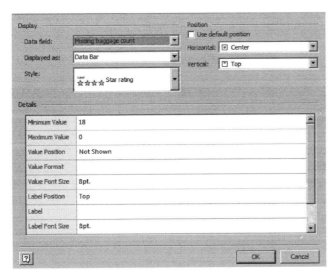

Figure 2–31. Choosing a style for Missing baggage count

21. Return to the New Data Graphic window and notice the two data field settings. If you click either Apply or OK, an alert asks "Do you want to apply this data graphic to the selected shapes? Click Yes to close the prompt.

22. Notice the two icon sets that are displayed for the British Airways flight; with the available data (Figure 2–32), the graphic must display ratings in the center top position and a frown icon in the right top corner.

Figure 2–32. Data graphics set to the shape

23. Select other shapes and link corresponding rows of information to them as described earlier.

■ **Tip** Alternatively, select each of the shapes in the diagram and set the Text property for each. Each Text value should have the same text as in the Title of the data source. For instance, if you want to set the first shape to British Airways, you have to make sure the *text* exactly matches the text in the Title column of the data source.

Use the Automatically Link button on the Data tab, and choose the *All Shapes on this page* option, then click Next. From the *Automatically link rows to shapes* window, choose Title from the Data Column and from the Shape Field select Shape Text. Leave the default option of *Replace existing links* and click Next. View the final summary window and click the Finish button. Data source rows are now automatically linked to shapes.

After performing these steps, you'd see that star ratings and frown icons Styles are set for all the other shapes according to the data, as shown in Figure 2–33.

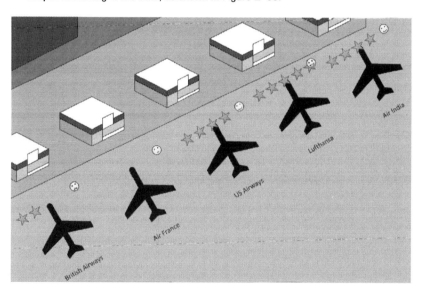

Figure 2–33. Completed Visio diagram with data graphics set

24. Now that your Visio diagram is ready, go ahead and publish it to your SharePoint environment.

25. From the File menu, select *Save & Send*. Choose the *Save to SharePoint* option, select the *Web Drawing File* Type, and click the *Save As* button. Choose the previously saved location, and save the file as Airport.vdw, overwriting the existing file.

■ **Tip** You can decide to not overwrite the file it by choosing another file name, such as Airport_with_data.vdw.

26. Access your SharePoint site and open the Visio Library document library.

27. Click on Add document, then browse and choose the .vdw file and click OK.

28. Click on the .vdw document and notice that the Visio diagram opens in a full browser window with the diagram and shapes connected to the SharePoint list data.

■ **Note** You will see a *Refresh Disabled* warning the first time you open a diagram driven with data. You can either *Enable (this session)* to refresh the current instance, or *Enable (always)* to always refresh the data.

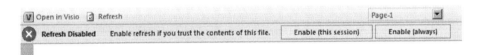

Figure 2–34. Visio drawing Refresh status prompt

26. Return to the Airport Flight Stats custom list and edit the Lufthansa item. Change the *Arrival delays* value to 14 and *Missing baggage count* to 15 and click on Save.

27. Return to the *Visio Library* document library and click on the airport.vdw drawing file. Notice that the Lufthansa flight data graphic styles have changed based on the new values.

■ **Note** In order to get real-time values, you'll want to set the Minimum and Maximum Cache Age Value to zero. You'll find these under Global Settings for Visio Graphics Service on the Central Administration screen (explained later in this chapter).

You've already seen how to view Visio diagrams in the SharePoint environment by clicking on the .vdw file in the document library; this opens the diagram in full-screen mode in the browser. Well, this may not be what you want in every situation. You might want to display diagrams on a page with other web parts or you may be connecting to information with other web parts. For such cases, you can use the *Visio Web Access web part.*

Using the Visio Web Access Web Part

To have this functionality, be sure to activate the *SharePoint Server Enterprise Site Collection Feature* feature. You can access the *Visio Web Access (VWA) web part,* which is available out of the box, under the Business Data Category. To add this web part, click on Edit Page icon.. Click on web part zone and then on the Insert menu under Editing Tools tab on the ribbon. Press the Web Part button, select Office Client Applications, and then Visio Web Access web part. Now click Add to add the Web Access web part to the page. The VWA web part seeks the .vdw file path to display the drawings. Use the *Click here to open the tool pane* link and choose the .vdw file from your Visio Library as shown in Figure 2–35, then click OK.

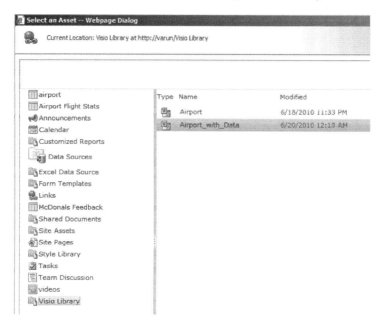

Figure 2–35. *Choosing a Visio drawing file for the Visio Web Access web part*

On the tool pane, leave all the defaults as is and click the OK button at the bottom. The .vdw file is now loaded and you can view the diagram with data as in Figure 2–36.

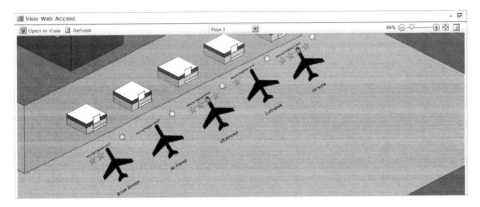

Figure 2–36. Visio web drawing file loaded using Visio Web Access web part

The Visio Web Access web part header includes a number of options:

- *Open in Visio:* opens the file in either Read-Only or Edit mode, assuming you have the Visio client installed on your machine.

- *Refresh:* refreshes the data on the current page of the diagram. You can have more than one page in a diagram.

- *Choose Page:* displays any page from the web drawing.

- *Zoom in/out:* zooms the image from 10-400 percent.

- *Zoom to fit page to view:* fits the diagram to the web part height and width.

- *Shape Information:* displays a Shape Information pane (movable on the diagram) that provides Shape Data and any hyperlinks on the shape.

■ **Note** You can move the image in any direction by clicking and holding the left mouse button. You can use the scroll button on your mouse to zoom the diagram in or out.

Visio Web Access Web Part Connections

Visio Web Access web parts support two-way communications, providing rich interaction with other web parts on the page. They can act as both consumer and provider. Web part connections can be directly configured in the browser.

■ **Tip** After configuring the connections, if you use the view source option of the browser to view the page, you'll notice that these web part connections are built using JavaScript.

There are many scenarios in which these connections can be helpful. You have already seen how to use a VWA web part that can load a .vwd file and connect to a SharePoint list. Let's use the same SharePoint list and try to filter the information and reveal the shape that results from the filter criteria.

1.   Create a new site page (Airport Stats.aspx in this case) and add the VWA web part. Configure it to load the airport_with_data.vwd drawing file or the Airport.vwd file if you haven't saved the file with a different name. Also add the list web part (Airport Flight Stats) as shown in Figure 2–37.

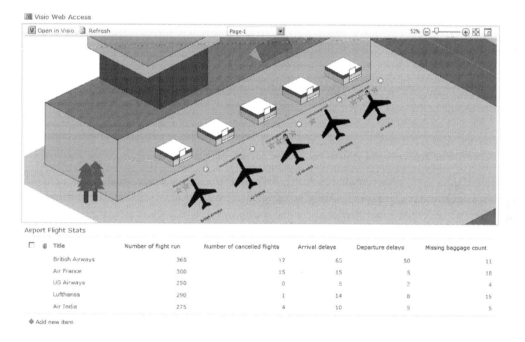

Figure 2–37. Adding the drawing file (using a VWA web part) and custom list to the page

2.   From the VWA web part menu, click on 'Edit Web Part' link. Once again from the VWA web part menu, choose *Connections* ➤ *Get Filter Results From* ➤ *Airport Flight Stats,* as shown in Figure 2–38.

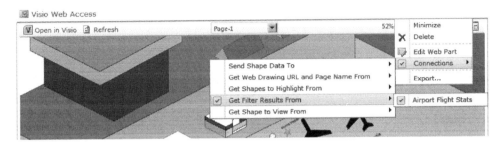

Figure 2–38. *Visio Web Access web part connections*

3. Click on Apply or OK on the editor pane.

4. Now apply the filter on *the Airport Flight Stats* list for the *Number of cancelled flights* column and choose 15.

5. As soon as the filter is applied, notice that the shape with corresponding value is selected, as Figure 2–39 shows.

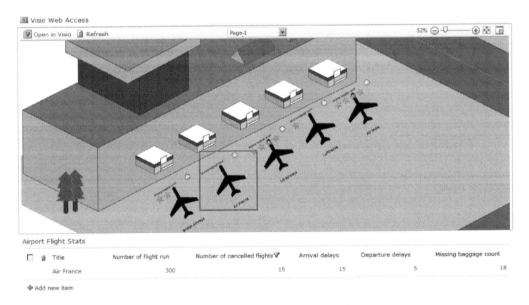

Figure 2–39. *Visio Web Access web part connections with filtered data*

▓ **Tip** You can use web part connections with any list to obtain filtered data results on the drawing, assuming there is information to filter. If there's no filtered information, you will not see any results.

Here are the various connection options:

- *Send Shape Data To (provider):* sends shape data to any other web part on the page.

- *Get Web Drawing URL and Page Name From (consumer):* gets diagram URL from another web part on the page to render.

- *Get Shapes to Highlight From (consumer):* gets shape name from another web part to highlight the corresponding shape.

- *Get Filter Results From (consumer):* gets shape data values from another web part to highlight the shapes based on the values provided.

- *Get Shape to View:* gets and zooms to the shape provided.

▓ **Note** If you need to configure advanced options, you might have to use SharePoint Designer. You can extend and build custom interfaces to address connections to other web parts on the page using the `IWebPartParameters` interface. For more details, visit `msdn.microsoft.com/en-us/library/system.web.ui.webcontrols.webparts.iwebpartparameters.aspx`.

So far you've seen publishing Visio drawings either with data (using a SharePoint list) or without data. Now let's see how to connect using SQL Server as a data source, publish the diagrams to SharePoint, and configure security options.

Using a SQL Server Data Source

Now that you've seen how to establish a data connection with a SharePoint list, let's try to connect a Visio diagram to a SQL Server table. First, of course, you'll need to create a database table and then populate the table with some data.

PROBLEM CASE

Display Washington, D.C. mall monuments with the number of visitors in a year and the landmarks' popularity ratings. Publish this diagram to SharePoint and use Visio Services to display real-time data.

Solution

1. Create a new database named VisioServices.

2. Create a table named "tblLandmarks" in the new database and create the columns shown in Figure 2–40. Populate the columns with data as shown in Figure 2–41.

Figure 2–40. Design a custom SQL table structure

	LandmarkID	Landmark	YearBuilt	Details	Ratings	Visitors
1	1	White House	1792	The White House is the official residence and princip...	5	614000
2	2	Federal Triangle	1900	The Federal Triangle is an area just North of the Nati...	5	412000
3	3	Museum of American History	1964	The National Museum of American History is an ever ...	5	525765
4	4	Gallery of Art	1937	The National Gallery of Art houses a permanent colle...	4	435000
5	5	US Capitol	1793	The US Capitol is the meeting place of the United St...	5	415732
6	6	Washington Monument	1840	The Wahington Monument is one of the many famou...	4	785455
7	7	Museum of Natural History	1910	National Museum of Natural History houses the majori...	4	121548
8	8	Freer Gallery of Art	1923	The Freer Gallery of Art contains art from East Asia, S...	4	154547
9	9	Hirshhorn Museum	1974	The Hishhorn Museum contains over 10,000 paintings	4	245623
10	10	Air and Space Museum	1976	Washington's National Air and Space Museum attrac...	5	554564
11	11	Museum of the American Indian	2004	An exciting new museum that tells the story of the US...	4	440546
12	12	Arts and Industries	1879	The Arts and Industries building is the second oldest ...	3	457524

Figure 2–41. Populating the custom table with sample data

3. Open Visio 2010 and create a new diagram. From More Shapes > Maps and Floor Plans > Map, choose Landmark Shapes (US Units) and add some of the available shapes to the page. Provide Titles for all the shapes either by using the Shape Data window or the shape's label. When you create each label, make sure it matches the values in the *Landmark* column in Figure 2–41.

4. Use *Link Data to Shapes* and choose the Microsoft SQL Server database option, then click Next.

5. In the Data Connection wizard, enter the Server name and the Log-on credentials, either Windows Authentication or User Name and Password. Click Next to continue.

▦ **Note** While communicating with SQL Server through Visio Services, you'll need to configure an additional setting. If you're using SQL Server with Windows Authentication, you'd connect using:

Kerberos/Integrated Windows Authentication. This setting uses the current logged-in user account, which requires Kerberos delegation to authenticate to the database server. For more information on Kerberos, see `http://technet.microsoft.com/en-us/magazine/ee914605.aspx`.

Secure Store Service (SSS). This setting uses either an individual user or group that's mapped for authentication while using an office data connection file (*.ODC). SSS is explained in more detail later in this chapter.

Unattended Service Account. This is a low-privilege Windows account mapped to a target application that is impersonated while connecting to the database. (This is also what you'd use with SQL Authentication.) We will be using this model with SSS while connecting to SQL Server as a data source.

---

6. From the available databases choose VisioServices and select the tblLandmarks table. Click Next to continue.

7. The next step gives you the option to save the data connection file (.odc) as a physical file. Click on Browse to choose where to save the .odc[6] file (or skip this step by clicking on Finish). Provide a friendly name for the file and click Finish to complete the wizard.

---

[6] The .odc file can be repurposed to create a new data source connection from the *Data Selector* window by choosing the option Previously created connection.

▓ **Note** To create a data-refreshable web drawing (.vdw), you have to save the .odc file to the same SharePoint site location as the data connection library.

---

8. Under 'Data Selector' screen, choose the columns and rows to include and click Next to continue. After a successful import message, click on Finish.

9. The External Data window will now load and display the data from the selected database table.

10. Make sure that the text in the *Landmark* column is identical to the *Title* of the shapes. Drag row data from the External Data window to the shape on the page. If the column text is identical to the shape text, the link will be created successfully and you can then create the data graphics for the shape.

11. Create the Data Graphics as explained earlier and choose the *Ratings* data field. Uncheck Use default position and set the custom position for the Data Bar Style as horizontally Center and vertically Above Shape.

12. Add the Visitors data field and choose the Thermometer Data Bar Style. Position it Far Right horizontally and Middle vertically. Click OK to close the data graphics wizard.

13. Use the *Automatically Link all shapes* option to connect all the rows of data to the respective shapes. Choose the data column Landmark to match the shape field Shape Text and click on Finish button.

14. Now use the Insert Legend option to name the page "DC Landmarks."

15. The web drawing should now look like the one in Figure 2–42.

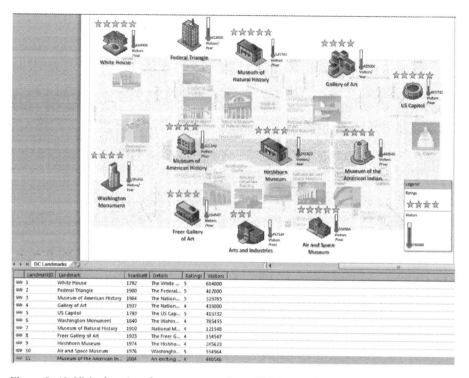

Figure 2–42. Visio drawing shapes connected to a SQL Server database table

▨ **Tip** I created the diagram in Figure 2–42 on a blank stencil using images and shapes from Landmark Shapes (US units).

16. If the data changes and you want to make sure the drawing reflects the updates, choose either of *Refresh All* or *Refresh* Data on the Data tab.

17. Choosing either of these opens the Refresh Data window (Figure 2–43), which displays all data sources related to this diagram. You can refresh one data source or all of them together. To configure a data source, just select it and choose Configure. Close the window when you're finished.

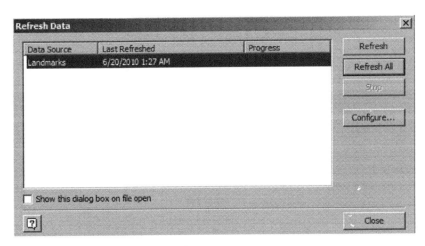

Figure 2–43. The Refresh Data window

18. Now that you finished the diagram, go ahead and publish it to the SharePoint environment. Choose File ➤ Save & Send ➤ Save to SharePoint ➤ Web Drawing ➤ Save As to save the file physically to your disk as Mall.vwd.

19. Open the SharePoint site and upload Mall.vwd to the Visio Library.

20. Click on the Visio drawing you uploaded and view the drawing that is rendered in the browser.

21. If SQL Server is on the same machine, the drawing will render correctly. However, if you are accessing SQL Server from a different machine or if you are on a domain controller, you'll see the error shown in Figure 2–44.

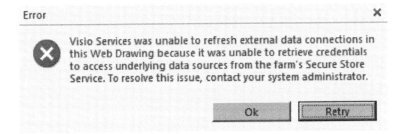

Figure 2–44. Error refreshing the data connection in the Web drawing

If you encounter this error, it's because of a scenario well-known as the *double-hop issue.*

The Double-Hop Issue

Take a look at the error message in Figure 2–44. Basically it means that although you can use impersonated credentials locally, Windows won't forward impersonated credentials to a remote resource (the second hop), so the user's identity is lost even before he reaches the back end. And in this scenario SharePoint can't pass the credentials of the logged-in user all the way to the back end via the services.

What you need is a mechanism by which the logged-in user is impersonated "as someone else" to use Visio services and connect to the back end data. You can achieve this by using the Secure Store Services (SSS) in SharePoint.

Secure Store Services

You can consider Secure Store Services the next generation of the single sign-on service in MOSS 2007. SSS is a credential store that saves account information securely in the database.

You can create and set these credentials on a per application basis associated to an Application Id and use this Application Id for different services that are subject to the double-hop issue. You can consider SSS as a gatekeeper service for authenticating a user (or a group) against an application. You can also set ID for each target application at the farm level.

Configuring Secure Store Services

1. Make sure you are a Farm Administrator and log on to the Central Administration site.

2. Click on Application Management and choose Manage Service Applications from the Service Applications group (Figure 2–45).

Web Applications
Manage web applications | Configure alternate access mappings

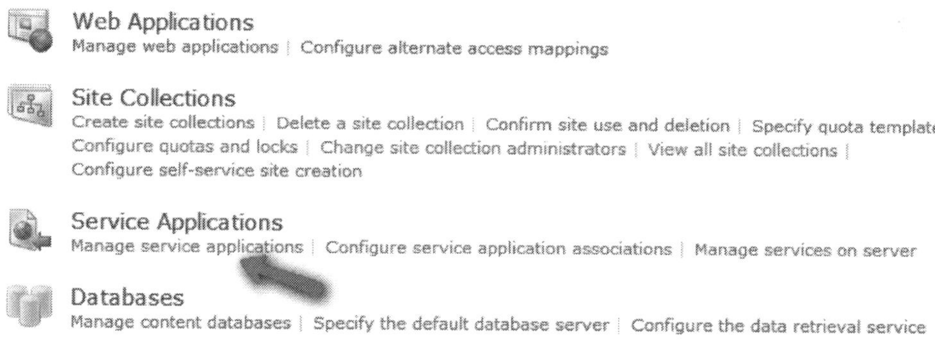

Site Collections
Create site collections | Delete a site collection | Confirm site use and deletion | Specify quota templates |
Configure quotas and locks | Change site collection administrators | View all site collections |
Configure self-service site creation

Service Applications
Manage service applications | Configure service application associations | Manage services on server

Databases
Manage content databases | Specify the default database server | Configure the data retrieval service

Figure 2–45. Choose Manage service applications on the Central Administration site.

3. From the list of available services, click on the Secure Store Service (Figure 2–46).

Figure 2–46. Choose Secure Store Service

On the Secure Store Service page, set the following options:

- *Generate New Key:* Before beginning to create a new target application, you need to generate a new key from a pass phrase (Figure 2–47). This key is used to encrypt and decrypt credentials that are stored in the database. You must have Administrator rights to create a key.

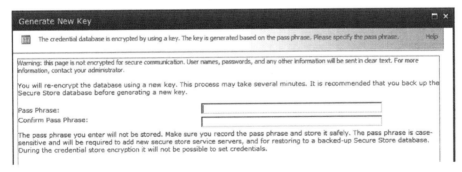

Figure 2–47. The Generate New Key dialog

- *Refresh Key:* To refresh a key (Figure 2–48), you again need Administrator rights, as well as the pass phrase you set when you created the key.

▓ **Note** Refreshing a key will be necessary if you add a new application server to the existing server farm, or if you restore a secure store service database, or if you receive errors such as "Unable to get master key."

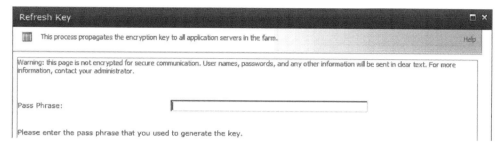

Figure 2–48. Enter the pass phrase to refresh a key.

▓ **Caution** Secure Store Services has its own database. Whenever you create a new key or refresh an existing key, be sure to back up the database.

---

4. After you have successfully created the new key, click the New button under Manage Target Applications on the Edit tab of the ribbon and provide the following information in the Target Application Settings window.

    •   *Target Application ID:* A unique identifier that will be used in service applications as the unattended service account reference for authentication. You can't change the Target Application ID once created.

    •   *Display Name:* A name used for display purpose only.

    •   *Contact E-mail:* The primary e-mail for this Application ID.

    •   *Target Application Type:* Specify Individual for individual users and Group for group credentials.

    •   *Target Application Page URL:* Selecting *Use default page* will use the sign-up page *http://yoursite/_layouts/SecureStoreSetCredentials.aspx?TargetAppId=<application Id>*; this option is only available when you select the Individual Target Application Type. If you select Use custom page, you need to create a page first and provide its URL. This page is used to authenticate users. Choose None if you don't want a sign-up page.

5. Enter VisioServices for the Target Application ID; SSS for Visio Services for the Display Name; <YourValidEmailAddress> for the Contact E-mail; Individual for the Target Application Type; Use default page for the Target Application Page URL (see Figure 2–49). Click Next.

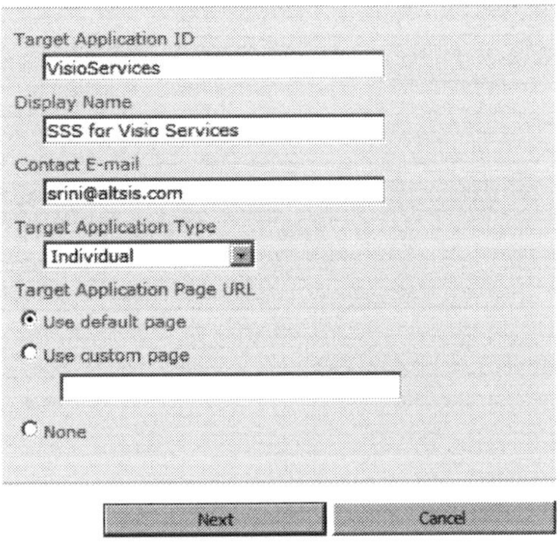

Target Application ID
VisioServices
Display Name
SSS for Visio Services
Contact E-mail
srini@altsis.com
Target Application Type
Individual
Target Application Page URL
⦿ Use default page
○ Use custom page

○ None

Next   Cancel

Figure 2–49. Configuring target application settings for SSS

6. In the Add Field window (Figure 2–50), leave the defaults as is and click on Next to continue.

Figure 2–50. Secure Store Service fields

7. Add administrator users who need to have access to this *Application ID* on the Target Application Administrators and click OK.

8. Return to the Secure Store Services window and choose the *Target Application ID* created in the previous step. Click the *Set* button on the Credentials tab of the Edit tab, as shown in Figure 2–51.

Figure 2–51. Set Secure Store Service Application ID credentials.

9. On the Set Credentials for Secure Store Target Application screen (Figure 2–52), enter the Credential Owner, Windows user name and password (and confirm password) and click OK. Credential owners are the members (individuals or group) of the target application that will impersonate credentials when accessing external data.

Figure 2–52. Setting credentials for target application.

▓ **Note** Since you will be using SSS for your Visio diagram to connect to the SQL server, you need to enter the user credentials of those who have permissions to the VisioServices database from where you will load data. It must be a low-privilege user, not an administrator.

The previous step creates a new SSS Application ID that can be used to connect to SQL Server from service applications that require additional authentication to retrieve data.

Using Visio with SQL Server and SSS

Now let's configure Visio Services to use the new Application ID.

1. Go to Central Administration ➤ Application Management ➤ Service Applications ➤ Manage Service Applications and choose Visio Graphics Service.

2. Click on the Global Settings in the External Data section and enter VisioServices under Application ID (Figure 2–53). Click OK.

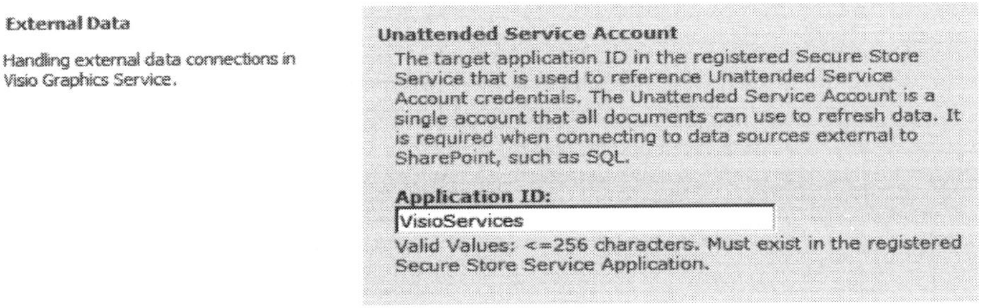

External Data

Handling external data connections in
Visio Graphics Service.

Unattended Service Account

The target application ID in the registered Secure Store
Service that is used to reference Unattended Service
Account credentials. The Unattended Service Account is a
single account that all documents can use to refresh data. It
is required when connecting to data sources external to
SharePoint, such as SQL.

Application ID:

VisioServices

Valid Values: <=256 characters. Must exist in the registered
Secure Store Service Application.

Figure 2–53. Set the External Data Unattended Service Account Applicaion ID.

■ **Note** Application IDs are set for each service application, such as Visio Graphics Service. You can also have two Visio Graphics Service applications set for one Web application, one default and the other a Custom Visio Graphics service application. For that, create a new Application ID with different credentials and set them to a new Custom Service Application. You can then add the new custom service application to the web application Service Connections.

This sets the authorization proxy for the Visio Graphics Services to connect to the SQL Server database and retrieve data without losing the user context.

■ **Note** Other settings on Visio Graphics Services under *Global Settings* include:

Maximum Web Drawing Size: This is the size of web drawing file that can be set, between 1-50MB. The bigger the file size, the slower the rendering and performance.

Minimum Cache Age: This is the minimum duration in minutes each drawing is cached in memory. Set the value to zero if you need real-time data. However, setting this value to zero or too low puts a load on CPU and memory usage. The allowable range is 0-34560. This parameter is valid only for data-driven web drawings.

Maximum Cache Age: This is the value in minutes after which the cached drawings are removed from memory. You need to set this to zero (in addition to setting the Minimum Cache Age value to zero) to get real-time data. Setting this value too high will increase memory consumption but it decreases file I/O and load on the CPU. This parameter is valid only for static web drawings.

Maximum Recalc Duration: This is the value in seconds of the period before an operation times out before a data refresh. The allowable range is between 10 –120.

3. Open your SharePoint site and click on Mall.vdw in the Visio Library document library to open the Visio diagram in full-screen mode.

4. Since you have set the SSS, data should display accurately from the database, with the data graphics populating the correct information on the shapes.

5. On SQL Server, go to the *tblLandmarks* table and change the data in the rows.

6. Return to the SharePoint site and refresh the Visio diagram to view the real-time changes in the diagram for the shapes as shown in Figure 2–54.

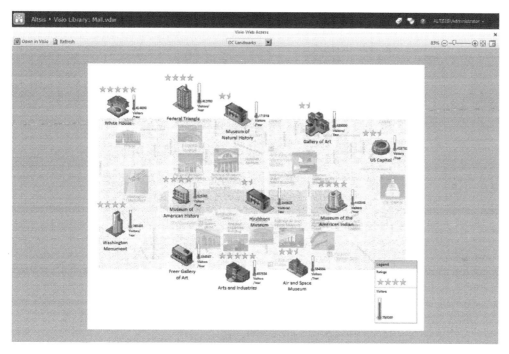

Figure 2–54. Visio drawing connected to a SQL Server data source and published to SharePoint

You can also interact with these Visio diagrams and shapes. For example, suppose you want to get more information by clicking on a shape or to pass the information from a shape to another web part. You can achieve these scenarios by using the JavaScript API with Visio Services.

Visio Services JavaScript Mashup API

The Visio Services JavaScript Mashup API provides great functionality for accessing or manipulating the shapes of published diagrams. Using the API, you can alter data, shapes, and pages to make the diagrams more interactive. There are many operations you can perform on the drawings, some of which are discussed below:

- *At the Control level*, you can retrieve the version, display mode (Silverlight or Image), active page, and events such as shape selection changed, diagram render complete, etc.

- *At the Page level*, you can get the available shapes, selected shape, shape, position, and other details.

- *At the Shape Collection level*, you can get the count, items, and metadata, etc.

- *At the Shape level*, you can get the shape data and hyperlink, and set highlighting to the shape, overlays, etc.

The Visio Services JavaScript Mashup API lets you create a rich user interface that combines shapes, data, and events.

The API consists of a hierarchy of classes, methods, and events as shown in Figure 2–55. To obtain the reference of the Visio Web Access web part on a page you need to get the corresponding object, which can be accessed via the *Vwa.VwaControl* object. The next level would be the Page object.

■ **Note** It is very important to understand that the page object in this context is the active web drawing page that is inside VWA web part—not the .aspx page.

On the page, you can have one or more shapes that can be retrieved using the ShapeCollection object. And, finally, you can access the individual shape from the shape collection and its properties.

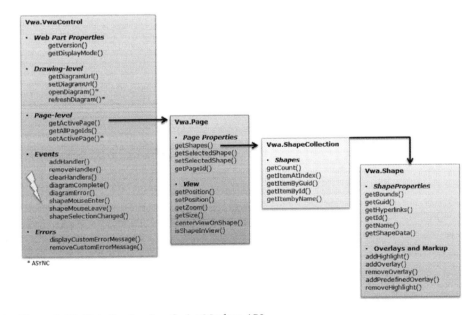

Figure 2–55. Visio Services JavaScript Mashup API

To use the JavaScript Mashup API and understand it more clearly, let's begin with a simple exercise.

PROBLEM CASE

Using the previously created Mall.vdw, display the details of each monument by clicking the shape.

Solution

1. Create a new page under the site pages and name it Mall.aspx

2. From Insert on the Editing Tools tab, under the web parts section, select Web Part and insert a Visio Web Access web part from the Business Data Categories. Add a web part to the page.

3. After you add the web part, make sure the page is in edit mode and click the link that says *Click here to open the tool pane*.

4. From the Visio Web Access configuration window, choose Mall.vdw from the Visio Library document library and click OK.

5. Click OK on the configuration window.

6. Save and close the page to view the Visio diagram rendered on the web page.

7. Right-click on the browser, click View Source on the context menu, and search for the text `class="VisioWebAccess"`.

8. Find the corresponding id of the `td` that you should find just above the `div`. Usually, it will be `WebPartWPQ2` on a freshly created site page.

9. Open Notepad and paste the code in Listing 2–1 into it. Save this as the file assets.js.

Listing 2–1. Assets.js

```
<script language="javascript">
var _application = Sys.Application;
var _visioWebPart;
var onShapeSelectionChanged = null;
_application.add_load(onApplicationLoad);
function onApplicationLoad()
{
    _visioWebPart= new Vwa.VwaControl("WebPartWPQ2"); // Change the control id based on the
code on your page
    _visioWebPart.addHandler("diagramcomplete", onDiagramComplete);
    _visioWebPart.addHandler("shapeselectionchanged", onShapeSelectionChanged);
}
function onDiagramComplete()
{
    var _page = _visioWebPart.getActivePage();
    _page.setZoom(85);
```

```
}
onShapeSelectionChanged = function(source, args)
{
    var _activePage = _visioWebPart.getActivePage();
    var _shape = _activePage.getShapes();
    var _shapeItem = _shape.getItemById(args);
    var _shapeData = _shapeItem.getShapeData();
    var _description = "";

    for (var j = 0; j < _shapeData.length; j++)
    {
        if (_shapeData[j].label == "Details")
        {
            _description = _shapeData[j].value;
            continue;
        }
    }
    document.getElementById('landmarkDetails').firstChild.data = _description;
}
</SCRIPT>
<div id="landmarkDetails" style="font-family: Verdana; font-style: bold; font-size:14pt;
color:red;">landmark details...</div>
```

10. Upload the assets.js file into the *Visio Library* document library.

11. Right-click on assets.js and by using the Copy Shortcut menu, copy the URL to the clipboard.

12. Open the Mall.aspx site page in edit mode and add the *Content Editor Web part* from the Media and Content category as shown in Figure 2–56.

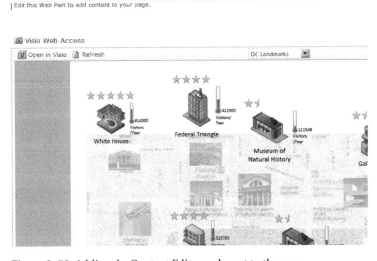

Figure 2–56. Adding the Content Editor web part to the page

13. Edit the Content Editor web part and paste the link to assets.js in the Content Link textbox.

14. Verify the link by clicking on Test link URL below the textbox. If the URL is accurate, the assets.js file will be downloaded to your disk.

15. Click Apply and OK on the editor part pane to return the page to normal mode.

16. Save and close the page.

17. You should now see that the Content Editor web part displays "landmark details..." text in red, as shown in Figure 2–57.

Figure 2–57. The Cntent Editor web part with the Visio Web Access web part

18. Click on any shape—for instance on the White House—and see that the text on the Content Editor web part changes to the White House details, as shown in Figure 2–58. Try clicking on other shapes. Notice that the text changes on the Content Editor web part instantly without a page refresh.

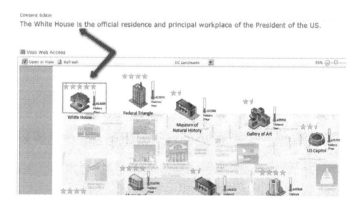

Figure 2–58. Interacting with the VWA web part and the drawing using the JavaScript Mashup API

Now that you have successfully created a simple JavaScript mashup with a Visio diagram, let's understand the code. One of the major reasons JavaScript was chosen to build the API is because of its simplicity.

Understanding the assets.js Code

First we need to get to the application object and create the event handler for the application load.

```
_application.add_load(onApplicationLoad);
```

Once the application loads, we get the instance of the Visio web access from the page and add two more event handlers—one when the diagram completes loading and the other when the shape selection is changed. In the life cycle of these events, the onDiagramComplete event fires first, and onShapeSelectionChanged is the last event.

```
_visioWebPart= new Vwa.VwaControl("WebPartWPQ2");
_visioWebPart.addHandler("diagramcomplete", onDiagramComplete);
_visioWebPart.addHandler("shapeselectionchanged", onShapeSelectionChanged);
```

After the diagram loads, all the objects are available and the diagram is rendered to the browser. This means that the diagram is completely available on the page and we can get to the page-level properties and methods. For example, we can set the diagram current page zoom value percentage:

```
var _page = _visioWebPart.getActivePage();
_page.setZoom(85);
```

Alright, once any shape is selected or changed on the active page, we need the corresponding shape and the shape data. We need to get to Shape Data in order to get the column values. We use the method getItemById() that's submitted through the event arguments.

```
var _activePage = _visioWebPart.getActivePage();
var _shape = _activePage.getShapes();
var _shapeItem = _shape.getItemById(args);
var _shapeData = _shapeItem.getShapeData();
var _description = "";
for (var j = 0; j < _shapeData.length; j++)
    {
    if (_shapeData[j].label == "Details"){
            _description = _shapeData[j].value;
            continue;
        }
    }
```

Finally, we get the description and assign it to the div text, like so:

```
document.getElementById('landmarkDetails').firstChild.data = _description;
```

Now, suppose your business analyst wants to create a simple workflow using a Visio diagram? Is there a way to connect this diagram to one of the available workflows easily?

Working with SharePoint Designer 2010

The answer is yes. This scenario can be achieved using Visio 2010 diagrams with SharePoint Designer 2010, which now allows importing and exporting Visio diagrams, attaching workflows to them, and then publishing to SharePoint environment.

PROBLEM CASE

One of the leading fast food chain (let's call it "Tasty Foods") wants to collect feedback from its customers on various food items. The feedback form must be filled out by the customer using an online web application. Customers must enter their full name, food item, e-mail address, and they must leave comments. If the customer doesn't enter a comment, the workflow status will be *rejected;* if he does, the status will be *approved*.

There are three major components that will be used in this case.

- A SharePoint list, used as the feedback form (*responsibility of the developer*).

- A Visio diagram to create the workflow design (*responsibility of the business analyst*).

- SharePoint Designer to enable the workflow and deploy (attach) it to the list (*responsibility of the developer*).

Solution:

1. Create a custom list, add a few columns as shown in Figure 2–59, and save it as *Tasty Foods Feedback*.

Columns

A column stores information about each item in the list. The following columns are currently available in this list:

Column (click to edit)	Type	Required
Title	Single line of text	✔
Full Name	Single line of text	
FoodItem	Choice	
Email Address	Single line of text	
Comments	Multiple lines of text	
Created By	Person or Group	
Modified By	Person or Group	

Figure 2–59. The Tasty Foods custom list

The Fooditem Choice column can contain items such as sandwiches, chicken, breakfast, salads, snacks and sides, beverages, coffee, desserts, shakes, etc.

2. Open Visio 2010 and create a new Visio diagram using Shape Stencils *SharePoint Workflow Actions (US units)* and *SharePoint Workflow Terminators (US units)*. You'll find these in the Flowchart section.

3. Create a simple workflow as shown in Figure 2–60, using shapes that compare the data source, send e-mail, and set the workflow status.

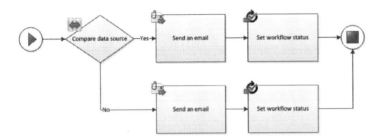

Figure 2–60. Simple workflow designed in Visio using SharePoint templates

4. From the File menu, save the diagram (as a .vsd file) to your local file system.

5. On the Process tab of the ribbon, click the Export button as shown in the Figure 2–61.

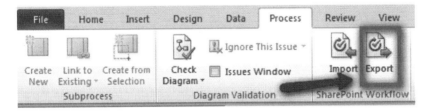

Figure 2–61. Exporting a Visio diagram as a SharePoint workflow

6. Save the file to your local disk as a *Visio Workflow Interchange* (.vwi) file.

7. Close Visio and open the SharePoint Designer 2010 client.

8. Open the SharePoint site where you created the *Tasty Foods Feedback* custom list.

9. From the Site Objects menu, click on Workflows.

10. Click on the *Import from Visio* icon on the Workflow tab of the ribbon. In the *Choose a Visio drawing to import* wizard (Figure 2–62), browse and select the previously exported .vwi file, then click Next to continue.

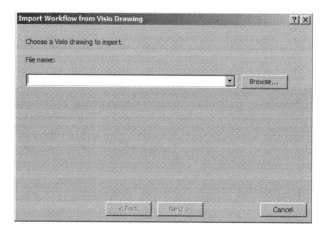

Figure 2–62. Importing a Visio workflow interchange file to SharePoint Designer

11. Provide a proper workflow name and choose List Workflow as the type of workflow to import. Select the custom list you created earlier for the feedback and click Finish, as shown in Figure 2–63.

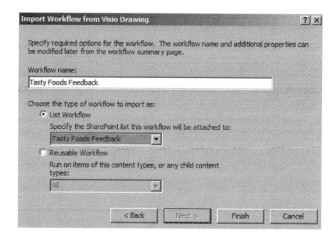

Figure 2–63. Setting the workflow name and selecting the list to attach to the workflow

12. This creates a simple workflow screen that is built from the workflow framework created from Visio (see Figure 2–64).

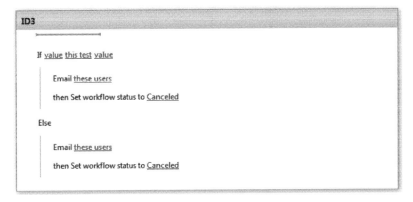

Figure 2–64. *Visio workflow intechange file (.vwi) loaded in the SharePoint Designer workflow editor*

13. As you can see in Figure 2–64, two conditions are automatically created under the editor as there are two flows when comparing the data (refer to Figure 2–60). This includes the *send e-mail process* step, *change the workflow status,* and the *end the process step* for both flows.

14. Modify each of the conditions to meet the requirements. For instance, under the If condition (Figure 2–64), set the value to look up from the custom list datasource and choose the field (Comments) for looking up the value. Set the this.test value to "is empty".

15. If this condition is true, then set the Email "these users" to Current Item:Email Address. Configure Subject and message and then Set workflow status to "Rejected" from the look-up values.

16. Under the "Else" condition, set Email "these users" to Current Item:Email Address. Configure Subject and message and then Set workflow to "Approved".

17. Finally, set the Title of the workflow as "Tasty Foods Feedback Workflow" as shown in Figure 2–65.

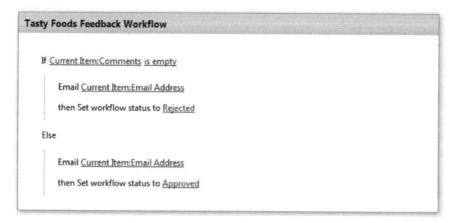

Figure 2–65. Setting up the workflow conditions in SharePoint Designer

18. In the Start Options, under *View and manage settings for this workflow page,* you can choose to start the workflow automatically either when the item is created or when it is changed (see Figure 2–66).

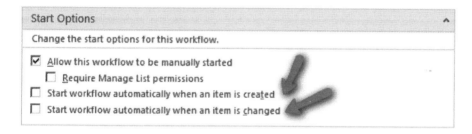

Figure 2–66. Setting workflow start-up options in SharePoint Designer

19. From the Workflow tab on the ribbon, click the Check for Errors button and then save the workflow (Figure 2–67).

20. Publish this workflow to the list using the Publish button on the Workflow tab.

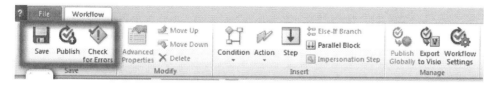

Figure 2–67. Save and Publish the workflow to SharePoint list

These steps will validate and publish the workflow to the corresponding list.

21. Open the SharePoint site and the <u>Tasty Foods Feedback</u> list.

22. Go to List ➤ List Settings and click on the Workflow Settings in the Permissions and Management section. You can also access the Workflow settings from List Tools ➤ List ➤ Settings ➤ Workflow Settings.

Locate the Workflow you just submitted. If the workflow is published more than once, a new version is created.

23. Return to the list and click Add new item, which pops up the New Item screen as shown in Figure 2–68.

24. Create two items, one with comments and one without comments. Since the workflow hasn't been set to start automatically, you'll have to start it manually after any item is created. Choose the item on which you'd like to run the Workflow and click the *Workflows* button on the Items tab, as shown in Figure 2–69.

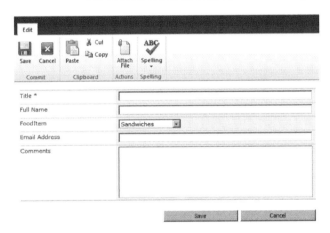

Figure 2–68. Adding a new item to the feedback form

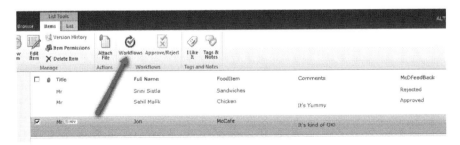

Figure 2–69. Starting a workflow for the list item

This opens the *Start a New Workflow* window, displaying the available workflows, as Figure 2–70 shows.

Start a New Workflow

Ⓖ Tasty Foods Feedback

Workflows

Select a workflow for more details on the current status or history. Show my workflows only.

Name	Started	Ended	Status

Running Workflows

There are no currently running workflows on this item.

Figure 2–70. Starting a new workflow

25. Click on the Tasty Foods Feedback workflow link, and then on the Start button on the next screen. This will execute the rules underlying the workflow and apply any changes to the respective columns

26. Notice that under the Tasty Foods Feedback column (Figure 2–71), the status is set based the on the comments provided by customer. The status would be Approved when the customer fills in the Comments field and Rejected when the customer doesn't add any comments.

☐	ⓘ	Title	Full Name	FoodItem	Comments	Tasty Foods Feedback
		Mr ☑ NEW	Srini Sistla	Sandwiches		Rejected
		Mr ☑ NEW	Sahil Malik	Chicken	It's Yummy	Approved
		Mr ☑ NEW	Jon	Coffee	It's good!	Approved

✚ Add new item

Figure 2–71. Workflow status after items are added

■ **Caution** You can now visualize the status of the Visio workflow using the workflow visualization web part. However, to use this functionality you need to set *Show workflow visualization* on the status page from SharePoint Designer.

In some instances, the requirement may not be as simple as just connecting to an Excel file or SharePoint list or even using a SQL Server database. A more interesting scenario would be consuming data from a web service or from a different data source that Visio Services doesn't support natively. In such cases, you would have to write a custom data provider.

Creating Your Own Custom Data Providers

The Visio Services API provides features to build custom data modules or custom data providers. Using the API you can create custom data sources and refresh the data on the Visio diagrams that are deployed to a SharePoint site.

Let's take a look now at how to support non-natively supported data sources by designing a custom data provider.

PROBLEM CASE

Display the status of the test environment servers whether they are online or offline. Note that current status information is in a SQL Server database and can be retrieved using WCF services. We will need to get the data and connect to the shapes.

Solution

The major components in this scenario are SQL Server, WCF Service, Visio, and Security.

- Let's begin with a SQL Server database and then write a WCF Service to retrieve data from the database table.

- We'll write a VBA script to create the data source and connect the data source to the shapes in the Visio diagram.

- We'll deploy the .vdw file to a SharePoint environment and view the output.

- We'll write a custom data provider and configure its settings in the Central Administration site of the SharePoint environment.

    1. Create a table named *tblServerStatus* with columns as shown in Figure 2–72 in the VisioServices database you created earlier.

Figure 2–72. Server Status Table in SQL Server

> 2. Populate a few rows of information into this table as in Figure 2–73.

SINo	ServerName	ServerIP	ServerStatus
1	Vajra	192.168.2.1	1
2	Varun	192.168.2.2	1
3	Asura	192.168.2.3	0
NULL	*NULL*	*NULL*	*NULL*

Figure 2–73. Populating data for the server status table in SQL Server

> 3. Create a stored procedure named uspGetServerDetails that will execute the
>   SQL query to retrieve the values from the table in Figure 2–73. Listing 2–2 shows
>   the code.

Listing 2–2. The uspGetServerDetails Stored Procedure

```
USE [VisioServices]
GO
/****** Object:  StoredProcedure [dbo].[uspGetServerDetails]     Script Date: 06/11/2010
22:10:31 ******/
SET ANSI_NULLS ON
GO
SET QUOTED_IDENTIFIER ON
GO
-- =============================================
-- Author:          <Author,,Name>
-- Create date: <Create Date,,>
-- Description:     <Description,,>
-- =============================================
CREATE PROCEDURE [dbo].[uspGetServerDetails]
```

```
AS
BEGIN
    -- SET NOCOUNT ON added to prevent extra result sets from
    -- interfering with SELECT statements.
    SET NOCOUNT ON;
    -- Insert statements for procedure here
    SELECT ServerName, ServerIP, ServerStatus from tblServerStatus
END
```

▦ **Note** The stored procedure code is explained toward the end of this chapter in the section "Understanding the Custom Data Provider Code."

Writing the WCF Service library and Hosting it in IIS

4. Open Microsoft Visual Studio 2010, choose to create a new project, and from the available templates select Visual C# ➤ WCF ➤ WCF *Service Application,* and provide a proper Name and Location. Make sure you pick .NET Framework 3.5. This creates a service class (Service1.svc) and an interface (IService1.cs).

5. Rename the default Service1.svc file and the interface class to *ServerStatus.svc* and *IServerStatus.cs* respectively. Ensure that all the references under the project reflect this name change.

6. After completing these steps, your project should look like the one in Figure 2–74.

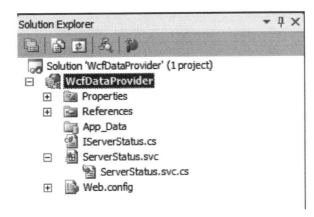

Figure 2–74. Setting up a WCF service application project in Visual Studio 2010

7. Open the *Web.config* file and add an entry under the connectionStrings section—your SQL Server connection string as follows:

```
<connectionStrings>
```

```
      <add name="VisioServicesConnectionString" connectionString="Data
Source=ServerName;Initial Catalog=VisioServices;Integrated Security=SSPI;User
Id=userId;Password=pwd" providerName="System.Data.SqlClient"/>
      </connectionStrings>
```

8. Open the *ServerStatus.svc.cs* file and paste the code from Listing 2–3 in it.

■ **Note** The code in Listing 2–3 is explained toward the end of this chapter in the section "Understanding the Custom Data provider code."

Listing 2–3. WCF Service Library class to retreive Server Status

```
using System;
using System.Collections.Generic;
using System.Linq;
using System.Runtime.Serialization;
using System.ServiceModel;
using System.Text;
using System.Data;
using System.Data.Sql;
using System.Data.SqlClient;
using System.Configuration;
namespace WcfDataProvider
{

    public class ServerStatus : IServerStatus
    {
        [OperationBehavior]
        public DataTable GetServerStatusDetails()
        {
            DataSet dataSet = new DataSet();
            SqlConnection connection = new
SqlConnection(ConfigurationManager.ConnectionStrings["VisioServicesConnectionString"].Co
nnectionString);

            SqlCommand command = new SqlCommand("uspGetServerDetails", connection);
            command.CommandType = CommandType.StoredProcedure;
            SqlDataAdapter dataAdapter = new SqlDataAdapter(command);

            dataAdapter.Fill(dataSet);
            connection.Close();
            return dataSet.Tables[0];
        }
    }
}
```

9. Now copy the code in Listing 2–4, open the *IServerStatus.cs* file and paste the
    code in it.

▓ **Best Practice**: It is a good practice to add a Test Project for any projects you create as this would perform the first level of unit testing for your projects.

Listing 2–4. WCF Service library Interface Class

```
using System;
using System.Collections.Generic;
using System.Linq;
using System.Runtime.Serialization;
using System.ServiceModel;
using System.Text;
using System.Data;
namespace WcfDataProvider
{
    // NOTE: You can use the "Rename" command on the "Refactor" menu to change the
interface name "IServerStatus" in both code and config file together.
    [ServiceContract]
    public interface IServerStatus
    {
        [OperationContract]
        DataTable GetServerStatusDetails();
    }
}
```

10. Build the WCF project in release mode and make sure you have no errors.

11. Create a local folder in your file system under C:\ and name it *wcfServicehost*.

12. Make a folder called *bin*.

13. Copy the WcfDataProvider.dll file to the bin folder.

14. Make sure Network Service and IIS_IUSRS users have Read & Execute permissions on the root folder.

15. Create a file named *VisioWcfService.svc* under the wcfServicehost folder and add the following text:

```
<% @ServiceHost Service="WcfDataProvider.ServerStatus" %>
```

16. Create a Web.config file in the same folder and copy the code from Listing 2–5 to it.

Listing 2–5. WCF data provider Web.config file settings

```
<?xml version="1.0" encoding="utf-8"?>
  <configuration>
    <system.serviceModel>
      <services>
        <service behaviorConfiguration="WcfDataProvider.ServerStatusBehavior"
name="WcfDataProvider.ServerStatus">
          <endpoint address="" binding="basicHttpBinding"
contract="WcfDataProvider.IServerStatus" />
                    <host>
              <baseAddresses>
```

```
          <add baseAddress="http://localhost:<portnumber>/visiowcfservices.svc" />
        </baseAddresses>
      </host>
    </service>
  </services>
  <behaviors>
    <serviceBehaviors>
      <behavior name="WcfDataProvider.ServerStatusBehavior">
        <serviceMetadata httpGetEnabled="true" />
        <serviceDebug includeExceptionDetailInFaults="false" />
      </behavior>
    </serviceBehaviors>
  </behaviors>
  </system.serviceModel>
<connectionStrings>
    <add name="VisioServicesConnectionString" connectionString="Data
Source=vajra;Initial Catalog=ServerName;Integrated Security=SSPI;User
Id=uid;Password=pwd" providerName="System.Data.SqlClient"/>
  </connectionStrings>
</configuration>
```

After completing the above steps, your folder structure and files should look similar to those in Figure 2–75.

Figure 2–75. WCF service host folder

17. Open IIS and create an application pool by providing a Name, .NET Framework version, and pipeline mode.

18. Create a new web site. Choose the app pool you just created, provide a site name, and choose the local folder where you copied the .dll file as the physical path. Under binding, provide a Port number that's not in use.

19. Open the browser and type the URL `http://localhost:<portnumber>/ VisioWcfServices.svc;` to see the output shown in Figure 2–76.

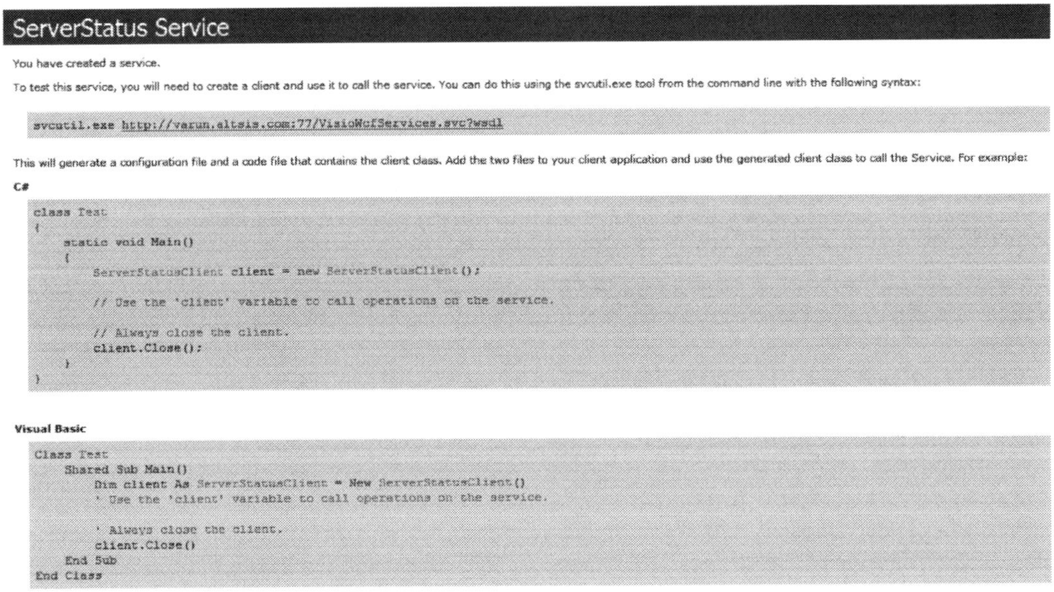

ServerStatus Service

You have created a service.

To test this service, you will need to create a client and use it to call the service. You can do this using the svcutil.exe tool from the command line with the following syntax:

```
svcutil.exe http://varun.altsis.com:77/VisioWcfServices.svc?wsdl
```

This will generate a configuration file and a code file that contains the client class. Add the two files to your client application and use the generated client class to call the Service. For example:

C#

```csharp
class Test
{
    static void Main()
    {
        ServerStatusClient client = new ServerStatusClient();

        // Use the 'client' variable to call operations on the service.

        // Always close the client.
        client.Close();
    }
}
```

Visual Basic

```vb
Class Test
    Shared Sub Main()
        Dim client As ServerStatusClient = New ServerStatusClient()
        ' Use the 'client' variable to call operations on the service.

        ' Always close the client.
        client.Close()
    End Sub
End Class
```

Figure 2–76. *Accessing the WCF service*

■ **Note** For more information on how to create WCF services, go to `http://blah.winsmarts.com/2008-4-Host_a_WCF_Service_in_IIS_7_-and-amp;_Windows_2008_-_The_right_way.aspx`.

Creating the custom data provider project

20. Open Microsoft Visual Studio 2010, create a new project, and from the available templates pick Visual C# ➤ SharePoint ➤ 2010 ➤ Empty SharePoint Project. Make sure you choose .NET Framework 3.5. Provide a Name, Location, and Solution Name, and click OK. Create the project name as *VisioDataService*.

21. In the next screen, enter the SharePoint site URL for debugging and choose *Deploy as a farm solution* for the trust level. Click on Finish.

22. Right-click on the project, select the properties, and make sure the Assembly name and default namespace fit your situation.

23. Right-click on the project again and click on Add Class. Name the class as *VisioDataService.cs*.

24. Right-click on the project and choose Add Service Reference....

25. From the wizard, click Discover and make sure there's a reference to the WCF service you built earlier. Alternatively, you can enter the WCF URL (`http://localhost:<portnumber>/VisioWcfServices.svc`) in the Address text box. Provide the namespace as `WcfDataService` and click OK.

26. Right-click on the project and choose Add Reference.... From the Add Reference window .NET tab, choose the System.Web component and click OK.

27. Right-click on the project again and choose Add Reference.... From the Add Reference window Browse tab, browse to the folder `C:\Windows\assembly\GAC_MSIL\Microsoft.Office.Visio.Server\14.0.0.0_71e9bce111e9429c\` and choose the file Microsoft.Office.Visio.Server.dll and click OK.

At this stage, the project structure should resemble the one in Figure 2-77.

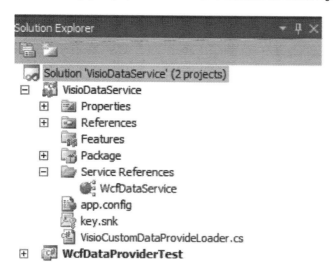

Figure 2–77. WCF consumer project structure

28. Open the VisioDataService.cs file from the VisioDataService project and copy the code in Listing 2–6 into the file. Make sure you have the correct namespaces as per your project settings.

Note: The code in Listing 2–6 is explained toward the end of this chapter in the section "Understanding the Custom Data provider code."

29. Open Microsoft Visual Studio 2010, create a new project, and from the available templates pick Visual C# ➤ SharePoint ➤ 2010 ➤ Empty SharePoint Project. Make sure you choose .NET Framework 3.5. Provide a Name, Location, and Solution Name, and click OK. Create the project name as *VisioDataService*.

30. In the next screen, enter the SharePoint site URL for debugging and choose *Deploy as a farm solution* for the trust level. Click on Finish.

31. Right-click on the project, select the properties, and make sure the Assembly name and default namespace fit your situation.

32. Right-click on the project again and click on Add Class. Name the class as *VisioDataService.cs.*

33. Right-click on the project and choose Add Service Reference....

34. From the wizard, click Discover and make sure there's a reference to the WCF service you built earlier. Alternatively, you can enter the WCF URL (`http://localhost:<portnumber>/VisioWcfServices.svc`) in the Address text box. Provide the namespace as `WcfDataService` and click OK.

35. Right-click on the project and choose Add Reference.... From the Add Reference window .NET tab, choose the System.Web component and click OK.

36. Right-click on the project again and choose Add Reference.... From the Add Reference window Browse tab, browse to the folder `C:\Windows\assembly\GAC_MSIL\Microsoft.Office.Visio.Server\14.0.0.0_ _71e9bce111e9429c\` and choose the file Microsoft.Office.Visio.Server.dll and click OK.

37. At this stage, the project structure should resemble the one in Figure 2–77.

Listing 2–6. Visio Custom Data Provider Service Class Code

```
using System;
using System.Data;
using System.Threading;
using System.Xml;
using System.Web;
using Microsoft.Office.Visio.Server;
using VisioDataService.WcfDataService;
namespace Altsis
{
    public class VisioDataService : AddonDataHandler, IAsyncResult
    {
        private object _asyncState;
        private bool _completeStatus;

        WaitHandle IAsyncResult.AsyncWaitHandle
        {
            get { return null; }
        }
        object IAsyncResult.AsyncState
        {
            get { return _asyncState; }
        }
        bool IAsyncResult.IsCompleted
```

```
        {
            get { return this._completeStatus; }
        }
        bool IAsyncResult.CompletedSynchronously
        {
            get { return false; }
        }
        public override IAsyncResult BeginGetData(HttpContext httpContext, AsyncCallback
callback, object asyncState)
        {
            _asyncState = asyncState;
            ThreadPool.QueueUserWorkItem(new WaitCallback(GetData), callback);
            return this;
        }
        public override DataSet EndGetData(IAsyncResult asyncResult)
        {
            return this.Data;
        }
        public override void Cancel()
        {
            // Not implemented
        }
        private void GetData(object state)
        {
            AsyncCallback asyncCallback = (AsyncCallback)state;
            try
            {
                ServerStatusClient oServerStatus = new ServerStatusClient();
                DataTable dt = oServerStatus.GetServerStatusDetails();
                this.Data.Reset();
                this.Data.Tables.Add(dt);
                this.Data.AcceptChanges();
            }
            catch (Exception ex)
            {
                this.Error = new AddonDataHandlerException(ex.Message);
            }
            asyncCallback(this);
            _completeStatus = true;

        }
    }
}
```

Now build the project. Once the build is successful, right-click on the VisioDataService project, then click on Package to create the WSP file under the project bin folder.

■ **Tip** If you are performing this step on your local development machine, try the Deploy option from the project properties.

---

38. Deploy the WSP using either STSADM or Windows PowerShell commands to add the solution to your SharePoint site.

39. Open Central Administration ➤ Application Management ➤ Manage Service Applications ➤ Visio Graphics Service.

40. Click on Trusted Data Providers and then on Add a new Trusted Data Provider.

41. Under *Trusted Data Provider ID*, enter the fully qualified assembly signature (in my case it is `Altsis.VisioDataService,VisioDataService, Version=1.0.0.0, Culture=neutral, PublicKeyToken=<publickeytoken>`). Please see `http://blah.winsmarts.com/2009-12-SharePoint_Productivity Tip_of_the_day.aspx` for a convenient way to extract assembly signatures.

42. Under Trusted Data Provider Type, enter the value 6 (for Visio Custom Data Providers).

43. Under Trusted Data Provider Description, enter a valid description such as Visio Custom Data Services Provider and click OK.

44. Your service provider is now ready and will display in the available service provider list.

45. Open the Web.config file that belongs to your SharePoint web application and paste the settings in Listing 2–7 under the `system.serviceModel` section.

Listing 2–7. Service Model section setting values under web.config file

```
<bindings>
    <basicHttpBinding>
        <binding name="BasicHttpBinding_IServerStatus" closeTimeout="00:01:00"
            openTimeout="00:01:00" receiveTimeout="00:10:00" sendTimeout="00:01:00"
            allowCookies="false" bypassProxyOnLocal="false"
hostNameComparisonMode="StrongWildcard"
            maxBufferSize="65536" maxBufferPoolSize="524288"
maxReceivedMessageSize="65536"
            messageEncoding="Text" textEncoding="utf-8" transferMode="Buffered"
            useDefaultWebProxy="true">
            <readerQuotas maxDepth="32" maxStringContentLength="8192"
maxArrayLength="16384"
                maxBytesPerRead="4096" maxNameTableCharCount="16384" />
            <security mode="None">
                <transport clientCredentialType="None" proxyCredentialType="None"
                    realm="" />
```

```
          <message clientCredentialType="UserName" algorithmSuite="Default" />
        </security>
      </binding>
    </basicHttpBinding>
  </bindings>
  <client>
    <endpoint address="http://varun.altsis.com:77/VisioWcfServices.svc"
        binding="basicHttpBinding"
bindingConfiguration="BasicHttpBinding_IServerStatus"
        contract="WcfDataService.IServerStatus" name="BasicHttpBinding_IServerStatus"
/>
  </client>
```

Designing the Visio Diagram

46. Open Visio 2010 and create a blank diagram. Choose the Network ➤ Servers (US units) stencil from More Shapes ➤ Network.

47. From the Insert tab, Add a Container block from the *diagram parts,* and add three servers: *Web Server, Database Server, and Application Server.* Give a name to the Container block as shown in Figure 2–78.

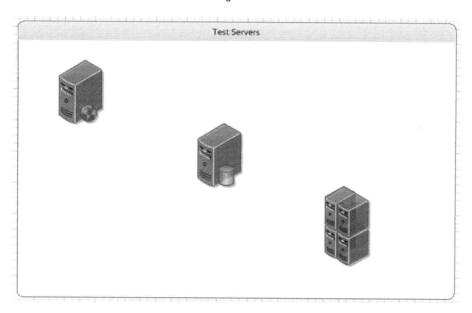

Figure 2–78. Designing a Visio diagram for test servers

Right now, there is no data source configured. While your Visio diagram is open, press Alt+F11 to open Microsoft Visual Basic for Applications. In the Project window, double-click on *ThisDocument* under Visio Objects to open the code view. Paste the code in Listing 2–8 into the code area.

■ **Note** The code below is explained towards the end of this chapter in the section "Understanding the Custom Data provider code." You need to customize the connection string and the Data module assembly details in the below code.

Listing 2–8. Using Visual Basic for applications to retreive data from SQL Server data source

```
Sub LoadData()
    Dim diagramServices As Integer
    Dim vsoDataRecordset As Visio.dataRecordset

    Dim connectionString As String
    Dim commandText As String

    diagramServices = ActiveDocument.DiagramServicesEnabled
    ActiveDocument.DiagramServicesEnabled = visServiceVersion140
    Application.ActiveWindow.Windows.ItemFromID(visWinIDExternalData).Visible = True

    commandText = "SELECT ServerName, ServerIP, ServerStatus FROM tblServerStatus"
    connectionString = "Provider=SQLOLEDB;Data Source=<YourDataSourceName>;Initial
Catalog=VisioServices;Integrated Security=SSPI;"
    Set vsoDataRecordset = ActiveDocument.DataRecordsets.Add(connectionString,
commandText, 0, "Server Status Details")
    vsoDataRecordset.DataConnection.connectionString =
"DataModule=Altsis.VisioDataService,VisioDataService;"

    ActiveDocument.DiagramServicesEnabled = diagramServices
End Sub
```

The Microsoft Visual Basic for Applications window should look like the one in Figure 2–79.

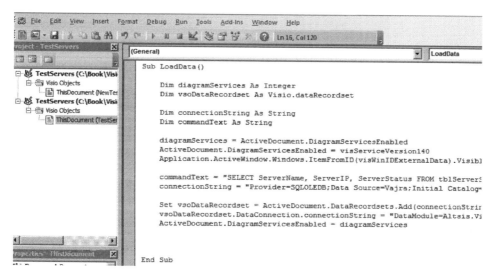

Figure 2–79. *Microsoft Visual Basic for Applications*

48. Press **F5** or click on the *Run* button on the menu to execute the `LoadData()` subroutine. Pressing **Alt+F11** will toggle back to the Visio diagram. Under the External Data tab, the data will be loaded as shown in Figure 2–80.

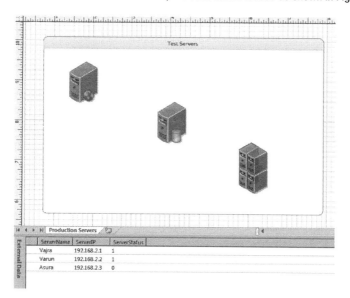

Figure 2–80. *The Visio diagram loading external data using VBA code*

49. Drag and drop row data to the respective shapes or set the *Text* property to the shapes that match the *ServerName* column and use the option *Automatically Link all.*

50. Set the data graphics to display *ServerIP* and *ServerName* as Text, and *ServerStatus* as *Color by Value* (Figure 2–81), such that if the value is 0 (*server is down*) the server shows red and if the value is 1 (server is live), it show green.

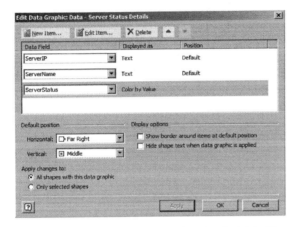

Figure 2–81. Setting up Data Graphics for the Visio diagram

Your final Visio diagram before saving should look like the one in Figure 2–82.

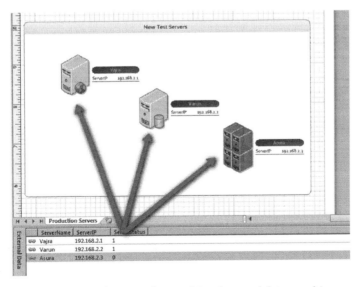

Figure 2–82. Visio diagram after applying data and data graphics

51. Save the Visio diagram to the local file system.

52. From the File menu, click on Save & Send ➤ Save to SharePoint ➤ Web Drawing ➤ Save As .vdw file.

53. Open the SharePoint site and open the Visio Library Document library. Click on Add document, browse to the saved .vdw file, and click OK.

54. Click on the .vdw file to open the diagram in the browser to display the results from the database.

55. Change the values in the database and notice the server status. If the cache age values on the general settings of the Visio Graphics Service are set to zero, the values reflect instantly on the diagram (Figure 2–83).

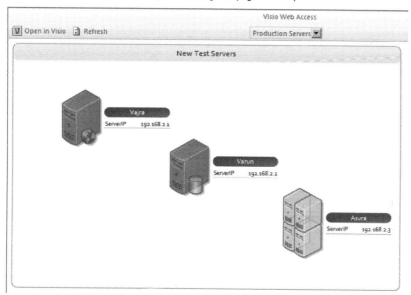

Figure 2–83. Visio diagram loaded using a custom data provider

Make sure the following are correct to avoid the error shown in Figure 2–84.

56. Assembly details are accurate when you add the custom data providers in the Central Administration.

57. The WCF services are properly hosted and can communicate with the Custom Data Providers.

58. Your configuration files (Web.config) have the right binding settings for the WCF.

59. As discussed earlier, you might encounter the double-hop issue while connecting to data sources via WCF. If so, you might need to set the credentials under the Secure Store Service.

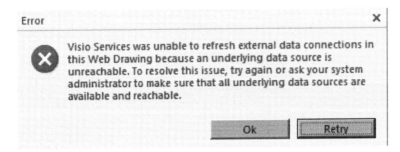

Figure 2–84. *External data connection refresh error*

UNDERSTANDING THE CUSTOM DATA PROVIDER CODE

uspGetServerDetails Stored Procedure (Listing 2–2):

This stored procedure contains a simple T-SQL statement that retrieves all rows of data from the table `tblServerStatus`.

```
SELECT ServerName, ServerIP, ServerStatus from tblServerStatus
```

WCF Service Library (and Interface) Class (Listings 2–3 and 2–4):

Consider this a data access layer class that would call the `uspGetServerDetails` stored procedure and return the output as a data table.

When the WCF application project is created, a service class and corresponding interface template are added to the project. Declare the Service Contract and Operation Contract (as shown below) interface class that will be implemented in your derived class. Since the intention is to retrieve a data table from this service, the data contract method will be of type `DataTable`.

```
[ServiceContract]
public interface IServerStatus
{
    [OperationContract]
    DataTable GetServerStatusDetails();
}
```

Under the derived class in the implemented method `GetServerStatusDetails`, create the data objects needed for the output:

```
DataSet dataSet = new DataSet();
```

Next, create the SQL Connection using the connection string from Web.config:

```
SqlConnection connection = new
SqlConnection(ConfigurationManager.ConnectionStrings["VisioServicesConnectionString"].Co
nnectionString);
```

Create the command object by calling the stored procedure with the help of the SQL Connection and set the command type to StoredProcedure.

```
SqlCommand command = new SqlCommand("uspGetServerDetails", connection);
command.CommandType = CommandType.StoredProcedure;
```

Finally, create the data adapter, load the command, and fill the data set using the data adapter.

```
SqlDataAdapter dataAdapter = new SqlDataAdapter(command);
dataAdapter.Fill(dataSet);
```

Close the connection and return the output:

```
connection.Close();
return dataSet.Tables[0];
```

■ **Tip** If you are a novice WCF developer, simply start from here: http://blah.winsmarts.com/2008-4-Writing_the_WCF_Hello_World_App.aspx.

Custom Data Provider Class (Listing 2–6):

Before beginning, it is important to understand some of the key concepts. First, prepare to query data from those data sources that are not natively supported. Second, these operations must be asynchronous in order to perform the tasks in a timely fashion. And most importantly, methods used must be thread safe.

Microsoft.Office.Visio.Server assembly provides these functionalities with its abstract class AddonDataHandler and its abstract methods that deal with all the necessary data module implementations.

Add a reference to Microsoft.Office.Visio.Server as the derived class will be inheriting the AddonDataHandler abstract class. It needs to also inherit the IAsyncResult interface from the System namespace to get the result of the asynchronous operation. Though there are many methods to override, the most important to understand are BeginGetData and EndGetData.

Visio Services calls the custom data provider's BeginGetData() method as soon as the request begins. Under the BeginData() method, create a thread and delegate a method to it. Create a callback method to be aware of when the thread completes its job.

```
ThreadPool.QueueUserWorkItem(new WaitCallback(GetData), callback);
```

In the GetData() method, create an instance to the WCF service object and call the GetServerStatusDetails method to retrieve the Server Status details

```
ServerStatusClient oServerStatus = new ServerStatusClient();
DataTable dt = oServerStatus.GetServerStatusDetails();
this.Data.Reset();
```

```
this.Data.Tables.Add(dt);
this.Data.AcceptChanges();
```

After the set operation completes its job by retrieving the data, Visio Services calls the `EndGetData()` and returns the `Data` object as DataSet.

```
return this.Data;
```

VBA Code (Listing 2–8):

The VBA code is used it to create and populate a data source that can be used by the Visio diagrams. This is similar to creating a data source using macros.

The code is very simple. It begins by initializing the data objects such as recordset, connection strings, command text, etc.

```
Dim diagramServices As Integer
Dim vsoDataRecordset As Visio.dataRecordset
Dim dataRecordset As Visio.dataRecordset
Dim connectionString As String
Dim commandText As String
```

First, get to the instance of the diagram services of the active document, which is the page. Set the Visio Services Version and the visibility of the external data sources window to true:

```
diagramServices = ActiveDocument.DiagramServicesEnabled
ActiveDocument.DiagramServicesEnabled = visServiceVersion140
Application.ActiveWindow.Windows.ItemFromID(visWinIDExternalData).Visible = True
```

The following steps are optional here. They are to populate the external data source with values to facilitate if designer wants to bind the row data to the shapes in design mode. Connect to the SQL store, retrieve the recordset, and add the recordset to the active document data record set collection.

```
commandText = "SELECT ServerName, ServerIP, ServerStatus FROM tblServerStatus"
connectionString = "Provider=SQLOLEDB;Data Source=<YourDataSourceName>;Initial
Catalog=VisioServices;Integrated Security=SSPI; "
Set vsoDataRecordset = ActiveDocument.DataRecordsets.Add(connectionString, commandText,
0, "Server Status Details")
```

Set the custom data provider assembly details to the recordset command string. Set and enable the diagram services to the active document:

```
vsoDataRecordset.DataConnection.connectionString =
"DataModule=Altsis.VisioDataService,VisioDataService;"
ActiveDocument.DiagramServicesEnabled = diagramServices
```

So far, you've seen a lot of information on Visio and Visio Services. Now it's time to get to know some more references and information. You have seen the administration of Visio services using the UI in Central Administration. Now, you will learn more options for administering Visio Services using both CA and Windows PowerShell.

Administration of Visio Services

Creating a New Visio Graphics Service Application

Administering Visio Services can be done using both Central Administration (CA) or using PowerShell (PS).

▓ **Tip** To access PowerShell, simply click on Start ➤ All programs ➤ Microsoft SharePoint 2010 Products ➤ SharePoint 2010 Management Shell.

▓ **Best Practice:**

1. Set up an application pool and a managed account before you begin; most of the settings and configurations require both application pool accounts and managed accounts and you really don't want to go back to create them in the middle of operation. Plan ahead and make a list of all these accounts before you begin setting up your farm/application.

2. Make sure you are member of the Administrators group. Again, you definitely need to be the localadministrator for many obvious reasons. You don't want to start your application with a low privilege account and get access denied for an administration job.

From CA: from Application Management ➤ Manage Service Applications, click New and choose Visio Graphics Service. Provide the application name, choose application pool or create a new one, and choose or not to create an application proxy (add to default group) and click OK.

Using PS: at the PS prompt type:

```
New-SPVisioServiceApplication <ServiceApplicationName> - serviceapplicationpool
<ServiceApplicationPoolName> -AddToDefaultGroup
```

Deleting an Existing Visio Graphics Service Application

From CA: from Application Management ➤ Manage Service Applications, choose the Visio Graphics Service application name, then click on the Delete button on the ribbon.

Using PS: at the PS prompt type:

```
Remove-SPServiceApplication <VisioServiceApplicationName>
```

List all Existing Visio Graphics Service Applications

From CA: from Application Management ➤ Click on Manage Service Applications to view all Visio Services Service applications.

Using PS: at the PS Prompt type:

```
Get-SPVisioServiceApplication
```

Creating a New Visio Graphics Service Application Proxy

From CA: You can only create an application proxy when creating a new Service application.
   Using PS: at the PS prompt type:

```
New-SPVisioServiceApplicationProxy <ServiceApplicationName>
```

▓ **Note** Service application proxies stand as the gateway or channel for connecting with service applications. They are deployed along with the service applications and encapsulate the components used to execute the calls on the service application.

Delete an Existing Visio Graphics Service Application Proxy

From CA: from Application Management ➤ Manage Service Applications, from the available Visio Service Proxies select the proxy from the list and Click Delete button from the ribbon.
   Using PS: At the PS Prompt type:

```
Remove-SPServiceApplicationProxy <ProxyID>
```

List All Existing Visio Graphics Service Application Proxies

From CA: from Application Management ➤ Click on Manage Service Applications to view all available Visio Service Application Proxies under the selected Service Application.
   Using PS: At the PS Prompt type:

```
Get-SPVisioServiceApplicationProxy
```

Setting Up Visio Graphics Service Global Settings

From CA: from Application Management ➤ Manage Service Application, choose Visio Graphics Service ➤ Global Settings. You can now set Maximum Diagram Size, Minimum Cache Age, Maximum Cache Age, Maximum Recalc Duration, External Data.
   Using PS: To set the performance parameters, at the PS Prompt type:

```
Set-SPVisioPeformance –MaxDiagramCacheAge <InMinutes> -MaxDiagramSize <SizeInMB> -
MaxRecalcDuration <InSeconds> -MinDiagramCacheAge <InMinutes> - VisioServiceApplication
<VisioServiceApplicationName>
```

   To set the data configuration, at the PS Prompt type

```
Set-SPVisioExternalData –VisioServiceApplication <VisioServiceApplicationName> -
UnattendedServiceAccountApplicationID <ApplicationID>
```

Setting Up a Graphics Service Trusted Data Provider

From CA: from Application Management ➤ Manage Service Application, choose Visio Graphics Service ➤ Trusted Data Providers. Now add a new, edit, or delete a Trusted Data Provider (for the how-to, refer to the SSS Section of this chapter).

Using PS: To create a new Trusted Data Provider, at the PS Prompt type

```
New-SPVisioSafeDataProvider –DataProviderId <ProviderID> -DataProviderType <Int32> -
VIsioServiceApplication <VisioServiceApplication>
```

To edit an existing Trusted Data Provider, at the PS prompt type

```
Set-SPVisioSafeDataProvider –DataProviderId <ProviderId> -DataProviderType <Int32> -
Description <String> -VisioServiceApplication <VisioServiceAPplicationName>
```

To delete an existing Trusted Data Provider, at the PS Prompt type

```
Remove-SPVisioSafeDataProvider –DataProviderId <ProviderId> -DataProviderType <Int32> -
VisioServiceApplication <VisioServiceApplicationName>
```

Factors Affecting the Performance of Visio Services

Many factors are involved in the performance of the Visio Services. One of the key factors is often the infrastructure itself. If the following items don't help you achieve optimum performance, keep in mind that the weakest link may well be your infrastructure.

- Complexity of the drawing. This involves the number of shapes, data sources, and pages used, and so forth.

- Number of users accessing the drawing. The number of end users accessing a drawing simultaneously, especially during peak load hours, affect performance.

- Size of the drawing. The size of the drawing itself can be a factor; the more complex the drawing, the greater the size and this takes more time to render.

- Data source performance. External data sources connectivity, access, and performance all influence performance.

- Data refresh settings. As we discussed earlier, when you have a smaller data refresh interval, you get more real-time access and less from the cache, which can hit performance badly.

▓ **Note** For more information please read the TechNet article "Plan Visio Services deployment" at http://technet.microsoft.com/en-us/library/ff356849.aspx.

Summary

In this chapter we have looked at the following (see Figure 2–83):

- Why we should use Visio and what the new Visio Services in SharePoint Server 2010 are.

- The Visio client and its new features.

- Integrating Visio with SharePoint using a Visio Web Access (VWA) web part and the JavaScript Mashup API.

- Implementing Secure Store Services and using it in conjunction with Visio, SQL server, and SharePoint.

- Designing custom data providers with Visio Services.

- Administering Visio Services.

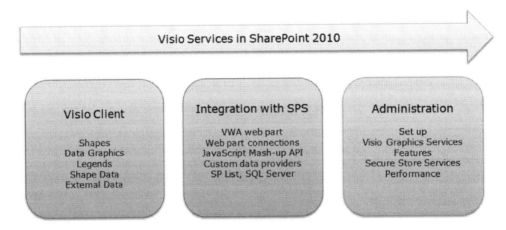

Figure 2–83. Visio Services in SharePoint 2010

What's Next?

In the next chapter, you will learn about Reporting Services in SQL Server 2008 R2, architecture and installation, Reporting Services Add-in, data source management, Report authoring tools, and integration of Reporting Services with SharePoint. You will also learn about publishing reports in native and SharePoint mode, Access Services, and managing Reporting Services.

CHAPTER 3

Reporting Services

One of the most vital aspects of Business Intelligence is reporting. Organizations rely on reporting engines to deliver key information in a timely fashion. These engines need to allow users to create and deliver a variety of reports based on customer requirements. SQL Server 2008 R2 Reporting Services (SSRS) provides a complete range of tools and services to meet those customer requirements.

If you've designed reports using any version of SSRS, you'll probably be familiar with some of the topics. However, if you are new to SSRS 2008 R2, we recommend you read the overview of SSRS beginning at msdn.microsoft.com/en-us/library/ms159106(v=SQL.100).aspx.

What Will You Learn in This Chapter?

- Introduction to Reporting Services

- Architecture of Reporting Services

- Installation and configuration

- Data source management

- Authoring reports using reporting tools

- Publishing and subscribing to reports

- Integration with SharePoint

- Introduction to Access Services

- Reporting with Access Services

Software Prerequisites

- SharePoint Server 2010 Enterprise Edition

- SQL Server 2008 R2 x64 / SQL Server 2008 x64

- Adventure Works Database (SQL Server 2008 or R2), downloadable at http://msftdbprodsamples.codeplex.com/.

- SQL Server 2008 R2 Reporting Services Add-in for SharePoint Technologies downloadable at www.microsoft.com/downloads/en/ details.aspx?FamilyID=B3BEBF9D-D86D-48CD-94E2-0639A846BE80.

- SQL Server 2008 R2 Business Intelligence Development Studio
- Office Access 2010 x64 – included in Office 2010 Professional Plus edition

Introduction

Reporting Services is a server-based platform that facilitates reporting with ready-to-use tools to author, manage, deploy, and deliver reports using Web or Windows applications. Using Reporting Services, you can retrieve data from various data sources, publish reports, and view or export them in various formats. Reporting Services also includes a central management capability through which you can manage reports and report security.

Reporting Services delivers end-to-end processing and management of reports, with solutions that address a wide range of scenarios. You can take advantage of the out-of-the-box features using built-in tools, or write custom code using the API. In this way the product meets the needs of different audience—report administrators, report authors, and business users. While they all essentially share same tools, the Reporting Services API helps developers extend the features and functionality.

Here are some of the key features of Reporting Services.

- Builds reports from a range of data sources and data sources types.
- Creates a variety of reports, including tabular, matrix, and charts, to meet different needs, such as column-based, with summarized data, with graphical data, and more, using built-in templates.
- Supports ad hoc reporting with report models and report templates using a ClickOnce application called Report Designer.
- Lets users create reports, save them locally, publish them to a SharePoint site or Report Server and subscribe to these reports
- Supports interactivity, drilldown, and linking to sub reports
- Supports seven presentation formats—HTML, MHTML, PDF, XML, CSV, TIFF, Word, and Excel to open or export a report.
- Allows embedding custom or third-party controls with custom report extension(s) in reports.
- Allows adding bookmarks and document maps in large reports.
- Aggregates and summarizes data using controls and expressions.
- Supports embedding images and external content.

Now let's take a look at the Reporting Services architecture.

Architecture

Reporting Services Architecture consists of three major components:

Report Manager: This is the front end of Report Services, the UI that provides access to the Reporting Services web service, which in turn connects to the Report Server database.

Web Service Components: These components handle and process all on-demand and interactive requests from report manager and the other tools. They act as a programmatic interface for any custom development and interact with background processing applications.

Background Processing Applications: These are Windows service components that process reports triggered from a schedule and deliver them based on *processing extensions.* There are several processing extensions to support different operations:

- *Security extensions* handle authentication and authorization of users and groups. While the default security extension is Windows authentication, you can write a custom authentication model and replace the default.

- *Data processing extensions* are used to interact with different data sources. They perform query operations as they process query requests from the report processor component. While default data processing extensions are used to connect to many data source types, you can also write your own custom data processing extension.

- *Rendering Extensions* are those that render data and the layout of the report from the report processor in one of the seven supported formats mentioned earlier. Report Server processes tables, charts, matrices, and more by default. When you need to add a custom feature to a report, you can design and create a custom *report processing extension.*

- *Delivery extensions* are used to deliver reports to specific destinations. For instance, an *e-mail delivery extension* delivers a scheduled report to specified e-mail address through SMTP.

All of these extensions allow users to create custom features in the product. For example, you can create and install a custom rendering extension to support a new output format. Given all these extensions, on a high level the Reporting Services service and component architecture looks like what's shown in Figure 3–1.

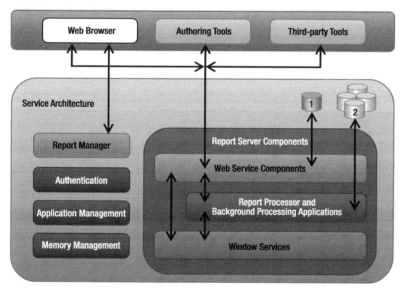

1: Report Server Database; 2: Data Sources

Figure 3–1. Reporting Services service and component architecture

141

Information about reports, report properties, and objects are stored in a SQL Server database, which also holds report models, published reports, and the folder hierarchy managed by Report Server. This database provides internal storage information for single or multiple report servers. This all arrives as an installation package with SQL Server 2008 R2.

Choosing the Right SSRS Mode

SSRS operates in two modes, *native* and *SharePoint integrated*. With native mode, Report Server takes the lead and manages all the functions of reporting services. If there is no plan for implementing SharePoint or for integrating with SharePoint, then choosing native mode is appropriate. However, there are significant advantages to using SharePoint integrated mode. Here are some of them.

- Familiar user interface with consistent look and feel

- Document libraries to host reports and data sources

- Single security model for all reports since they are deployed as items in a document library

- BI dashboards designed with reports

- SharePoint features for collaboration

- Publishing and subscription of reports

- Delivery of reports in chosen formats

░░ **Note** There are performance issues associated with SharePoint integrated mode, so native mode is better if there is no need for ad hoc report management; native mode is faster and easier to manage.

Reporting Services supports multiple instances of Report Server and you can have both modes running on a single server. However, to integrate with SharePoint, additional configuration steps are needed. And it is also important to understand what changes occur to the infrastructure after installing SSRS and integrating with SharePoint. Since the SharePoint platform provides the necessary infrastructure when you choose SharePoint integrated mode, you no longer have the functions such as Report Manager, Management Studio, My Reports, Linked Reports, and Job Management that are available in native mode. Also, there's no way to migrate reports designed in native mode to SharePoint integrated mode. You have republish them to SharePoint manually.

Installing and setting up SQL Server Reporting Services and SharePoint 2010 is quite easy, but you might find yourself in one of the following situations.

1. Your environment is yet to be built. SQL Server 2008, SharePoint Foundation 2010 or SharePoint Server 2010 and Reporting Services are not installed.

2. Your infrastructure is installed with SQL Server 2008 and SharePoint Foundation 2010 or SharePoint Server 2010, but Reporting Services is not installed.

In either of these situations, configuration can be done post installation. Reporting Services comes as a package with SQL Server. Though you can choose to install any edition of SQL Server 2008 R2, in this chapter we will walk you through installing and configuring Enterprise edition.

■ **Note** To understand the differences in the feature set of various SQL Server 2008 R2 editions, see the information at www.microsoft.com/sqlserver/2008/en/us/compare-std-ent.aspx.

Installation

After you've finished the basic steps for installing SQL Server, such as verification, entering the product key, accepting licensing terms, and installing setup support files, you can then choose features as shown in Figure 3–2. If you are installing SQL Server for the first time, you can select Reporting Services, along with Database Engine Services and others features. If SQL Server is already installed and you are setting up Reporting Services now, rerun the SQL Server setup and choose Reporting Services in the Features pane.

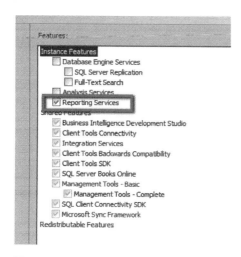

Figure 3–2. Choosing SQL Server features to install

In the next several steps, you configure a number of items, including the installation rules, the SQL Server instance, and the service account for the server. When you've completed the basic installation, you then go through Database Engine Configuration, Analysis Services Configuration, and Reporting Services configuration. For Reporting Services Configuration, you can choose among three options as shown in Figure 3–3.

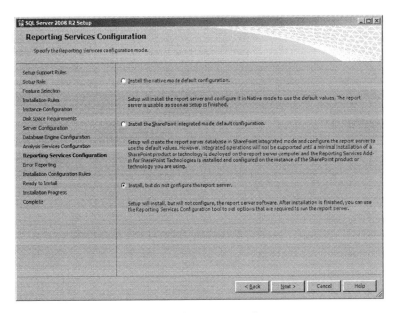

Figure 3–3. Reporting Services configuration modes

Install the native mode default configuration – select this option to install Report Server in its native mode, irrespective of SharePoint. If you choose this option, though you can technically use Report Server after installation, you can't run it in a SharePoint environment. However, the Report Viewer Web Part can load native-mode reports. Skip this option since we will be using Reporting Services integrated with SharePoint.

Install the SharePoint integrated mode default configuration – choose this option to install Report Server in SharePoint integrated mode. You will also need to install and configure the Reporting Services Add-in for SharePoint Products. For this mode to be operational, SharePoint must be available on the same computer. If not, choose the next option.

Install, but do not configure the report server – choose this option to install but not configure Report Services. When you decide to configure, you can simply run the Reporting Services Configuration tool to set the various options.

■ **Note** You can install Reporting Services without the Database Engine on a computer and configure it for SharePoint. In this case, you'll have to set the service account information (Figure 3–4) that Reporting Services uses to run. You might also need to plan for a scale-out deployment consisting of two or more Report Server instances and a load-balancing cluster to increase scalability and handle concurrent users. You'll find guidance at http://technet.microsoft.com/en-us/library/ms159114.aspx.

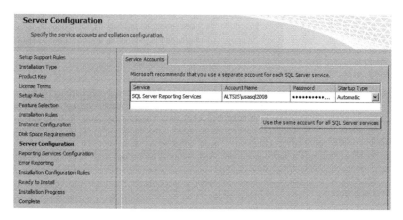

Figure 3–4. Reporting Services service account configuration

After completing the installation, you'll need to configure both Report Server and SharePoint Server.

Configure Report Server

1. Launch Reporting Services Configuration Manager. Locate the database you wish to configure and connect to it as shown in Figure 3–5.

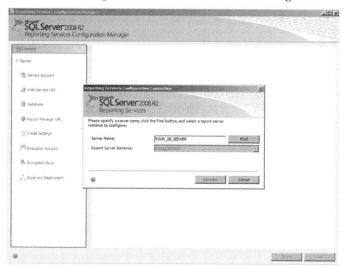

Figure 3–5. Reporting Services Configuration Manager

2. In the Report Server Status window, you'll see key information regarding the SQL Server instance, database name, Report Server mode, and status of Report Server (Figure 3–6). If you've already configured Report Server, all these fields display corresponding values. Report Server Configuration Manager provides the necessary interface to

   a. Configure the Service Account that is used to run Reporting Services. Though it is the same account selected during set up, you have the option to change it if required.

   b. Create or manage the Web Service URL for Report Server and Report Manager (this is not available in SharePoint integrated mode). These are ASP.NET applications and you can configure single or multiple URLs for them.

   c. If this is the first installation of Report Services, set the Report Server database. You are allowed to change it if necessary at a later stage.

   d. Set the SMTP server and e-mail settings. You use the SMTP server to deliver reports or report processing notifications via e-mail.

   e. Set the unattended domain account to execute report data sources in order to connect with remote servers and access data sources used in reports. For security concerns, make sure this service account has only minimal permissions to execute.

   f. Reporting Services generates a symmetric key to encrypt the credentials and data that is stored in the Report Server database. You can manage these keys— back up or restore keys, replace the key with a new one, or delete encrypted content.

   g. Scale out your deployment by connecting multiple Report Server instances to one shared report server database.

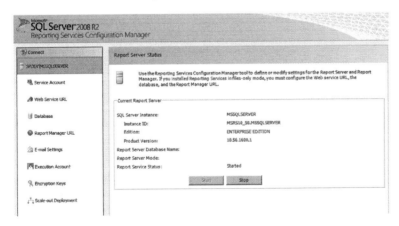

Figure 3–6. *Report Server Status*

Let's get to the most important features and configure them.

3. Click on Web Service URL on the quick-launch menu. As mentioned earlier, both Report Server and Report Manager[1] are available as ASP.NET applications after configuration. Enter a Virtual Directory name as shown in Figure 3–7. The default value is ReportServer. Based on the virtual directory name entered, a URL is generated that will be used to access reports stored on the report server.

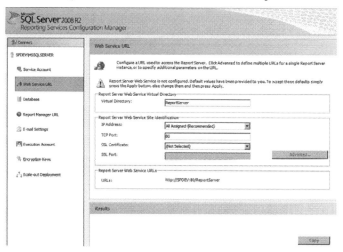

Figure 3–7. Report Server Web Service URL configurations

■ **Tip** You are allowed to configure multiple URLs for a single Report Server instance by clicking on the Advanced button and setting different URLs and Host Headers.

---

4. Click on the Database link on the quick launch, then click the Change Database button as shown in Figure 3–8. We will now configure the report server database.

---

[1] Report Manager is not available in SharePoint integrated mode.

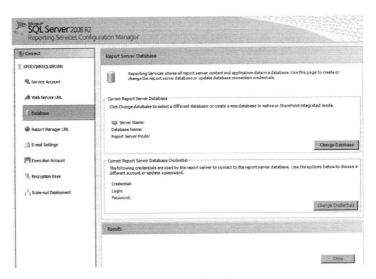

Figure 3–8. Configure the report server database

5. The Change Database window allows you to create a new Report Server database or use an existing one. Since we haven't yet created one, select "Create a new report server database" and click Next as shown in Figure 3–9.

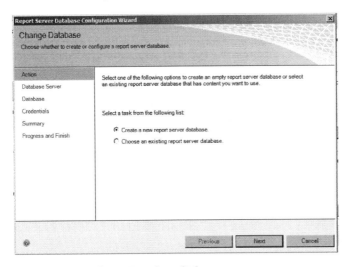

Figure 3–9. The Change Database dialog

6. From the previous step, the Server Name field will be prepopulated as shown in Figure 3–10. A server contains one or more instances of report server. You can change the server name if you like, to create a report server database on a different server. However, be aware that in this type of setting, the connected database will load Report Server settings from a different database. Click Next to continue.

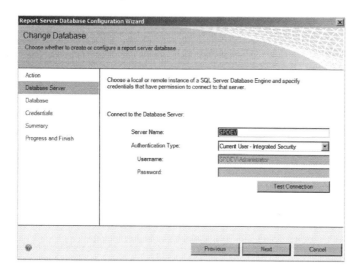

Figure 3–10. *Report server database configuration*

7. In the following screen (see Figure 3–11), provide the database name and the language and choose either native or SharePoint Integrated for Report Server Mode.

As noted earlier, *native mode* is the default for a report server instance. In this mode, report server is a stand-alone application server that provides all reporting functions. It also supports scale-out deployments, including servers with or without the SQL Server database engine loaded. If you choose this option, as soon as installation and setup are complete, Report Server is readily available and needs no further configuration. It contains all necessary resources to manage the data related to your reports, configuration, and so forth.

Choosing *SharePoint Integrated Mode* is required when you are intended to work in a SharePoint environment. In this case, report server properties, report execution snapshots, history, schedules, and subscription definitions, secondary copy of reports, models, and shared data sources are stored in a report server database and the primary copy of the report documents are stored in SharePoint content databases. For our example, select SharePoint Integrated Mode and click Next, as shown in Figure 3–11.

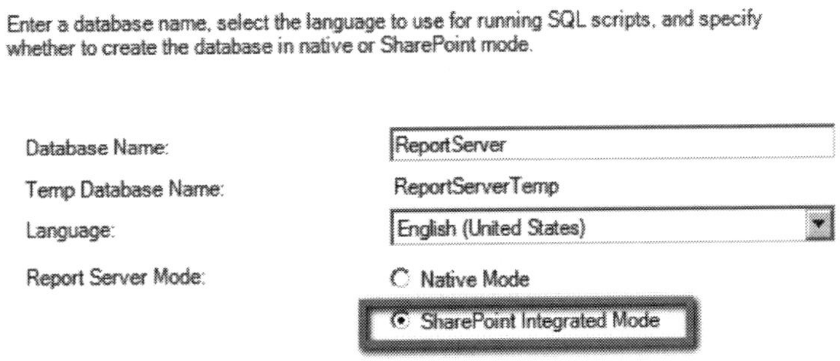

Enter a database name, select the language to use for running SQL scripts, and specify
whether to create the database in native or SharePoint mode.

Database Name: ReportServer

Temp Database Name: ReportServerTemp

Language: English (United States)

Report Server Mode:
- ○ Native Mode
- ● SharePoint Integrated Mode

Figure 3–11. Report Server Mode configuration

■ **Tip** You can always change the Report Server Mode later; see msdn.microsoft.com/en-
us/library/bb326407.aspx to learn how to switch modes.

---

8. On the Credentials screen (Figure 3–12), provide the authentication type. Select
    SQL Server Credentials and set the user name and password. These credentials
    will be used by report server to connect with the report server database.

Specify the credentials of an existing account that the report server will use to connect to
the report server database. Permission to access the report server database will be
automatically granted to the account you specify.

Credentials:

Authentication Type: SQL Server Credentials

User name: usassrs

Password: ••••••••••••••

Figure 3–12. Set Reporting Services credentials

9. Click Next on the Credentials screen to display a summary and selected
    options. Ensure that they are accurate; click the Previous button if you need to
    change anything. Clicking Next on the summary screen run scripts and makes
    modifications according to the options selected. Click on Finish to close the
    wizard. When you return to the Report Server Status window, it should display
    the database information, its name, mode, and status, as in Figure 3–13. If
    everything is correct, click the Exit button to leave the application.

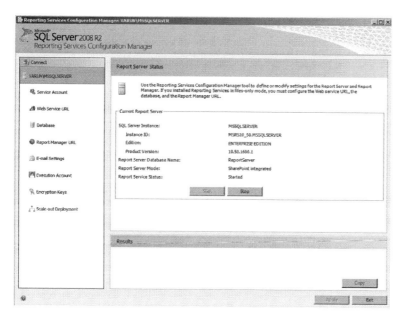

Figure 3–13. *Current report server status*

To integrate Reporting Services with SharePoint server, you have some additional steps and configurations, including installing the add-in that integrates the two. Download SQL Server 2008R2 Reporting Services Add-in for SharePoint Products and Technologies from `www.microsoft.com/downloads/en/details.aspx?FamilyID=B3BEBF9D-D86D-48CD-94E2-0639A846BE80` and install it on the computer where SharePoint is installed.

▓ **Note** It is highly recommended to install the SharePoint product - first.

Let's see what this add-in provides, and what new features it offers.

Reporting Services Add-In Features

- The Report Viewer Web part that can load and render report files.

- Support for both SPS 2010 and SPF 2010 capabilities including collaboration, document management, and security.

- Ability to create subscriptions and schedules, item-level security, manage reports, data sources, alerts, version control, and filters.

- Publish reports using BIDS Report Designer to SharePoint libraries.

151

- Open reports published to document library using Report Builder.

- Manage report server content using a SOAP endpoint.

Reporting Services Add-in New Features in SQL Server 2008 R2

- You can now install the add-in either before or after the SharePoint product installation.

- Steps to configure report server are greatly reduced.

- You can use SharePoint list data as data source and generate reports from list data.

- There is support for the SharePoint user token and claims-based authentication.

- There is support for SharePoint Universal Logging Service.

- You can run reports generated using Microsoft Access 2010 and Reporting Services SharePoint list data extension in local mode.

- There is support for multiple languages, officially up to 37.

In the context of SharePoint Server, Reporting Services can run in either connected mode or local mode. Connected mode is the default and includes SharePoint Server, the SSRS add-in, and SQL Server 2008 R2 Report Server. It enables end-to-end reporting, collaboration, and server-based features such as subscriptions. However, after installing the SSRS add-in, you have to configure your SharePoint server.

Local mode is newly introduced in this version; it is very lightweight and integrates Reporting Services with SharePoint Server. It consists of SharePoint Server and the SSRS add-in, but does not require report server. Since report server is not available, users can view the reports but have no access to server-side features such as subscriptions. In local mode, reports are rendered locally from a SharePoint document library. In order to run local mode reporting you need to enable ASP.NET session state.

Figure 3–14 shows how the Reporting Services Add-in and report server are connected.

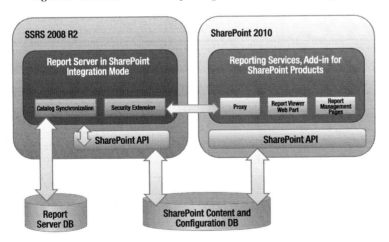

Figure 3–14. Server integration architecture

When a user requests a report on the SharePoint site, the report server proxy endpoint creates a session and connects to the report server. It prepares for the processing the report, and on the report layout delivers the data and displays it using the Report View web part. There are other processing instructions that help in exporting the report in the selected output format, and provide drilldown capabilities, delivery on subscription, and so forth.

A key item to note in Figure 3–14 is the SharePoint API. You can program and create custom delivery extensions, extend the data processing, transform data, and create custom rendering extensions. You can also build a custom security extension to support your own authentication needs. Furthermore, you can use the SOAP API to access report server and the web service programmatically.

Now that report server is configured and the add-in installed, you can configure your SharePoint environment for Reporting Services.

Configure SharePoint Server for Reporting Services

After installing the Reporting Services add-in for SharePoint products, you will see a Reporting Services section in the General Application Settings on your Central Administration web application, as shown in Figure 3–15.

Figure 3–15. *Reporting Services configuration in SharePoint Central Administration*

Configuring Reporting Services takes three simple steps. Click on *the Reporting Services Integration* link in the Reporting Services section (Figure 3–15) to launch the settings screen shown in Figure 3–16. On this screen, you'll use same settings you used when completing the SQL Server Report Server Configuration.

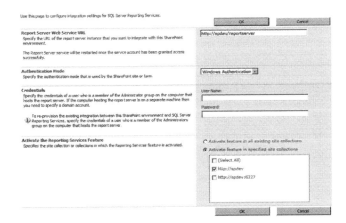

Figure 3–16. Configure integration settings for SQL Server Reporting Services

Reporting Services Integration Settings

Enter the Report Server Web Service URL that you configured earlier. In this case, it will be
`http://<your_reportserver_url_configured>/reportserver` or equivalent. For the Authentication Mode,
choose between a trusted domain account and a Windows account that can be assumed to be trusted
and is used by SharePoint site. In the Credentials section, specify the credentials of a user who belongs
to the administrator group on the local computer where report server is set up. If report server is on a
different machine, use a domain user account. And, finally, specify the site collections in which you want
to activate Reporting Services. After you click OK, you will see the status of feature activation on the sites.
Click Close to return to the General Application Settings page.

Add a Report Server to the Integration

In Reporting Services on the General Application Settings page, click Add a Report Server to the
Integration. In the Report Server section, enter a name for the server on which you set up report server.
Set the instance type to either a default or named instance as shown in Figure 3–17. This step is very
important as it ensures that service accounts used for the report server instance will be granted access to
SharePoint databases. Once service accounts are granted access, the report server service will be
restarted.

Figure 3–17. Report Server integration with SharePoint

After clicking OK, you will be prompted to enter credentials for the service accounts used in the previous step that have access to Reporting Services. Once the credentials are validated, the results (success or failure) of Reporting Services integration are displayed as shown in Figure 3–18.

Figure 3–18. *Reporting Services integrated with SharePoint*

Set Server Defaults

On returning to the General Application Settings page, click on the Set Server defaults link to manage default server settings (Figure 3–19) for Reporting Services. You can leave the settings as is, but it is important to understand them.

Report History Snapshots: This value limits the number of snapshots to retain. When you set this value, it applies to the entire site.

Report Processing Time-out: This sets the time report processing can run on the report server before being stopped. Note that this value does not include the actual query processing time that happens on your database server. However, ensure that this value does account for both report server processing and database data processing.

Report Processing Log: Enable this if report server needs to generate trace log files. Also set a value in days until which old log entries will not be removed. These log files are stored in %Program Files%Microsoft SQL Server\MSRS10_50.MSSQLSERVER\Reporting Services\LogFiles\.

Windows Integrated Security : Enable this setting to use the user's Windows security token for the report data source.

Ad-Hoc Reporting: Enable this if ad-hoc queries can be run from a Report Builder report.

Client-Side Printing: Enable the RSClientPrint ActiveX control for users to download for client-side control of printing options.

Report Builder Download : Enable this to allow users to download Report Builder from sites in SharePoint farm.

Custom Report Builder Launch URL: This is an optional value and when blank, the default Report Builder URL is used. Specify this value only when Report Builder doesn't use default URL.

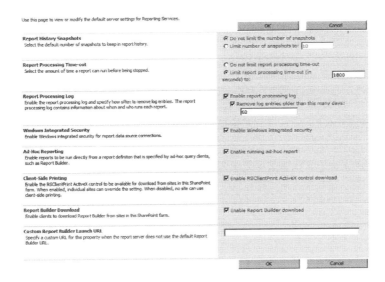

Figure 3–19. *Modifying default settings for Reporting Services*

You have now configured Reporting Services in your SharePoint environment. Before authoring your first report, you'll need to consider some basic information about the report life cycle and data sources.

Report Life Cycle

There are three general steps to consider with any report you want to generate.

1. *Authoring or creating reports,* in which you create a report definition file (.rdl) using SQL Server 2008 BIDS Report Designer or Report Builder 3.0. These report files use data sources that are either embedded or shared and can be published to a report server that is either integrated or not integrated with your SharePoint environment.

2. *Managing reports,* which involves the administration of reports, defining security, managing data-source connections, setting properties, scheduling operations, and so forth.

3. *Delivering reports,* which can be by various means. The delivery mechanism can be either on-demand or subscription-based.

Data Source Management

In order to consume data or add it to your reports, you will have to create connection to data source. To create a data source connection, you need three elements—a data source type, connection information, and credential information. A data source type is connection type, such as a Microsoft SQL Server, SharePoint List. Connection information contains details about the name and location of the data source. And Credentials with permissions over the data source are required, in order to access the data.

Data sources can be either shared or embedded. Shared data sources are necessary when a data source is used often by more than one report. Embedded data sources are part of report itself and can't be shared with others. Table 3–1 compares shared and embedded data sources.

Table 3–1. Comparison of Shared and Embedded Data Sources

Shared Data Source	Embedded Data Source
Available on report server or SharePoint site	Defined inside a report
Can be used by multiple reports	Can only be used by a specific report
Managed on report server	Managed on report server
Can't be created with Report Builder 3.0	Can be created using Report Builder 3.0
Required for shared datasets	Not required

Authoring Tools

You can author reports with data sources using either Report Builder 3.0 (or 2.0 / 1.0) or Report Designer from SQL Server 2008 R2 Business Intelligence Development Studio. The key difference between the two is that in Report Builder you use the ribbon to insert and configure report items while in Report Designer you use the BIDS toolbox to perform those tasks. However, both tools generate reports in report definition language (rdl). Table 3–2 compares the tools.

Table 3–2. Comparison of Report Designer and ReportBuilder

BIDS Report Designer	Report Builder 3.0
Reports authored using BI development studio by connecting with various data sources.	Does not use BI development studio and is a separate application
Source control system compatible.	Though it is not directly compatible, reports can be source controlled from the application. For instance, you can source control report files using SharePoint document library versioning.
Used mostly by advanced users and developers	Used by business users for easy report generation
Capable of multiple deployments	Not capable of multiple deployments
Can embed a data source and create shared data sources	Add report models.
Can view RDL file source	Can't view RDL file source
Can import reports from Access database	Can't import reports from Access database

Even a brief glance at the products, as in Table 3–2, suggests that BIDS Report Designer provides many more features than Report Builder 3.0. To get more details about the features of both, visit http://msdn.microsoft.com/en-us/library/dd207010.aspx. Now, let's author a basic report using BIDS.

Building and Publishing a Basic Report

When you're authoring a report and publishing it to your SharePoint environment, it is important to choose the right tool. We will use BIDS Report Designer for the following example and later edit the published report using Report Builder.

PROBLEM CASE

Use BIDS Report Designer to author a report that retrieves data from the Adventure Works DW 2008 R2 cube and publish the report to a SharePoint environment.

Solution:

1. Launch SQL Server Business Intelligence Studio and, from the File menu, click on New Project

2. In the New Project window, select Report Server Project from the available templates. Select the .NET Framework version as 3.5, and set Name, Location and Solution Name and click OK. In this example, let's name this project as 'Report Project Sample'. In the Solution Explorer window, right-click on the Reports folder and then on Add New Report.

3. Click Next on the Report Wizard Welcome screen. In the Select the Data Source window (Figure 3–20), choose the "New data source" option and enter a valid Name for the data source. Under type, select Microsoft SQL Server Analysis Services from the drop-down.

4. Click the Edit button and in the Connection Properties window, enter the Server Name and choose or enter a database name in the "Connect to a database" drop-down. For this example, choose Adventure Works DW 2008R2 as your database.

5. Click the Advanced button if you need to configure security options, such as integrated security or extended advanced options. Return to the Connection Properties window by clicking OK.

6. Verify the connection by clicking on Test Connection, then click OK.

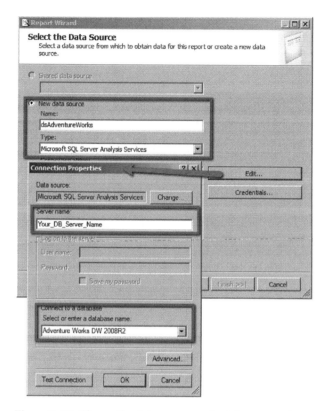

Figure 3–20. Choose the data source and set the connection properties

7. When you return to the Select the data source window, click Next to continue.

8. In the Design the Query window, click the Query Builder button, then in the Query Designer window, from the Measure Group drop-down select Internet Sales.

9. Expand Measures and select Internet Sales ➤ Internet Sales Amount. Drag and drop Internet Sales Amount to the grid pane.

10. Expand the Date dimension and Fiscal. Select Date.Fiscal year and drag and drop it to the Dimension grid pane. Under Filter Expression, select All Periods and click OK.

11. Expand the Product dimension and drag and drop the attributes Category, Subcategory, and Product on to the grid pane. Your final Query Designer window should look like Figure 3–21.

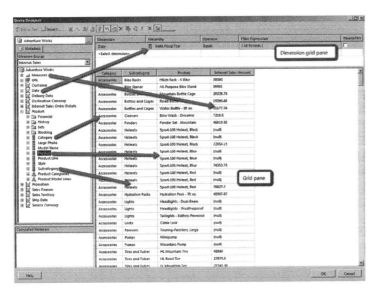

Figure 3–21. Query Designer

12. Click OK to return to the Design the Query window.

As a result of previous step, a *Query string* will be build for you that is nothing but an MDX query[2] that retrieves data from the Adventure Works cube. You can also use query mode by simply clicking on the Design Mode icon (which toggles between design mode and query mode) from the *Query Designer* window and write your own MDX query.

13. Click Next to continue. In the Select the Report Type window, select Tabular and click Next.

In the Design the Table window, you can choose where to place the fields on the report. The Page option displays fields at the page level, which means that for any field added to this section, all pages would see the value. A classic example in this case would be the Title field.

Use the Group option to view other fields grouped with a selected field in the report table. For instance, you can use this option when you want to group items by some category or by date.

Finally, choose Details to view the fields in the Details section of the report table. In this example, since our aim is to display Internet Sales Amount grouped by Category and Subcategory of Products, you can simply use the Group and Details options shown in Figure 3–22.

14. From the "Available fields list, select the Category, Subcategory, and Product fields and click on the Group button.

---

[2] Refer to the MDX Scripting topic in Chapter 1 of this book for more details.

15. Now select Internet_Sales_Amount and click the Details button. Click Next to continue.

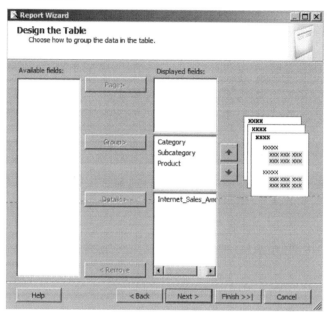

Figure 3–22. Designing the table in Report Wizard

16. In the Choose the Table Layout window, select the Stepped option and click the "Enable drilldown" checkbox. Click Next to continue.

17. From the Choose the Table Style window, select Corporate and click Next to continue.

18. Finally, provide the report name as "rptInternetSales" and click Finish. You can choose to preview the report by checking the Preview report option before clicking Finish.

If you have opted to preview, your report will now open in preview mode. To toggle design mode, simply click on the design tab. Since the title of the report table will automatically inherit the report name, you have to manually change it if you want to display a proper name. Set the title to "Product Internet Sales" in design mode. Adjust the table column widths so they fit values without wrapping.

19. In the Internet Sales Amount column, right-click on the field [Internet_Sales_Amount] and choose Text Box Properties. In the Text Box Properties window, select the Number property and choose the Currency category as shown in Figure 3–23. You can leave the other values at the defaults and click OK.

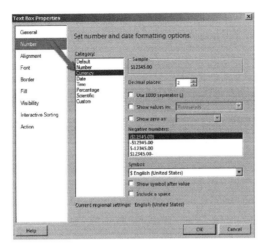

Figure 3–23.Choose Text Box Properties for a specific column field

Your final design-mode window should look like what's shown in Figure 3–24.

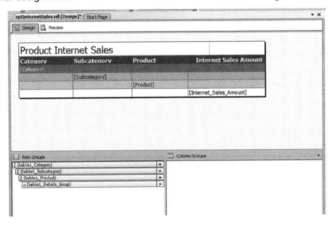

Figure 3–24. BIDS Report Designer design-mode window

Before you deploy this report to your SharePoint environment, you need to adjust some settings on the BIDS project and create some libraries to host the report and data source if it is shared.

20. Fire up your SharePoint site and from Site Actions ➤ More Options… select Data Connection Library. For the Name, use RS Data Connections and click Create. This is the location where your data source will be published.

21. After successful creation, your new data connection library opens. From Library Tools ➤ Documents, click on New Folder. Set the name to Data Sources and click

Save. Similarly create two other folders named Datasets and Report Parts as shown in Figure 3–25.

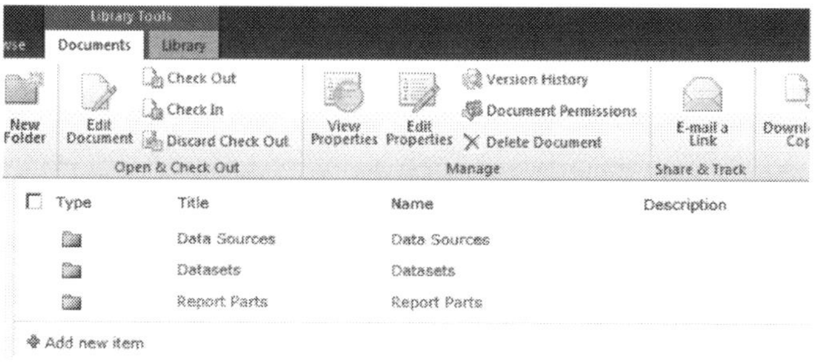

Figure 3–25. *Create New Folders in the data connection library*

This data connection library and the corresponding folders will be used as place holders for the data sources, datasets, and report parts you design in the report. These will be used only when you have shared any data sources, datasets, and report parts in your report. If you don't share, these libraries will be empty even after deploying the reports. Create one more document library to publish the report itself.

22. From Site Actions ➤ More Options… select the Document Library template, name it Report Library, and click Create.

Ok! Your infrastructure is ready. You can now publish your report and its data source to SharePoint.

23. Return to BIDS and in Solution Explorer, right-click your Report project and select Properties. You need to set the deployment options on the Project Property Page to those in Listing 3–1.

Listing 3–1. *Basic Report Property Page settings*

```
Target Dataset Folder - http://yoursharepointsite/rs%20data%20connections/datasets
Target Data Source Folder -
http://yoursharepointsite/rs%20data%20connections/data%20sources
Target Report Folder - http://yoursharepointsite/report%20library
Target Report Part Folder -
http://yoursharepointsite/rs%20data%20connections/report%20parts
Target Server URL - http://yoursharepointsite/
```

24. Leave all the other options as is and click OK to close the window.

25. Right-click the project in Solution Explorer, choose Build, and ensure there are no errors. Again, right-click on the project and this time choose the Deploy option. Verify that deployment is successful as shown in Figure 3–26.

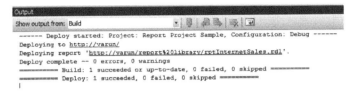

Figure 3–26. Deployment status output window

Deployment uses the target library settings indicated in Listing 3–1 and will deploy the report to Report Library. Return to your SharePoint site and access the Report Library document library. You should now see the rptInternetSales.rdl file in the document library. Since the data source is embedded in this example, nothing will be deployed to the dataset or data source folders.

▓ **Note** If you created a shared data source, it would be deployed to the report server data connections/data sources library folder.

To view the report, simply click on the rptInternetSales.rdl file to render the report in the browser as shown in Figure 3–27. Since the report you authored has drilldown capabilities, you can expand a group under the product category and view the internet sales amount value for a given product.

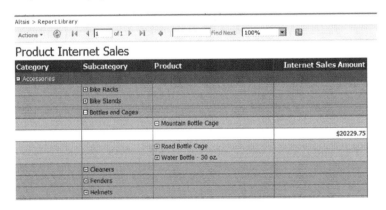

Figure 3–27. Report rendered in browser in a SharePoint enviroment

Take a look at the report viewer URL. The URL consists of the Report viewer page and arguments passed to the page that include the relative path of the report, source document library, and the default view option of the report indicating whether to open in the client application or browser.

```
http://yoursharepointsite/_layouts/ReportServer/RSViewerPage.aspx?
rv:RelativeReportUrl=/Report%20Library/rptInternetSales.rdl&
Source=http%3A%2F%2Fvarun%2FReport%2520Library%2FForms%2FAllItems%2Easpx&
DefaultItemOpen=1
```

Now that you know how to construct a URL for a specific report, you can use it to load the report in any web or Windows application. For instance, on a different web page, you can use this URL within an iframe to load the report. As mentioned earlier, you can use Report Builder to edit published reports, as we'll see in the next section.

Using Report Builder to Edit a Published Report

Now you've seen how to author and publish a report using the BIDS Report Designer. You can edit the same published report using Report Builder 3.0. Published reports can be edited by clicking Edit in Report Builder from the ECB menu of the report item (Figure 3–28). You can also edit the report after you open it by clicking on Open with Report Builder from the Actions menu as shown in Figure 3–29.

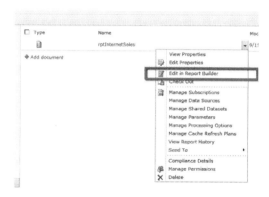

Figure 3–28. Edit in Report Builder from the ECB menu of the report

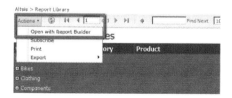

Figure 3–29. Opening Report Builder from the Actions menu

Once you choose one of those options, the click-once application (Figure 3–30) will launch Report Builder and request user permission to run the application, as shown in Figure 3–31.

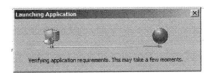

Figure 3–30. Launching Report Builder

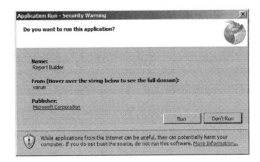

Figure 3–31. Asking user permission

Click the Run button to download and run the Report Builder application. Once it loads, you'll see the rptInternetSales.rdl file in open in design mode. Let's add some additional functionality to this report now.

1. Select the Insert tab on the ribbon and click on Chart from the Data Visualization section. Choose Chart Wizard… from the drop-down menu.

2. In the New Chart wizard window, select the option "Choose an existing dataset in this report or a shared dataset" and click on DataSet1. Click Next to continue.

3. Select chart type as Pie and click Next to continue.

4. In the "Arrange chart fields" window, from the Available fields, select Internet_Sales_Amount and drag it to the Sum Values section as shown in Figure 3–32. Then select Subcategory and drag it to the Categories section and click on Next.

Arrange chart fields

Add data fields to the chart. For most chart types, a field in the Categories list is displayed on the x-axis. A field in the Values list shows aggregated data on the y-axis. A field in the Series list creates a new series in the chart.

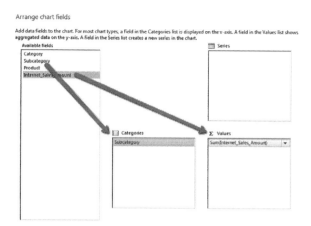

Figure 3–32. Arrange the chart fields for a report using Report Builder

5. Select Generic chart style in the Choose a style window and click the Finish button. Once the chart is added to the report canvas, adjust it to fit under the table that already exists, as shown in Figure 3–33.

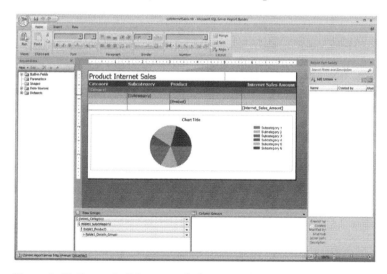

Figure 3–33. Report Builder 3.0 with the report file loaded

6. Click the Home tab, then the Run button in the Views section to preview the report. To return back to the design mode, simply click on Design button in the Views section of the Run tab.

7. From the File menu, click the Save button, then click on Exit Report Builder.

8. Return to Report Library on your SharePoint site and click on rptInternetSales item to view the output, as shown in Figure 3–34.

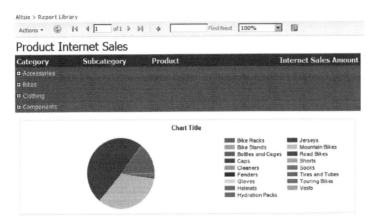

Figure 3–34. Report rendered in the browser using the Reporting Services viewer

Although this report is loaded and rendered using the Reporting Services viewer page, some situations might require you add the report to a specific custom page instead. In that case you can load the report to any page using the Report Viewer web part, which is available when you install the Reporting Services Add-in to your server. The Report Viewer web part provides the same functionalities as the Reporting Services viewer page, such as opening with Report Builder, subscribing to the report, retrieving a report rss feed, and so forth. Let's see how to load reports using Report View web part.

Loading Reports using the Report Viewer Web Part

1. Create a site page from Site Actions ➤ New Page by providing a page name in the New Page creation window.

2. Once the page is created, from Editing Tools ➤ Insert, click the Web Part button from the Web Parts section on the menu.

3. From the Categories section, select SQL Server Reporting. In the available web parts section, select the SQL Server Reporting Services Report Viewer web part and click Add.

4. After the Report Viewer web part is added to the page, as shown in Figure 3–35, you can configure the options.

Figure 3–35. SSRS Report Viewer

5. Click the link that reads "Click here to open the tool pane" and in the editor window, click the Browse button next to the Report input text box.

6. Browse to the Report Library document library, choose the rptInternetSales.rdl file, and click OK.

7. Expand the View settings in the editor window and choose the options you'd like for the report viewer. For now, let's leave them at the default values.

8. Click OK.

9. Save and close the page and notice that the report is loaded in the report viewer as shown in Figure 3–36.

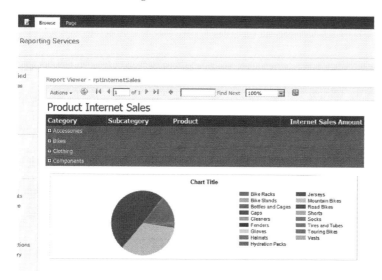

Figure 3–36. The SSRS Report Viewer with the Internet Sales report loaded

Is there a way to create a new report using Report Builder? Yes! And it's quite simple, too. When you install Reporting Services in SharePoint integrated mode, you will have Reporting Services predefined content types automatically enabled on the site. Let's see what different content types are available and how to use them on your SharePoint site.

Reporting Services Content Types

Reporting Services content types are enabled on SharePoint sites that are integrated with Reporting Services, which you can use to manage Report Builder models (.smdl), Report Builder reports (.rdl), and shared data sources (.rsds). You can enable these content types in a library so that you can create new documents of these types.

Before setting up these content types in a library, you will have to verify few things on the site. First, make sure you are a site collection administrator or have full permissions. Second, ensure that the Report Server Integration Feature is Active in the site collection feature of your site. This feature provides the necessary infrastructure, content types, and so forth for the site. This feature should have been activated when you configured your SharePoint site for Reporting Services earlier in this chapter (Figure 3–16).

You'll find the content types available under Report Server Content Types. Since you already created a Report Library document library earlier, let's go ahead and enable these content types on it.

1. Open the Report Library document library and from the Library tools ➤ Library tab menu on the ribbon, click Library Settings in the Settings group.

2. Click the Advanced Settings link under General Settings and ensure that "Yes" is checked for "Allow management of content types?" Click OK to return to the Document Library Settings window.

3. Click Add from existing site content types under Content Types.

4. From the Select Content Types section, in the Select site content types drop-down, choose Report Server Content Types.

5. Select Report Builder Model, Report Builder Report, and Report Data Source from the Available Site Content Types list box and click Add.

6. Click OK to return to the Document Library Settings window. Browse back to the Report Library.

7. Click the Documents tab under Library Tools tab. Under New click the New Document button to view the drop down that consists of links to create a Report Model, Report, or a Report Data Source.

8. Click on Report Builder Report to load Report Builder 3.0 and you can create a new report and publish it to this document library.

In the examples you've seen so far, we've used an embedded data source, which means the data source is very much specific to this report only. And as we discussed earlier in this chapter, when you want a data source that can be used in other reports, you need to create a shared data source. The connection information file can be either a report shared data source (.rsds) file or an office data connection (.odc) file that can be hosted in a SharePoint document library. An .rsds file is the same as an .rds file but it has a different schema. When you create a Report Data Source from a new file in a document library on SharePoint, an .rsds file is created. When you create an .rds file from the BIDS Report Designer and publish it to a SharePoint document library, it will be converted into .rsds file.

To create an .rsds file on your SharePoint site, open the document library where you used the Reporting Services content type earlier. On the Documents tab of the Library Tools tab, click on Report Data Source on the New Document menu. In the Data Source Properties window

1. Enter the Name of the shared data source (.rsds) file.

2. Select the data source type you'd like to use.

3. Under Connection String, enter the statement needed to connect with the selected data source type. For examples of connection strings, visit `msdn.microsoft.com/en-us/library/ms156450.aspx#Common`. For instance, if you'd like to connect to SQL Server and the Adventure Works database, your connection string would be `data source="(local)";initial catalog=AdventureWorks`.

4. Choose credentials for the report server to use to access the external data source.

   a. Use *Windows authentication* when you want to use users' credentials to access data in the report; this works well when Kerberos is in effect and it can't be used when Forms Based Authentication (FBA) is active on the site. The Windows authentication model doesn't fit when subscriptions are scheduled for the report since the user typically doesn't have exclusive permissions to the report data source.

   b. Choose *Prompt for credentials* when you want users to enter credentials every time they access the report.

   c. Choose *Stored credentials* for accessing data with a single set of credentials.

   d. Use *Credentials are not required* when you are specifying them in the connection string itself.

5. Click on Test Connection to ensure the credentials entered are accurate.

6. Under Availability, select Enable this data source to make the data source active.

7. Click OK to save the shared data source file.

The new data source can be accessed via a URL. Whenever you create a shared data source using BIDS Report Designer or Report Builder, you can enter the shared data source's URL to access it. To know if there are any dependent items using this shared data source, you can click View Dependent Items from the ECB menu of the shared data source item in the document library. You can certainly edit or delete this shared data source, but be aware that that will impact the reports using it.

Now, what if someone wants to subscribe to these reports and know how the data is changing over a course of time? Or maybe you want to save these reports in a particular output format on a scheduled basis? Reporting Services provides a mechanism to fetch these reports either on-demand or on a subscription basis. In the next section you'll see how to subscribe to reports that are published to a SharePoint environment.

Subscription to Reports

When you publish reports to a SharePoint environment integrated with Report Server, you have the option to subscribe to them as long as you have access to the reports. You can create subscriptions that can be delivered as follows:

1. *To a SharePoint document library* –Reports are delivered to a document library that is available on a SharePoint site integrated with Report Server running in SharePoint integrated mode. The delivered reports are static in this case.

2. *To a shared folder on file system* – Static reports can be delivered to a shared folder that is accessible from the network.

3. *To e-mail* –Reports are delivered as an e-mail attachment.

4. *Null* – You can preload ready-to-view parameterized reports into a cache for specific scenarios. They can be used by administrators with the data-driven subscription model.

▓ **Note** Data-driven subscriptions are used when you want to customize the distribution based on dynamic subscriber data at run time. For instance, you can distribute a report in any format either as is or filter data within your organization where subscribers list vary over time. To learn more about data-driven subscriptions, go to msdn.microsoft.com/en-us/library/ms169673.aspx.

Reports are delivered in one of the available formats you choose while subscribing, including xml, csv, tiff, pdf, mhtml, Excel and Word. For best results, it is recommended that you export reports in preview mode to see if they emerge correctly. If not, you can change them in design mode to make them look better.

An important aspect to note here is that reports delivered by subscription are not the original report files (.rdl). They are static reports and you can't use them with the Report Viewer web part. Even if you change the extension back to .rdl, you will not be successful in loading them.

▓ **Note** When versioning is enabled, only the major version will be created for the rendered output documents.

In the following example, let's try to subscribe to the Internet Sales report and deliver it to SharePoint document library as a web archive file format (.mhtml).

PROBLEM CASE

Subscribe to a published Internet Sales Report and have the report delivered to the document library in web archive file format.

Solution:

1. Open your SharePoint site and from the Site Actions menu, click on More Options...

2. From the available templates, choose Report Library[3], enter a valid name, in this case "Subscription Reports," and click Create. This will be the location where subscribed reports will render the output files.

---

[3] You can use any document library template as well.

3. Return to the Report Library document library where you previously published the Internet Sales report file (rptInternetSales).

4. From the ECB menu on the report file, choose Manage Subscriptions. On the Manage Subscriptions page, click Add Subscription (Figure 3–37).

Figure 3–37. Add subscription to report

Since credentials used to run the report are not stored and are embedded on the report, you will not be able to create a subscription and you'll see an error message as shown in Figure 3–38.

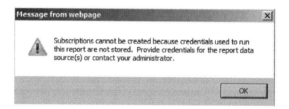

Figure 3–38. Error on adding a subscription to a report

5. Return to Report Library and right-click on the rptInternetSales item and from the ECB menu, choose Manage Data Sources.

6. Click on the dsAdventureWorks data source item. In the Credentials section on the Data Source Connection Information screen, select Stored credentials.

7. Enter your domain username for User Name and the corresponding password in the Password text box that has access to the data source. But most importantly, make sure you select the check box that says Use as Windows credentials. This ensures that the credentials act as if they are running in Windows Authentication mode, which is what is required for SSAS databases.

8. Click on Test Connection to ensure that the credentials have access to the data sources as shown in Figure 3–39. On verification, you will see the connection status under the Test Connection button.

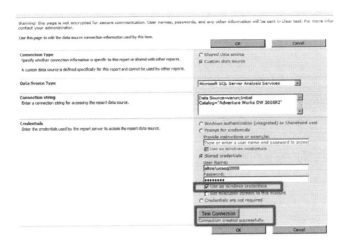

Figure 3–39. *Manage report data source connection credentials*

Click OK to return to the data source information page. Click the Close button to return to your Report Library document library. From the ECB menu, select Manage Subscriptions and click Add Subscription.

9. In the Subscription Properties window, select SharePoint Document Library as the Delivery Extension.

10. Enter the path of the document library or use the browse button next to the text box.

11. Under File Options, enter a valid file name. If you'd like to append the file extension, choose "Append file extension to name." The file extension is decided based on the output format you choose in the next setting. For instance, if you use "rptInternetSales" as the file name and choose the MHTML (web archive) format, the delivered subscription would have the filename rptInternetSales.mhtml. If you don't choose this option, the file will have no extension. If you'd like to set the Title property of the file, set its value in the Title input box.

12. Choose MHTML (web archive) as the output format from the drop down.

13. Under Overwrite Options, select Overwrite existing file or create new version of file.

14. Under Delivery Event, select On a custom schedule and click the Configure button

15. In the Schedule definition window, select the Frequency as Day. Under Schedule, select Repeat after this number of days and set the value as 1. Select the Start time as 8:00 A.M.

16. Under Start and End Dates, select Begin running this schedule on as the current date. If you'd like to run it forever, just leave "Stop running this schedule on" blank and click OK.

17. On returning to the Subscription Properties window, click OK.

■ **Note** To run Schedules, make sure that SQL Server Agent (MSSQLSERVER) is running.

18. You should now be able to view the newly created subscription in the Manage Subscriptions window as shown in Figure 3–40.

Figure 3–40. Manage subscriptions to a report

19. Return to the previously created subscription reports and you should see that a copy of the report is saved as shown in Figure 3–41.

Figure 3–41. Subscription report saved to Report Library

You can click and download the document to your local system and open it to view. However, you will notice that the drilldown capabilities don't work when you open these reports. This is one of the limitations of the delivered reports. To overcome this issue, you need to subscribe for e-mail delivery, which will contain a hyperlink to the generated report.

■ **Tip** Visit msdn.microsoft.com/en-us/library/bb283186.aspx to learn how to create a subscription for report server e-mail delivery.

There are three new data sources types in SQL Server 2008 R2 version: Microsoft SharePoint List, Microsoft SQL Azure, and Microsoft SQL Server Parallel Data Warehouse. You can view a complete list of available data connection types when creating a new data source or a report, as Figure 3–42 shows.

Figure 3–42. Data connection types available for report

In the previous example you saw how to use SQL Server Analysis Services as your data connection type. Authoring a report using a SharePoint list as a data source and publishing it to a SharePoint document library is similar. In the latter case, of course, you retrieve data from a SharePoint list.

Integration with SharePoint list

For this example, let's use the Airport Flight Stats custom list you created in Chapter 2. We will also author a new report using the same Report Project Sample you created using SQL Server 2008 R2 BIDS earlier in this chapter.

PROBLEM CASE

Author and publish a report using the Airport Flight Stats custom list.

Solution:

1. Launch SQL Server 2008 R2 BIDS and open the previously created Report Project Sample project. In Solution Explorer, right-click on the Reports folder, then click Add New Report.

2. On the Welcome screen, Click Next to continue. For Select the Data Source, choose New data source, enter the Name as dsAirportFlightStatus, and choose Microsoft SharePoint list under Type.

3. Click on Credentials… and select Use Windows Authentication (Integrated Security) and click OK. In the Select the Data Source window, enter `http://yoursharepointsiteurl/` as the Connection String and click Next.

4. In the Design the Query window, click the Query Builder... button. In the Query Designer window, from the available SharePoint Lists, select the Airport Flight Stats list as shown in Figure 3–43 and click OK.

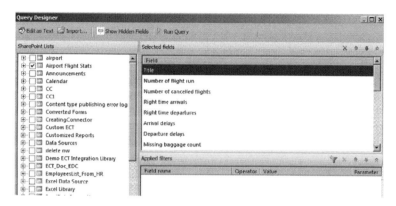

Figure 3–43. BIDS Report Designer Query Designer

5. The Query Builder window will close and return you to the Design the Query window. Notice that the Query string is now populated with field reference information. Click Next to continue.

6. In the Select the Report Type window, choose Tabular and click Next.

7. In the Design the Table window, from the Available fields, select Title, Number_of_flight_run, Number_of_cancelled_flights, Arrival_delays, and Missing_baggage_count and add them to Details ➤ display fields. Click Next and select Corporate style in the Choose the Table Style window.

8. In the Completing the Wizard window, enter the Report name as rptAirportFlightStats and click Finish.

9. In the Design window, adjust the column widths and provide a proper title for the table as shown in Figure 3–44.

Title	Number of flight run	Number of cancelled flights	Arrival delays	Missing baggage count
British Airways	365	12	65	11
Air France	300	15	15	18
US Airways	250	0	5	4
Lufthansa	290	1	14	15
Air India	275	4	10	5

Figure 3–44. Authoring a report using SharePoint List data

10. Since the project is already configured with deployment settings from our earlier project, right-click on the rptAirportFlightStats.rdl file and click Deploy. This step builds the project and deploys the report file to the Report Library.

11. Return to the SharePoint site and access the Report Library where the report was deployed.

12. Click the report file and view the report rendered in the browser as shown in Figure 3–45. Now that you have a published report, you can use the Report Viewer web part as well to load it to a specific page.

Altsis > Report Library

Actions ▾   ⊘   I◀ ◀ 1   of 1 ▶ ▶I   ◆   [   ]   Find Next   100%   ▾   🖫

Airport Flight Statistics

Title	Number of flight run	Number of cancelled flights	Arrival delays	Missing baggage count
British Airways	365	12	65	11
Air France	300	15	15	18
US Airways	250	0	5	4
Lufthansa	290	1	14	15
Air India	275	4	10	5

Figure 3–45. View a report authored using SharePoint list data

▓ **Tip** In the next chapter (Business Connectivity Services) you will learn how to create a list using Entity Content Types (ECT) with external data. When you finish that chapter, we encourage you to try to author reports against a list created using an ECT.

One of the most important features of Reporting Services is that it enables reports authored under Access Services.

Access Services

For years, the Access database has been used by individuals and organizations as their primary database. Its simplicity, the ease of table creation and the corresponding easy data entry makes it one of the most popular databases out there. Access is also considered a mini relational database, and it supports referential integrity, validation, query operations, and so forth. Though it is not meant to replace database servers such as SQL Server, it meets the basic requirement that users don't need much training to learn the simple functions.

In spite of its many advantages, Access does have limitations. For instance, it is not meant to run complex queries or store huge amount of data. Users tend to save Access databases locally, so generally there's no concept of centralizing the database. Hence, manageability can become a big challenge. Other significant issues relate to version control and backing up the database. Access also performs very poorly in multiuser and transaction-oriented scenarios.

These issues have been addressed in the form of *Access Services* running on SharePoint Server 2010. In order to run *Access Services* for SharePoint Server 2010, you need the SQL Server 2008 R2 Reporting Services Add-in for SharePoint Technologies 2010, which you installed earlier. With the add-in installed, you can use your Access 2010 databases under SharePoint site in two ways. One, you can save the database file in a document library and two, you can publish the database to Access Services.

There are good reasons to publish an Access 2010 database to Access Services rather than saving it as a document to a document library.

- Published databases can contain forms and reports that can run in both the browser and the Access client.

- Published databases are synchronized and efficient. For instance, local copies that you create and publish are properly synchronized with the server version. A database that is published to the server is actually serialized and is saved in a hidden SharePoint list. These databases are called as *web databases*.

- Published databases are more manageable than those stored in document libraries. Again, publishing is like storing it in a source control. This means you will get any changes between server and local copy. It has better management for object conflicts and provides greater administrative control.

Earlier in this chapter you learned about the connected and local modes in which Reporting Services runs. In the event you are using the default connected mode, you need to additionally configure Reporting Services to run Access Services reports.

Configuring Reporting Services for Access Services

Open the file rsreportserver.config at `c:\program files\microsoft sql server\msrs10_50.mssqlserver\reporting services\reportserver\`. In the <Data> section, in the <Extension> section, add the following ADS data extension.

```
<Extension Name="ADS" Type="Microsoft.Office.Access.Reports.DataProcessing.AdsConnection,
Microsoft.Office.Access.Server.DataServer, Version=14.0.0.0, Culture=Neutral,
PublicKeyToken=71e9bce111e9429c"/>
```

Open the file rssrvpolicy.config file at `c:\program files\microsoft sql server\msrs10_50.mssqlserver\reporting services\reportserver\`. In the <NamedPermissionSets> section, add the following XML code.

```
<PermissionSet class="NamedPermissionSet" version="1"
Name="ReportExpressionsDefaultPermissionSet">
<IPermission class="SecurityPermission" version="1" Flags="Execution" />
<IPermission class="Microsoft.Office.Access.Server.Security.AccessServicesPermission,
Microsoft.Office.Access.Server.Security,
     Version=14.0.0.0, Culture=neutral, PublicKeyToken=71e9bce111e9429c" version="1.0"
Flags="CalculationCallback" />
</PermissionSet>
```

In the <CodeGroup> section, in the following lines, change PermissionSetName from "**Execution**" to "**ReportExpressionsDefaultPermissionSet**".

```
<CodeGroup class="UnionCodeGroup" version="1" PermissionSetName="Execution"
Name="Report_Expressions_Default_Permissions"
 Description="This code group grants default permissions for code in report expressions and
Code element. ">
```

■ **Note** For optimum performance, it's best to install the x64 version of Office 2010. However, the 64-bit version does have some limitations, especially Access 2010. For more information about office versions, please visit http://office.microsoft.com/en-us/word-help/choose-the-32-bit-or-64-bit-version-of-microsoft-office-HA010369476.aspx#_Toc254341418.

Well, the bigger question is what is the relation between Reporting Services and Access? Reports that are authored inside Access are rendered using the Reporting Services on SharePoint server. If you closely observe, you'll notice that the rendering mechanism is similar to the rendering of a report authored using either Report Builder 3.0 or Report Designer from SQL Server 2008 R2 BIDS. However, the infrastructure is what differentiates them. Let's see what does this means.

When you author reports using Report Builder 3.0 or BIDS Report Designer and publish them to SharePoint server, they are saved as items in a document library. You can connect to various data sources such as SharePoint list, and you can use either a shared data source or have data sources embedded in the report.

In the case of an Access client, you are actually publishing the entire database to a SharePoint site. Database objects such as tables, forms, reports, queries, and macros will be posted to site either as lists or reports. When you use a SharePoint list as an external data source in the Access client, you have the option of converting it to a table before using its data. Even if you are using the SharePoint site as hosting site, you are actually dealing with database in this case.

Now that you have the high-level information, let's see how to author a report in Access and publish it to SharePoint integrated with Access Services.

PROBLEM CASE

Create an Access web database, import a SharePoint list as a table, generate a report with the table data, and publish the report to SharePoint.

Solution:

1. Launch the Access 2010 client and from the available templates select Blank web database. Enter a valid file name, "Acc_Rep_DB" in this case. Click on the browse icon and choose a location to save the Access database file as shown in Figure 3–46, then click on Create.

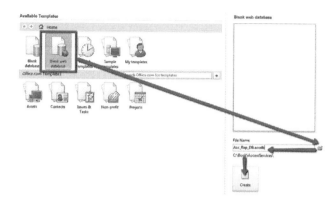

Figure 3–46. *Creating a blank web database in Access 2010*

2. By default, an empty table with the name Table1 will be created, which you can close without saving.

3. Click on the External Data tab and from the Import & Link menu, click the More button and choose SharePoint List.

4. In the Get External Data window, in Site Address textbox, enter the SharePoint site URL where the Airport Flight Stats list resides.

You have two options for importing the source data. First, you can import the source data structure and data as a new table in the database. In this case, any changes made to the source will not be reflected in the current database. Second, you can link to the data source by creating a linked table to the source data. This option will facilitate synchronization of any changes made between source and access database.

5. Select Import the source data into a new table in the current database and click Next.

6. In the Import data from list window, select the Airport Flight Stats list as shown in Figure 3–47 and click OK.

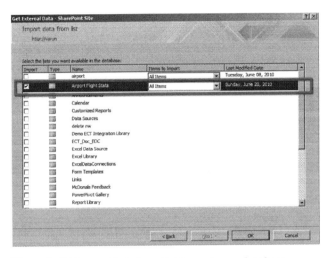

Figure 3–47. *Import data from list to an Access database*

7. Click Close on the Save Import Steps window. You should now see that the Airport Flight Stats list has been added to the objects list as a table. Double-click to open the table data.

8. Click on the Create tab and from the Reports section, click the Report button. If the table is selected when you click the Report button, a report is automatically generated for you as shown in Figure 3–48.

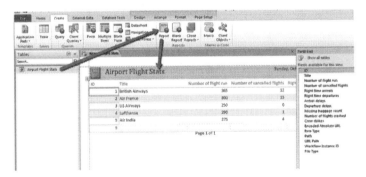

Figure 3–48. *Creating a report in Access*

9. You can also see the fields that are imported from the SharePoint list in the Field List window.

10. Remove unwanted columns by right-clicking on the column header and choosing Delete Column. Arrange the width of each column to fit the report to a single page. You can also change the column names and the title of the report.

11. To add a new column, right-click on a field's window and choose Add Field to View.

12. From the Report Layout Tools tab, click the Design menu. In the Themes section, select the theme Clarity and click the Save icon as shown in Figure 3–49.

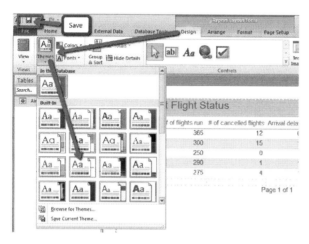

Figure 3–49. *Choose a theme for the report*

13. On the Save As dialogue, enter a valid name for the report, such as Airport Flight Statistics and click OK.

14. Click on the File menu and choose Save & Publish. In the Publish section, click on Publish to Access Services.

Whenever you create an Access Web Database, you can Check Web Compatibility before publishing to SharePoint. This provides necessary information about items and settings that aren't supported on the Web.

15. From the Access Services Overview section, click the button that says Run Compatibility Checker. This will ensure that database application items are Web-compatible and are supported.

16. In the Publish to Access Services section, provide a Server URL such as http://yoursharepointsite/ and a Site Name such as accsrv. A complete URL will be computed based the two entries and will be displayed as text for the Full URL a shown in Figure 3–50.

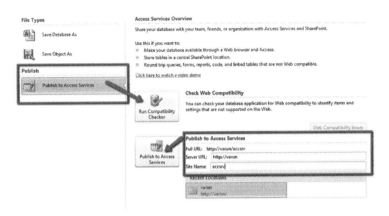

Figure 3–50. Publish an Access database to Access Services

17. Click the Publish to Access Services button to publish the database to the selected SharePoint site. You will notice that the Access 2010 client will attempt to synchronize all objects with the web application. When the database is successfully published, you'll a Publish Succeeded message as shown in Figure 3–51. Click OK to close the window.

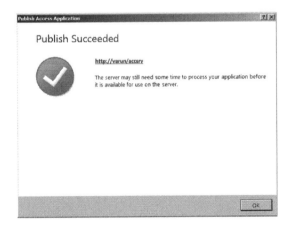

Figure 3–51. Publishing Access to SharePoint

In the previous step, a sub site is created with the site name you provided, which is your SharePoint root site collection, and your database is now synchronized with the SharePoint site. Hence you should see a Security Warning message just below the ribbon. You have to click on Enable Content in order to work with the database. From here on, in order to synchronize changes between database and published content on SharePoint site, you need to click on the Info button from the Backstage view. The Info screen (Figure 3–52) includes options such as Sync All, which sends and receives changes with the server; View Application

Log Table, which displays any errors, and Compact & Repair database, which helps in fixing any problems that occur if the database gets corrupted.

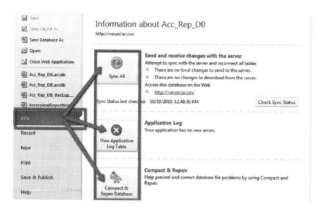

Figure 3–52. *Information about the Access web database*

Browse to the SharePoint site where you published your database and you can see that both the table and report are published to the site. From the ECB menu of the Airport Flight Statistics report, select View Airport Flight Statistics as shown in Figure 3–53.

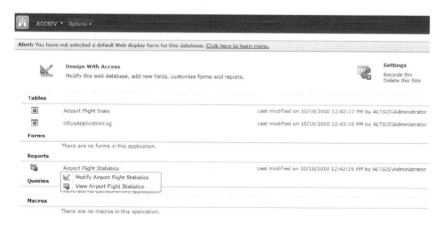

Figure 3–53. *The Access database was published to a SharePoint subsite .*

The selected report will be loaded on a page that is actually rendered using the ReportViewer Web part, as shown in Figure 3–54. You'll also see the Actions menu by which you can export the report to various available formats.

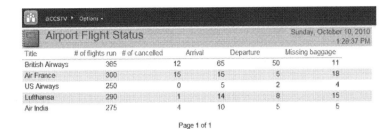

Figure 3–54. An Access database report rendered on the SharePoint site

As mentioned earlier, since the report is created from table that is newly created in the Access database, you will not be able to edit the table or the report. You will have to modify the Access database and then use the *Sync All* option instead.

You can access the published table as a data source using the site URL, and create a report using BIDS Report Designer.

Summary

As Figure 3–55 highlights, in this chapter you have learned the following

- Reporting Services architecture and installation
- Setting up Reporting Services
- Configuring SharePoint for Reporting Services
- Report life cycle
- Data source management
- Authoring tools for Reporting Services
- SharePoint integration
- Subscribing to reports
- Introduction to Access Services and creating an Access web database
- Authoring reports in an Access database and publishing to SharePoint

Figure 3–55. *Business Connectivity Services road map*

What's Next?

In the next chapter, you will learn about Business Connectivity Services and the improvements in the latest version. We will walk you through setting up BCS, the tools, and external content types (ECT). You will learn how to create an ECT using both SharePoint Designer and .NET Connector. And finally, you will learn about the BDC runtime and integration with Office applications such as Word and the SharePoint workspace.

CHAPTER 4

■■■

Business Connectivity Services

Business Connectivity Services (BCS) is a much-evolved version of the Business Data Catalog in MOSS 2007 (BDC). With BCS, you can now read as well as write to external systems. There are various ways to accomplish this, but to begin with you can simply define BCS with one simple equation as

Business Connectivity Services = Business Data Catalog (MOSS 2007) + much more!

What Will You Learn in This Chapter?

- BCS terminology

- Introduction to Business Connectivity Services

- Setting up BCS on your SharePoint 2010 installation

- Creating External Content Types (ECTs) using SharePoint Designer 2010

- Authoring ECTs using Visual Studio and a .NET assembly connector

- BDC runtime

- BDC and Office integration

- Relevant Windows PowerShell commands

Software Prerequisites

To get the most out of this chapter, you'll need the following software:

- SharePoint Server 2010 Enterprise Edition

- SharePoint Designer 2010 x64

- SQL Server 2008 R2 x64 or SQL Server 2008 x64

- Adventure Works Database (SQL Server 2008 or R2), downloadable at http://msftdbprodsamples.codeplex.com/

- Office Word 2010 Professional Plus

- SharePoint Workspace 2010 (Office Professional Plus)

It's a lot easier to learn about a new system if you're familiar with the terminology, so let's start with the common terms you'll encounter, in both their full and short form, in this chapter.

BCS Terminology

1. *Business Connectivity Services:* BCS is a *set of services* that facilitates the connection between SharePoint solutions and external systems. BCS architecture includes BDC services, BDC service data, Secure Store Services, the BDC runtime, and more.

2. *Business Data Connectivity (BDC) Service:* This is what used to be the Business Data Catalog in MOSS 2007. The BDC in SharePoint 2010 is a service that acts as a bridge between business data and a SharePoint site. However, it still depends on the Metadata Store and it helps you to design the external system model. The Metadata Store is used to bring external data into SharePoint or Office.

3. *External System:* This is your various databases, web services, and so forth.

4. *External Content Type (ECT):* Newly introduced in SharePoint 2010, the ECT is a much-evolved version of its predecessor, what was called an *entity* in MOSS 2007.

5. *External List:* Also new in SharePoint 2010, an external list is nothing but a SharePoint list that is used to display data from an external system in SharePoint.

6. *BDC Model:* This is basically an XML metadata file that contains definitions and details about connection settings, the authentication mode, and available ECTs. A BDC model file is uploaded to the BDC Metadata Store.

7. *BDC Model definition file:* The physical XML file that contains the metadata information mentioned in the BDC Model description.

8. *Type Descriptor:* A type descriptor, as the name suggests, describes a data type. Here, however, it is a data type that's specific to BCS and completely independent of WCF, SQL Server, or .NET connector data types. It is reusable across all data sources.

Introduction

If you've worked with the Business Data Catalog in MOSS 2007, you know that it facilitates presenting LOB[1] data within MOSS 2007. People often ask, '*Why use the BDC when the functionality can be achieved by writing custom code?*" But the BDC does a lot more than bringing LOB data into MOSS. If you are new to the BDC, see http://blah.winsmarts.com/2007-4-sharepoint_2007__bdc_-_the_business_data_catalog.aspx to learn the basics.

However, the BDC in MOSS 2007 does come with a few limitations.

1. *It's read-only* – BDC entities, web parts, lists, and so forth provide read-only functionality.

---

[1] Line-of-business

2. *Understanding the data isn't easy*– Implementers of the BDC need to have a thorough understanding of the underlying XML data structure and its elements.

3. *Insufficient tools* – Though there were a few tools available to build a BDC XML structure (model), it was not always easy.

4. *Lack of client integration* – There was no way to integrate data with rich client applications such as Word or Outlook.

Not only has Business Connectivity Services addressed these limitations, it also comes with additional features. Let's look at some of the major capabilities and enhancements in BCS.

1. *It's read / write capable* – You can perform CRUD[2] operations on the external systems either using Office applications or SharePoint external lists.

2. *Familiar UI* – In the earlier version, you had to rely on third-party tools to work with the BDC. Now you can work in an environment you are very familiar with, such as Office (Outlook, Word, and SharePoint workspaces) and SharePoint (lists, web parts, profile pages, and so forth).

3. *Good tools* – There has been significant improvement in tools, as well as some new ones that enable both no-code and code-based solutions.

    a. *No-code connectivity to external systems:* You can perform operations on external systems without writing any code for simple requirements using SharePoint Designer 2010. SharePoint Designer 2010 can perform many more operations compared with its predecessor.

    b. *Advanced and custom development:* You can use Visual Studio 2010 to meet more complex and specific custom requirements.

4. *Connectivity options* – There are more options to connect with data. You can use WCF services or .NET assembly connectors in addition to web services and databases.

5. *Rich-client integration* – You can use external lists[3] within Outlook, Word, or a SharePoint workspace.

6. *Offline Access* – You can work with data in offline or cache mode and synchronize with external system(s) when online.

7. *External data governance* – Using Business Data Connectivity you can access data securely and audit and perform management tasks from one central location.

8. *Search* – SharePoint enterprise search offers look up (discover) and index functionalities to the data in your external system.

Well, that looks pretty impressive doesn't it? But do you get all this functionality by installing any flavor of SharePoint 2010? And what do you have to configure to get it all to work?

---

[2] CRUD – Create, Read, Update and Delete

[3] You will learn more about *External Lists* later in this chapter.

■ **Note** When we say BDC, we are referring to Business Data Connectivity in SharePoint 2010, unless otherwise specified as MOSS 2007.

Setting Up Business Data Connectivity Services

BDC is part of the new Service Applications model in SharePoint. BDC arrives preactivated with installation of SharePoint, and it creates a specific database with name *Bdc_Service_DB_<guid>* on the same database server selected for SharePoint installation. Let's begin by creating a new BDC Service Application and then configure it.

Set Up a New BDC Service Application

To create a new BDC service application, you need to have Farm Administration privileges. Open Central Administration ➤ Application Management ➤ Service Applications and choose Business Data Connectivity Service from the New button on the Service Applications menu, as shown in Figure 4–1.

Figure 4–1. Creating a new BDC Service Application

In the Create New Business Data Connectivity Service Application window, enter a new Service Application Name, Database Server, and Database Name, and choose the Database authentication mode. Set the Failover Database Server[4] name, and choose an existing application pool or create a new one for the BDC service application to run in, as shown in Figure 4–2.

---

[4] A failover server is used in the case of SQL Server database mirroring.

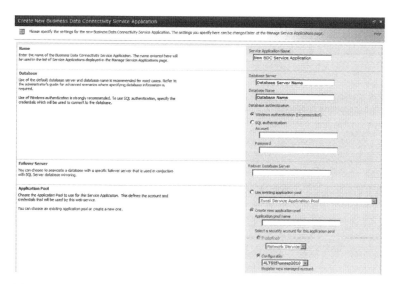

Figure 4–2. *Configuring a new BDC Service Application*

Once the new BDC Service Application is created, you can manage it through Central Administration ➤ Application Management ➤ Service Applications ➤ Manage Service Applications ➤ Business Data Connectivity Service. You'd follow the same steps to configure the default BDC Service Application.

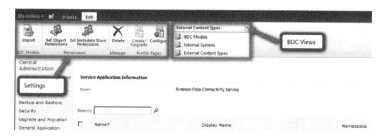

Figure 4–3. *Manage BDC Service*

You can manage BDC services using various settings, as Figure 4–3 shows. Let's discuss each of them. Notice that these menu items are contextual, based on the BDC View chosen.

Views

There are three views available, BDC Models, External Systems, and External Content Types, each showing or hiding various options. Let's look at the options each view presents.

BDC Models

Import, Export and Delete

You can import a BDC model definition file or a resource definition file that contains information about connection strings, authentication, and external content types related to the external system, as shown in Figure 4–4. You can also choose to Export a selected BDC Model or delete one or more existing models.

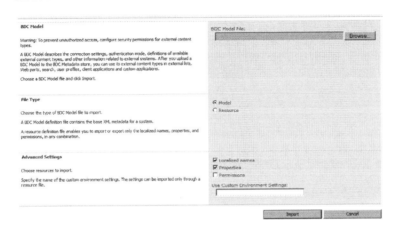

Figure 4–4. Importing a BDC Model file

Permissions

Set Object Permissions

You can add users and set permissions to Edit, Execute, Selectable In Clients, or Set Permissions for a particular object in a BDC Metadata Store. An object can be an External Content Type an External System. You can remove user permissions for a selected object if it's not required.

Set Metadata Store Permissions

The BDC Metadata Store includes models, external systems, ECTs, methods, etc. You can assign administrator(s) and set permissions to Edit, Execute, Selectable In Clients, or Set Permissions for the BDC Metadata Store itself. You can remove user permissions for the BDC Metadata Store if not required. If object permissions included in the store need to be overridden, select the option Propagate permissions to all BDC Models, External Systems, and External Content Types in the BDC Metadata Store. Doing so will overwrite existing permissions.

■ **Note** *Edit Permission* allows users or a group to edit an ECT. Handle this set of permissions very carefully as this has elevated privileges.

Execute Permission allows users or a group to execute CRUD operations. In the case of the metadata store, these permissions are related to metadata store child objects only.

Selectable In Clients allows users or a group to create external lists by choosing an ECT in the ECT item picker.

Set Permissions allows users or a group to set permissions on ECTs or child objects of the metadata store.

Manage

Settings

When an external system contains configurable properties to manage, you can alter them from the Settings menu.

Delete

Choose one or more from the list of available external content types or external systems to delete.

Profile Pages

Configure

Profile pages display data for an item that belongs to an ECT. For instance, it can display all fields of an Employee from the Employees table populated using the ECT. However, profile pages are not automatically created in this version and are available only with SharePoint Server Standard and Enterprise editions. To create a profile page, first you need to enable profile page creation and specify the host site URL.

Create or Upgrade

This setting is also available only with SharePoint Server Standard and Enterprise edition. Once you create a host site and enable profile page creation, you can create a new profile page for a particular ECT, and each ECT will then have a unique profile page or will upgrade existing profile pages from MOSS 2007. Default actions links will be created for these profile pages. For new profile pages, the default action is View Profile. For upgrades, a new action, View Profile (SharePoint 2007), is created. If you re-create a profile page, it overwrites a previous version of the same file.

BDC in MOSS 2007 is part of the enterprise licensing model. However, SharePoint 2010 brings good news for organizations and individuals who have budget restrictions and wouldn't purchase the

Enterprise edition but still want to use BCS. SharePoint Foundation 2010[5] comes with some of the BCS features that you can use to connect with external systems.

Figure 4–5 shows the different BCS features available across SharePoint editions. As you can see, SPF has the basic features. To obtain complete BCS functionality, you need the Enterprise edition.

BCS Feature	SPF 2010	SPS 2010 Std	SPS 2010 Ent
External List	✔	✔	✔
External Data Column	✔	✔	✔
BDC Service	✔	✔	✔
Connector Framework	✔	✔	✔
Secure Store Service	✘	✔	✔
External Data Search	✘	✔	✔
Profile Pages	✘	✔	✔
Business Data Web Parts	✘	✘	✔
Rich Client Integration Available only with Office Professional Plus 2010	✘	✘	✔

BDC: Business Data Connectivity; SPF: SharePoint Foundation; SPS: SharePoint Server; Std: Standard; Ent: Enterprise

Figure 4–5. BCS feature comparison

This comparison can also be depicted in a feature set view, as shown in Figure 4–6. BCS has an offline capability when connecting with an Office (Office Professional Plus 2010 only) client. However, you can sync data with an external system on a timely basis. For instance, the default sync time for SharePoint workspace with a SharePoint site is 10 minutes. You can, of course, choose to manually sync them at any time.

---

[5] SharePoint Foundation 2010 (SPF) is the new version of WSS 3.0

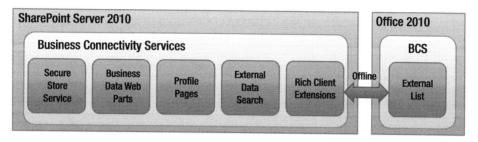

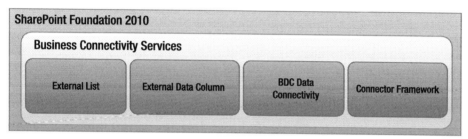

Figure 4–6. BCS feature sets

Let's see at a high level how all these components are connected. As you can see in Figure 4–7, there are three major participants—Business Connectivity Services, External Systems, and Rich Client Office applications. Note, however, that BCS is the connector for the other two layers.

Business Connectivity Services Layer

The BCS layer consists of two major blocks, the *BDC Metadata Store* and the *BCS Client Cache*. To understand what the BDC Metadata Store is, you need some background information. The BDC model contains metadata related to external content types, database connections, etc. It actually enables the API of an external system described in the metadata model with a much simplified BDC object model. A metadata model contains real information about methods, entities, and so forth, such as employee data, customer information, and sales orders.

BDC models are stored in SQL Server database tables and are loaded into memory before the BDC runtime[6] can use them. To perform operations such as load, modify, and so on, you make use of stored procedures. All these pieces form the BDC Metadata Store.

---

[6] You will learn more about the BDC runtime later in this chapter.

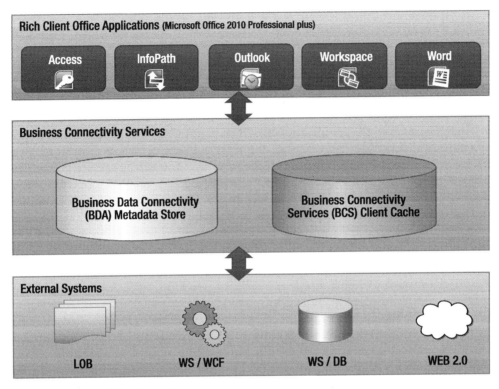

Figure 4–7. BCS High level overview

The BCS Client Cache essentially copies the external system data from the server and caches it for Office client solutions in the SQL Server Compact Edition database on the basis of per-user instances on the client computer. This facilitates the automatic copying and linking of client data with external systems either manually or by automatic synchronization, thus avoiding heavy transactions between the client and server data and improving the throughput of the application. This caching mechanism also enables offline disconnected mode.

External System Layer

This layer basically consists of the real meat—your data. The external system comprises the LOB system, database, and web service, WCF service, or .NET component. Data from this system is extracted using one of the mechanisms we will discuss later in this chapter, but ultimately is channeled into SharePoint site or Office client application using an ECT. As mentioned earlier, the BCS service and BCS client cache bridge the gap between the SharePoint site and the Office client.

Office Client Layer

The thick Office client application layer contains the client applications, such as Office, SharePoint Workspace, and Word. As discussed earlier, data from the external system is propagated to the client applications using the BCS client cache for automatic or manual sync and data refresh. This automatic cache refresh and synchronization is performed by a process on the client machine called BCSSync.exe, as indicated in Figure 4–8. BCSSync.exe comes as part of Office 2010 installation and is available in `%Program Files%Microsoft Office\Office14\`.

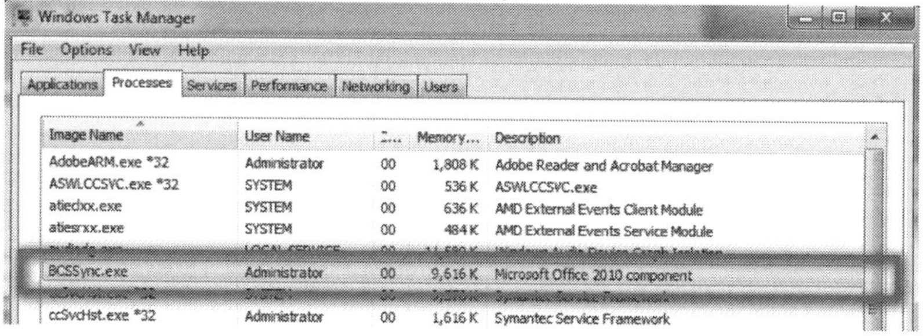

Figure 4–8. BCS synchronization process

So far we have discussed a little about terminology, fundamentals, and the core components of BCS. It's also important to see what tools should be used to work with BCS.

■ **Note** The client stack also consists of an additional component called *Dispatcher*, which will be aware of offline and online modes, is responsible for switching the connection to the external system for synchronization.

Tools Decision Tree

Based on the type of use and implementation, users can be categorized into two groups.

- Power users or RAD[7] developers who work with *out of the box* functionalities on both thin and thick clients. These are essentially simple solutions.

- Advanced developers who work with custom functionalities and design and develop complex applications with both thick and thin clients.

BCS tools are laid out so that each of these groups can take advantage of specific tools to accomplish their missions. For instance, as you can see in Figure 4–9, advanced solutions on the server side can be designed and developed using a custom .NET assembly connector to allow the use of external system data. At the same time, for a basic client solution, you can use Outlook, SharePoint Workspace, or Word.

---

[7] RAD – Rapid Application Development

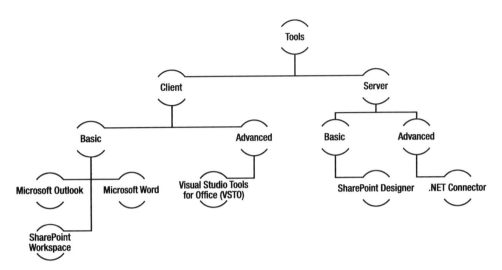

Figure 4–9. Tools decision tree

Now that we've introduced the concepts, let's roll with some examples. But wait; there is one last important concept you need to thoroughly understand in order to proceed.

External Content Types

You learned about ECTs at a very high level earlier. Now, let's take a deep dive. Anything and everything that is accomplished using BDC services is with the help of external content types. You can consider ECTs as the backbone for the entire BCS system. They are the content types that bring the external data sources, along with their schema, access capabilities, and behavior, into thin and thick clients, as shown in Figure 4–10. External content types contain business objects and can be created using either SharePoint Designer or by Visual Studio 2010.

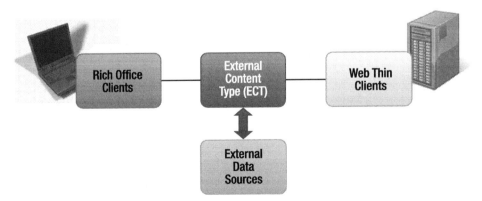

Figure 4–10. External content types bring external data sources to clients

Once you have ECTs, you can use them in many ways.

1. Use ECTs as data sources to drive an external list. External lists use metadata defined with the ECT and perform like any other SharePoint list.

2. Add data from the ECT modeled in BDC to an External Data Column and use the column in any standard SharePoint list.

3. External lists created using ECTs enable Read / Write operations on external system data, provided the external system allows this.

4. Display external system data using ECTs using BDC web parts—External Data List, External Data Item, External Data Item Builder, External Data Related List and External Data Connectivity Filter. However, BDC web parts are read-only and can't be used to write data back into external systems.

5. ECTs supplement profile pages that display ECT item data.

6. View or edit external system data using view and edit operations through the ECB menu[8] on the external lists.

7. Use parameterized query and filter capabilities on external lists using ECTs to prefilter the results.

Now you are ready to do a simple exercise. We will do the example first the no-code way, then achieve the same result by writing code.

■ **Note** In this chapter all the examples will use Employee table data from AdventureWorks database. This way, you'll see how different mechanisms can be used with one data source.

Creating Your First ECT Using SharePoint Designer

SharePoint Designer is the *no-code* mechanism by which you can design a simple ECT to bring external system data into SharePoint for read and write actions. This mechanism is primarily used by power users or RAD developers. By completing this exercise, you'll see how simple it is to build an ECT and how powerful SharePoint Designer is.

---

[8] ECB stands for Edit Control Button, which is available for items on a SharePoint list or a document library. The ECB menu is often called a context menu, which you can use to perform various operations, such as Edit, View, and Delete.

PROBLEM CASE

Create an ECT using SharePoint Designer—the no-code way. Retrieve Employee information from the AdventureWorks database Employees table. Facilitate insert, view, update, and delete operations on this data using external lists in SharePoint.

Solution:

1. Open SharePoint Designer and from the Backstage window, click on Sites and then on Open Site.

2. In the Site Name text box in the Open Site window, enter the SharePoint site URL, for example, `http://yoursiteurl,` then click Open.

3. From the Site Objects window, click on External Content Types as shown in Figure 4–11.

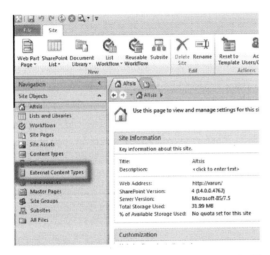

Figure 4–11. Creating External Content Types in SharePoint Designer

4. In the New section of the External Content Types menu, click on External Content Type.

5. In the New external content type section, click on External Content Type Information and set the Name and Display Name fields. For this exercise, set the Name as EmployeesList_From_HR.

6. Click the link "Click here to discover external data sources and define operations.", as shown in Figure 4–12.

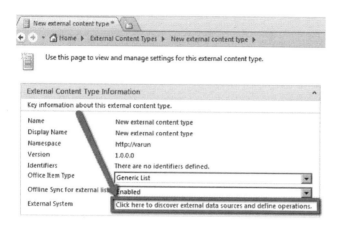

Figure 4–12. Discover external data sources

7. Clicking that link launches the Operation Designer window shown in Figure 4–13.

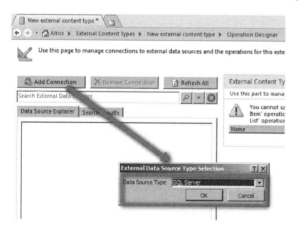

Figure 4–13. Manage connections for ECT

8. Click on Add Connection and from External Data Source Type Selection ➤ Data Source Type, select SQL Server and click OK.

9. Set Database Server, Database Name, and Optional Connection Name in the SQL Server Connection window. For this example, choose Connect with User's Identity and click OK. (Also, make sure the logged-in user has sufficient rights on the database selected.)

> ▓ **Note** In this example we will use the AdventureWorks database. However, note that we will be using the relational database this time, not cube data.

10. The selected data connection will be displayed in the *Data Source Explorer* section. Expand the Data source and Tables and, after right-clicking on the Employee table, select Create All Operations from the context menu. This launches a wizard you can use to create the required CRUD operations for the ECT, as shown in Figure 4–14. This also allows you to select columns you'd like to display and define any input or filter parameters.

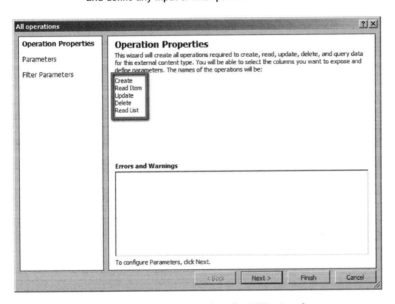

Figure 4–14. Create CRUD operations using the ECT wizard

In the All operations window, let's click on Finish without altering any other settings. The window will close and the External Content Type Operations section in the Operation Designer window will be populated with operations you created.

11. Return to the External Content Types ➤ EmployeesList_From_HR window and notice that the Identifiers value now says EmployeeID(Int32).

12. Leave the Office Item Type and Offline Sync for external list values as the defaults and click on Save from the Backstage window. All the changes to the ECT are saved to the BDC metadata store at this time.

13. After successful completion of these steps, the ECT EmployeesList_From_HR window should look similar to the one in Figure 4–15.

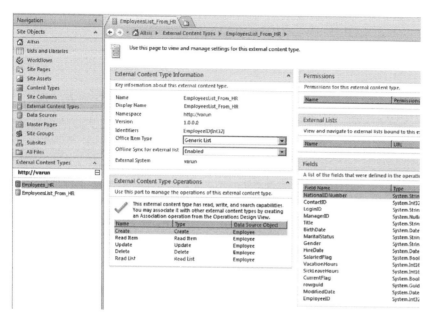

Figure 4–15. The ECT EmployeesList_From_HR window

The ECT is now ready and can be used in your SharePoint site. To access the external data source via the ECT, you need an *external list,* which is available out of the box in SPF/SPS 2010.

■ **Note** You can choose to create the external list either from SharePoint Designer or from the SharePoint site.

Click on the Create Lists & Form menu in the Lists & Forms section of the ribbon. On the Create List and Form for <ECT> ➤ Create New External List option, enter List Name and List Description. Leave the other settings at the defaults and click OK. This action creates a new external list on your SharePoint site. Notice that the External Lists section in the ECT designer window will now display the external list name and URL. You can return to your SharePoint site and view your new external list.

To create an external list from your SharePoint site, follow these steps:

1. Open your SharePoint site.

2. From Site Actions ➤ View All Site Content, click the Create button.

3. From the available templates, select External List and click on Create.

4. Enter Name, Description, and Navigation values.

5. In the Data source configuration section, for the External Content Type, click the Select External Content Type icon (second icon to the right of the input).

6. In the External Content Type Picker window, choose the ECT you created and click OK as shown in Figure 4–16. Click on the Create button in the Create External List window.

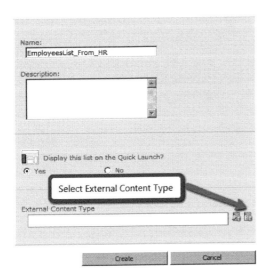

Figure 4–16. *Choosing the External Content Type*

On successful creation of the list, when a user attempts to open and view list data, he or she will receive an error "Access denied by Business Data Connectivity." There are two factors to understand here. First, the logged-in user needs to have permission to execute the ECT that created the list. Second, the logged-in user should have permissions on the SQL Server backend to read data from the AdventureWorks database Employee table. Let's see how to configure both of these settings.

Configure External Content Type Permissions

When an ECT is created, it is added to the BDC Metadata Store and can be accessed under BDC Metadata Store views, from which you need to manually configure the permissions related to the ECT. To do this, open Central Administration and from Application Management ➤ Service Applications ➤ Manage service applications, click on Business Data Connectivity Services. From the available list of ECTs, choose the ECT you created earlier then, from its ECB menu, click on Set Permissions (Figure 4–17).

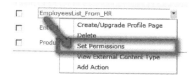

Figure 4–17. Setting permissions on an External Content Type

In the Set Object Permission window (Figure 4–18), in the Add an account box, enter a user account or group and click the Add button. In the Permissions section, choose the set of permissions you'd like to assign to the selected user. Choose or leave the value for propagating permissions and click OK.

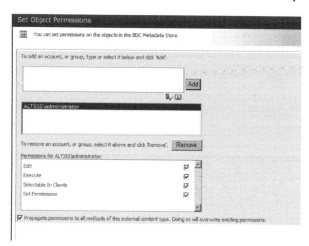

Figure 4–18. Setting object permissions to the external content type

Return to your SharePoint site and access the external list you created earlier. You should now see that list populated with Employee table details (Figure 4–19). To edit an item from the ECB menu on the EmployeeID, click on Edit Item. In the Edit Item window, change any value and click on Save, which results in a data update. Similarly, you can perform other operations, such as View Item, Delete Item, as well as create a New Item. Now, why do you have an ECB menu on the EmployeeID column? It's because EmployeeID was chosen as the identifier in this example.

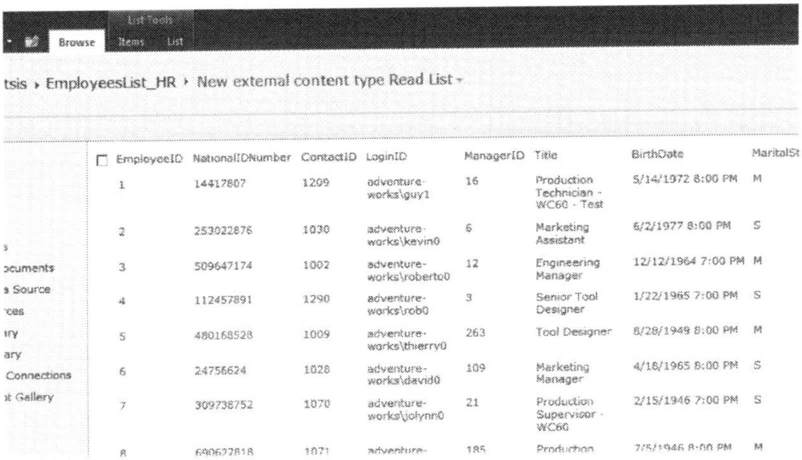

Figure 4–19. Employee details loaded in an external list

Note that in the example, the logged-in user is an Administrator who has the necessary rights on the SQL backend and so was able to view data. However, this will not be the case with every logged-in user. So do you end up giving access to every user of your database? Not a recommended practice.

You will have to set up an unattended service account that has access to the database and will impersonate the logged-in user. Secure Store Service comes to your rescue in such cases. As discussed in previous chapters, SSS replaces single sign-on and allows you configure an unattended service account to avoid authentication issues.

Configure ECT Data Connections with Secure Store Service

In this section, you'll learn how to configure ECT data connections with the Secure Store Service application. The steps are similar to those you performed in Chapter 2. You can either skim through this section or skip it if you want to.

1. Open Central Administration ➤ Application Management ➤ Service Applications ➤ Manage service applications and click on Secure Store Service. In the Secure Store Service management window, click the New button under Manage Target Applications section.

2. In the Target Application Settings window, set the Target Application ID (to BCS-SSS), the Display Name, and the Contact E-mail values. Choose the Target Application Type as "Individual" and the Target Application Page URL as "Use default page", and click Next.

3. In the Specify credential fields window, leave the defaults and click Next.

4. In the Members settings, add administrators to the Target Application Administrators list who should have full control on the target applications and click OK.

5. On returning to the Secure Store Services management window, select the Target Application ID created in the previous steps and click the Set button on the Credentials section of ribbon.

6. In the Set Credentials for Secure Store Target Application (Individual) window, enter a value for the Credential Owner as well as values for Windows User Name, Windows Password, and confirm Windows Password. Notice that in this case you are setting a domain account, not a SQL Server account. It is important that the user credentials you enter have permissions on SQL Server database tables. Click OK to close the window.

Launch SharePoint Designer and open your SharePoint site. On the Site Objects menu choose External Content Types and select the ECT you created (EmployeesList_From_HR). In the external content type manage settings window, click on either the Edit Connection Properties button on the ribbon in the Connection Properties section, or click on the External System link in the External Content Type Information Section.

In the Connection Properties windows, on the Default tab, choose Impersonate Windows Identity for the Authentication Mode. Enter the previously created Secure Store Service Application ID in the appropriate box as shown in Figure 4–20 and click OK.

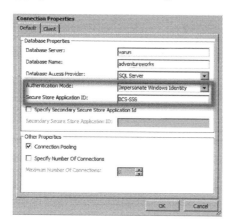

Figure 4–20. Set Secure Store Service Application ID for ECT database connection properties

When a user with insufficient permissions tries to access the external list, he will be presented with a link to authenticate, as shown in Figure 4–21.

Figure 4–21. Authenticate with credentials

On clicking the link, the user will be presented with window for entering his credentials (Figure 4–22), and on successful validation, he will have access to the backend system data.

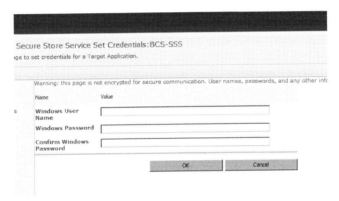

Figure 4–22 . Manage credentials for SSS target application

Now that you have configured ECT with the SSS Application ID, users can access external data via an external list in SharePoint without any issues.

■ **Note** You can't configure an ECT data source with SSS in SharePoint Foundation 2010. You have to use the User's Identity or Impersonated Windows Identity only.

Did you realize that you haven't seen or modified any XML file as you used to do in MOSS 2007? Do you now agree how simple and easy it is to create an ECT in SharePoint 2010? But wait! What if the data source is not a database but is actually a service that is delivering data, and this is the most common scenario your enterprise bus will have? If you use the tools decision tree (refer back to Figure 4–9), you'll see that for advanced solutions, you need to write a custom .NET assembly connector.

Authoring an ECT Using Visual Studio with a .NET Connector

Before you begin actually creating the .NET assembly connector for the ECT using Visual Studio, let's identify the essential steps. Here's what you'll need to do:

- Create stored procedures that enable the *get item, get collection,* and *set item* operations.

- Author an external content type.

- Develop a custom .NET Connector and associate the above-mentioned operations to the ECT.

PROBLEM CASE

Author an ECT using Visual Studio and generate actions — View and Edit for individual items. Develop a .NET assembly connector to Employee information in the Employees table in the AdventureWorks database. Enable the ECT to use the .NET assembly connector, and, finally, create an external list using this ECT.

Solution:

By the end of this exercise you will have

1. a .NET Type assembly connector and

2. an ECT

When you use the Visual Studio BDC template, you automatically obtain the BDC Model and External System along with an ECT. But first, using Listings 4–1, 4–2, and 4–3, create three stored procedures.

Listing 4–1. Stored Procedure for Retrieving All Employee Information

```
USE [AdventureWorks]
GO
SET ANSI_NULLS ON
GO
SET QUOTED_IDENTIFIER ON
GO
-- =============================================
-- Author:        <Author,,Name>
-- Create date: <Create Date,,>
-- Description:    <Description,,>
-- =============================================
CREATE PROCEDURE [dbo].[uspGetEmployees]
AS
BEGIN
     SET NOCOUNT ON;
     SELECT EmployeeID, NationalIDNumber, ContactID, LoginID, ManagerID, Title,
BirthDate, MaritalStatus,
```

```
        Gender, HireDate, SalariedFlag, VacationHours, SickLeaveHours, CurrentFlag,
    ModifiedDate
        FROM
        HumanResources.Employee
        WHERE ManagerID IS NOT NULL
    END
```

Listing 4–2. *Stored Procedure for Retrieving Specific Employee Information Using Employee ID*

```
USE [AdventureWorks]
GO
SET ANSI_NULLS ON
GO
SET QUOTED_IDENTIFIER ON
GO
-- ===============================================
-- Author:          <Author,,Name>
-- Create date: <Create Date,,>
-- Description:     <Description,,>
-- ===============================================
CREATE PROCEDURE [dbo].[uspGetEmployeesById]
@EmployeeID [int]
AS
BEGIN
    SET NOCOUNT ON;
    SELECT EmployeeID, NationalIDNumber, ContactID, LoginID, ManagerID, Title,
BirthDate, MaritalStatus,
        Gender, HireDate, SalariedFlag, VacationHours, SickLeaveHours, CurrentFlag,
ModifiedDate
    FROM
    HumanResources.Employee
    WHERE
    EmployeeID = @EmployeeID

END
```

Listing 4–3. Stored Procedure for Updating Specific Employee Information Based on Employee ID

```
USE [AdventureWorks]
GO
SET ANSI_NULLS ON
GO
SET QUOTED_IDENTIFIER ON
GO
-- ===============================================
-- Author:          <Author,,Name>
-- Create date: <Create Date,,>
-- Description:     <Description,,>
-- ===============================================
CREATE PROCEDURE [dbo].[uspSetEmployeesValueById]
@EmployeeID [int],
@NationalIDNumber nvarchar(15),
@ContactID [int],
@LoginID nvarchar(256),
```

```
@ManagerID [int],
@Title nvarchar(50),
@BirthDate DateTime,
@MaritalStatus nchar(1),
@Gender nchar(1),
@HireDate DateTime,
@SalariedFlag bit,
@VacationHours smallint,
@SickLeaveHours smallint,
@CurrentFlag bit,
@ModifiedDate DateTime
AS
BEGIN

    UPDATE HumanResources.Employee
    Set NationalIDNumber = @NationalIDNumber,
        LoginID = @LoginID,
        Title = @Title,
        BirthDate = @BirthDate,
        MaritalStatus = @MaritalStatus,
        Gender = @Gender,
        HireDate = @HireDate,
        SalariedFlag = @SalariedFlag,
        VacationHours = @VacationHours,
        SickLeaveHours = @SickLeaveHours,
        CurrentFlag = @CurrentFlag,
        ModifiedDate = @ModifiedDate
    WHERE
        EmployeeID = @EmployeeID
END
```

■ **Note** In Listing 4–3, which updates a specific selected item, we intentionally don't update the values of ContactID and ManagerID as they maintain reference keys with other tables.

Now that you have the necessary stored procedures, let's go ahead and create the project in Visual Studio 2010.

1. Open Visual Studio 2010 and from the File menu choose New Project.

2. From the installed templates under SharePoint 2010, select the Business Data Connectivity Model template. Provide the Name, Location, and Solution Name. Make sure to choose .NET Framework 3.5, and click OK to continue.

3. By default, the BDC Model template creates a farm solution[9] and doesn't support sandboxed solutions. Enter the SharePoint site URL as the site to use for debugging input. Click the Validate button before submitting to ensure the URL is accurate and the connection successful. Click Finish to continue.

4. After the project is successfully created, it will display windows that should look similar to those in Figure 4–23.

■ **Note** If you don't see the BDC Explorer window, you can launch it from View ➤ Other Windows ➤ BDC Explorer.

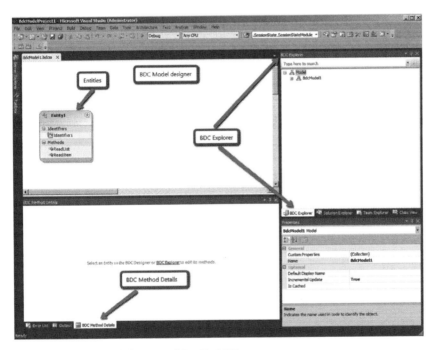

Figure 4–23. BDC model in Visual Studio 2010

---

[9] A Farm Solution is a full-trust solution that provides access to the entire SharePoint API, unrestricted data access, and all solution functionalities. Farm solutions, however, can only be deployed by farm administrators and are unmonitored.

5. Let's familiarize ourselves a little with important windows in the project, as indicated in Figure 4–23.

    a. *BDC Explorer*: This allows you to define a model, its entities, and their identifiers and methods. Methods can be configured with *in* and *out* parameters.

    b. *BDC Method Details*: This allow you to configure parameters both *in* and *out* and also to add new method templates such as *Blank, Creator, Deleter, Finder, Specific Finder,* and *Updater.*

    c. *BDC Model designer*: designer space where you can drag and drop Entities and create associations.

By default an entity (*Entity1*) is added to the model as shown in Figure 4–23. You will use it and configure it in this example. Entity1 consists of Identifier1 as its identifier and two methods, namely ReadList (*Finder* method) and ReadItem (*Specific Finder* method). While ReadList returns an entire entity collection, ReadItem returns only the specific collection item that matches the input filter parameter.

■ **Note** Visual Studio lets you add different stereotypes and methods for an entity of an external content type to perform the various operations noted below. All these methods are called by BDC shared service. As soon as you create these methods, Visual Studio adds corresponding empty and not implemented methods in the entity service class file.

Blank Method – Create a custom method to perform a specific operation in addition to the following methods.

Creator Method – Implement a method to create and return a new entity. This method is named Create.

Deleter Method – Implement a method to delete an existing entity instance. This method is named Delete.

Finder Method – Implement a method to query and return list or collection of entities. This method is named ReadList.

Specific Finder Method – Implement a method to query and return a specific entity. This method is named ReadItem.

Updater Method – Implement a method to edit an existing entity instance. This method is named Update.

In the Employees table, EmployeeID is the primary key and hence you need to configure the Entity1 Type Descriptor such that it can be mapped to EmployeeID. As you might have noticed, Identifier1 in this example is a Type Descriptor of type System.String. You need to set its type to System.Int32 in order to make it in conjunction with the EmployeeID data type.

6. Select Identifier1 under Entity1 in the designer window. In the properties window, change the Type Name to System.Int32.

7. Expand the BdcModel1 under the BDC Explorer. Go to the `ReadItem` and `ReadList` method *input* as well as *output* parameters and change Identifier1 Type Name to `System.Int32` as shown in Figure 4–24.

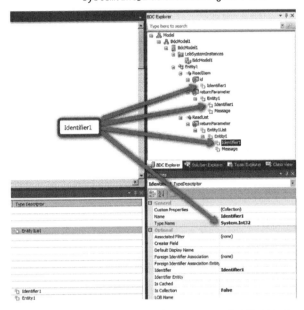

Figure 4–24. *Adding Identifier1's Type Name in BDC Explorer*

8. Delete the return parameter *Message* from both `ReadItem` and `ReadList`.

Since the idea is to retrieve and display columns from the Employees table, you need to create corresponding Type Descriptors related to the columns in the Employees table. Expand `returnParameter` under the `ReadItem` method. Right click on Entity1 and click Add Type Descriptor. In the properties window, set the Type Descriptor Name to the column name you'd like to map and set the Type Name to the corresponding data type of the column. For example, set Name to `NationalIDNumber` and Type to `System.String` since the column `NationalIDNumber` is an nvarchar(15) data type. Make sure you rename the existing return parameter Identifier1 to `EmployeeID`. Perform these steps for all the columns that you'd like to retrieve. Repeat the steps for `returnParameter` under `ReadList` method.

■ **Note** Columns chosen in this example are EmployeeID {int}, NationalIDNumber {nvarchar(15)}, ContactID {int}, LoginID {nvarchar(256)}, ManagerID {int}, Title {nvarchar(50)}, BirthDate {datetime}, MaritalStatus {nchar(1)}, Gender {nchar(1)}, HireDate {datetime}, SalariedFlag {Flag(bit)}, VacationHours {smallint}, SickLeaveHours {smallint}, CurrentFlag {Flag(bit)} and ModifiedDate {datetime}.

---

9. Switch to Solution Explorer, open the Entity1.cs file, and remove the lines of code for the Message property declaration.

10. Modify the public properties under Entity1 as shown in Listing 4–4.

Listing 4–4. Properties in the Entity1 Class

```
public Int32 EmployeeID { get; set; }
public string NationalIDNumber { get; set; }
public Int32 ContactID { get; set; }
public string LoginID { get; set; }
public Int32 ManagerID { get; set; }
public string Title { get; set; }
public DateTime BirthDate { get; set; }
public char MaritalStatus { get; set; }
public char Gender { get; set; }
public DateTime HireDate { get; set; }
public bool SalariedFlag { get; set; }
public Int16 VacationHours { get; set; }
public Int16 SickLeaveHours { get; set; }
public bool CurrentFlag { get; set; }
public DateTime ModifiedDate { get; set; }
```

11. In the Entity1Service.cs file, declare the namespace System.Data.SqlClient.

```
using System.Data.SqlClient;
```

12. Copy the code in Listing 4–5 for the ReadList method into the Entity1Service.cs file

Listing 4–5. The ReadList Method

```
List<Entity1> entityList = new List<Entity1>();
        using (SqlConnection conn = new SqlConnection("Data Source=<DB Server Name >;
Integrated Security=SSPI; Initial Catalog=AdventureWorks"))
            {
                conn.Open();
                using (SqlCommand cmd = new SqlCommand("uspGetEmployees", conn))
                {
                    cmd.CommandType = System.Data.CommandType.StoredProcedure;
                    SqlDataReader reader = cmd.ExecuteReader();
                    while (reader.Read())
                    {
                        entityList.Add(new Entity1
                        {
                            EmployeeID = Int32.Parse(reader[0].ToString()),
                            NationalIDNumber = reader.GetString(1),
                            ContactID = Int32.Parse(reader[2].ToString()),
                            LoginID = reader.GetString(3),
                            ManagerID =  Int32.Parse(reader[4].ToString()),
                            Title = reader.GetString(5),
                            BirthDate = DateTime.Parse(reader[6].ToString()),
                            MaritalStatus = char.Parse(reader[7].ToString()),
                            Gender = char.Parse(reader[8].ToString()),
                            HireDate = DateTime.Parse(reader[9].ToString()),
                            SalariedFlag = bool.Parse(reader[10].ToString()),
                            VacationHours = Int16.Parse(reader[11].ToString()),
                            SickLeaveHours = Int16.Parse(reader[12].ToString()),
                            CurrentFlag = bool.Parse(reader[10].ToString()),
                            ModifiedDate = DateTime.Parse(reader[14].ToString())
                        });
```

```
            }
            reader.Close();
        }
    }
    return entityList;
```

13. Copy the code in Listing 4–6 for the `ReadItem` method into the Entity1Service.cs
    file

Listing 4–6. The ReadItem Method

```
Entity1 entity = new Entity1();
        using (SqlConnection conn = new SqlConnection("Data Source=<DB Server Name >;
Integrated Security=SSPI; Initial Catalog=AdventureWorks"))
        {
            conn.Open();
            using (SqlCommand cmd = new SqlCommand("uspGetEmployeesById", conn))
            {
                cmd.CommandType = System.Data.CommandType.StoredProcedure;
                cmd.Parameters.Add("@EmployeeID", System.Data.SqlDbType.Int).Value =
id;
                SqlDataReader reader = cmd.ExecuteReader();
                while (reader.Read())
                {
                    entity.EmployeeID = Int32.Parse(reader[0].ToString());
                    entity.NationalIDNumber = reader.GetString(1);
                    entity.ContactID = Int32.Parse(reader[2].ToString());
                    entity.LoginID = reader.GetString(3);
                    entity.ManagerID = Int32.Parse(reader[4].ToString());
                    entity.Title = reader.GetString(5);
                    entity.BirthDate = DateTime.Parse(reader[6].ToString());
                    entity.MaritalStatus = char.Parse(reader[7].ToString());
                    entity.Gender = char.Parse(reader[8].ToString());
                    entity.HireDate = DateTime.Parse(reader[9].ToString());
                    entity.SalariedFlag = bool.Parse(reader[10].ToString());
                    entity.VacationHours = Int16.Parse(reader[11].ToString());
                    entity.SickLeaveHours = Int16.Parse(reader[12].ToString());
                    entity.CurrentFlag = bool.Parse(reader[13].ToString());
                    entity.ModifiedDate = DateTime.Parse(reader[14].ToString());
                }
            }
        }
        return entity;
```

■ **Note** As a recommended practice, add connection strings to the web.config file in the connectionStrings
section instead of including them in the code. Also, make sure to encrypt the connectionStrings element if you
have information such as username and password in the connection string.

14. Return to BDC Explorer and expand Entity1 under the `returnParameter` of the
    `ReadItem` method and select `EmployeeID`. From the properties window, ensure
    that the Identifier value is Identifier1. Check this for the `ReadList` method's
    `returnParameter` as well.

These steps provide you with the infrastructure for retrieving data as a list or a single item. The next step is to implement update functionality when a single item is selected.

15. In the BDC Explorer window, select Entity1. In the BDC Method Details window, click on Add a Method and choose Create Updater Method as shown in Figure 4–25.

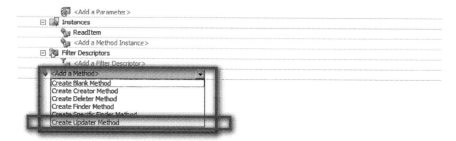

Figure 4–25. *Adding the Create Updater method*

This step automatically creates an empty *Update* method in the Entity1Service.cs file. Note that Entity1 would be an *In* parameter for this method. Add another parameter to serve as the selected row item.

16. Click on Add Parameter and choose Create Parameter in the Name column.

17. Choose the direction as *In* the Direction column.

18. Edit the parameter TypeDescriptor in the Type Descriptor column by clicking on the Edit link on the drop-down menu.

19. In the Type Descriptor Properties window,

    a. Set the Name property to EmployeeID and the Type Name as System.Int32. Select the Identifier as Identifier1.

    b. Set the Pre-Updater Field value to True. The Pre-Updater Field is a Boolean value that applies only to Type Descriptors and indicates if the TypeDescriptor object stores the latest business application data.

After completing this step, your BDC Model window should look similar to the one in Figure 4–26.

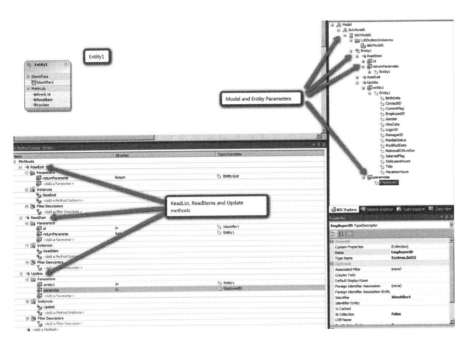

Figure 4–26. *The BDC Model*

    20. Switch to Solution Explorer and open the Entity1Service.cs file. Replace the code
         with the Update method code in Listing 4–7.

Listing 4–7. *The Update Method*

```
int ret = 0;
using (SqlConnection conn = new SqlConnection("Data Source=<DB Server Name>; Integrated
Security=SSPI; Initial Catalog=AdventureWorks"))
    {
        conn.Open();
        using (SqlCommand cmd = new SqlCommand("uspSetEmployeesValueById", conn))
        {
            cmd.CommandType = System.Data.CommandType.StoredProcedure;
            cmd.Parameters.Add("@EmployeeID", System.Data.SqlDbType.Int).Value = parameter;
            cmd.Parameters.Add("@NationalIDNumber", System.Data.SqlDbType.NVarChar).Value =
entity1.NationalIDNumber;
            cmd.Parameters.Add("@ContactID", System.Data.SqlDbType.Int).Value =
entity1.ContactID;
            cmd.Parameters.Add("@LoginID", System.Data.SqlDbType.NVarChar).Value =
entity1.LoginID;
            cmd.Parameters.Add("@ManagerID", System.Data.SqlDbType.Int).Value =
entity1.ManagerID;
            cmd.Parameters.Add("@Title", System.Data.SqlDbType.NVarChar).Value = entity1.Title;
            cmd.Parameters.Add("@BirthDate", System.Data.SqlDbType.DateTime).Value =
entity1.BirthDate;
            cmd.Parameters.Add("@MaritalStatus", System.Data.SqlDbType.NChar).Value =
entity1.MaritalStatus;
            cmd.Parameters.Add("@Gender", System.Data.SqlDbType.NChar).Value = entity1.Gender;
```

```
        cmd.Parameters.Add("@HireDate", System.Data.SqlDbType.DateTime).Value =
entity1.HireDate;
        cmd.Parameters.Add("@SalariedFlag", System.Data.SqlDbType.Bit).Value =
entity1.SalariedFlag;
        cmd.Parameters.Add("@VacationHours", System.Data.SqlDbType.SmallInt).Value =
entity1.VacationHours;
        cmd.Parameters.Add("@SickLeaveHours", System.Data.SqlDbType.SmallInt).Value =
entity1.SickLeaveHours;
        cmd.Parameters.Add("@CurrentFlag", System.Data.SqlDbType.Bit).Value =
entity1.CurrentFlag;
        cmd.Parameters.Add("@ModifiedDate", System.Data.SqlDbType.DateTime).Value =
entity1.ModifiedDate;
        ret = cmd.ExecuteNonQuery();
        }
    }
```

21. Your Solution Explorer should look like what's shown in Figure 4–27.

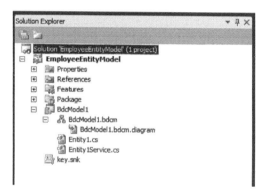

Figure 4–27.The .NET Connector Assembly in Solution Explorer

Finally, ensure that all classes and projects have the same namespace defined. If the namespace or assembly name is incorrect, you'll run into errors.

Now it's time to build, package, and deploy the solution to your SharePoint site. Right-click on the project and then click on Deploy. This essentially builds the project and deploys the package (.wsp) to your SharePoint site.

■ **Note** While building and packaging the project, if you encounter the message "Error: The default web application could not be determined", follow the instructions blogs.msdn.com/b/pandrew/archive/2010/04/08/ deploying-an-external-content-type-error-the-default-web-application-could-not-be-determined.aspx.

As mentioned earlier, the Business Data Connectivity Model template delivers two major pieces:

•   the BDC Model, which contains one or more Entities.

- an external content type that actually contains metadata information related to the external system.

    1. Open your Central Administration web application and go to Application Management ➤ Service Applications ➤ Manage service applications ➤ Business Data Connectivity Service.

    2. Observe the different views by choosing from the drop-down in the View section of the ribbon, as shown in Figure 4–28.

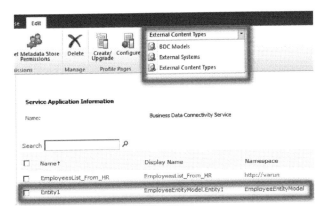

Figure 4–28. ECT deployed to BDC Service Application

    3. From the list of available ECTs, select the previously created and deployed ECT from the Visual Studio project.

    4. From the ECB menu on the entity, select Set Permissions. Enter a user account and click the Add button. You can add more than one user account and set object permissions.

    5. Select the added user and set any (Edit, Execute, Selectable In Clients, Set Permissions) or all permissions and click OK.

    6. Open your SharePoint site and from Site Actions ➤ More Options, select External List and click Create. In the Create New window, provide a Name and Description and choose whether or not to display the external list on the Quick launch.

    7. In the Data source configuration section, pick the ECT you created earlier by clicking on the Select External Content Type icon as shown in Figure 4–29. Then click on Create.

Figure 4–29. Choose the external content type through an external list

An external list will be created as shown in Figure 4–30. As you'll see, it is similar to the list you created using SharePoint Designer earlier in this chapter. In this case, however, the list is populated with data from the external data source using a .Net assembly connector code.

■ **Note** Columns might be ordered alphabetically. You can set the column order by editing the default view under the list settings or from the *List Tools* ➤ *List* ➤ *Modify View* option.

Figure 4–30. An external list with data populated using an ECT

Not only is the external list populated, you can also select an item to view and edit (Figure 4–31). When the View option is selected, the ReadItem method will be triggered and the selected identifier id (item id) is passed to the function as a parameter. When the Edit option is selected, the Update method is called and the identifier id (item id) and the entity (row data) are passed as parameters.

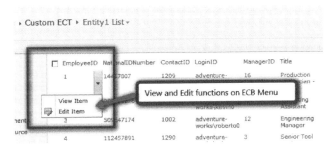

Figure 4–31. You can view or edit an item using the ECB menu on the external list

---

Note: When you change any entity value, type descriptor, assembly name, or namespaces and redeploy the solution on an existing ECT, it is recommended you delete the external list and recreate it. When you get an error, however, the first place to look is under %Program Files%Common Files\Microsoft Shared\Web Server Extensions\14\LOGSfolder.

You must have noticed that an external list looks similar to a normal SharePoint list, but it's not exactly the same. Table 4–1 indicates how they compare.

Table 4–1. External Lists vs. Normal SharePoint Lists

External List	**Normal / Custom SharePoint List**
Requires an external content type to create an external list and holds data related to the external source.	Can use existing content type and holds data related to data within the list.
Can read and write to external data	Can read and write to data within the list.
Can create an external list using SharePoint Designer or a SharePoint site.	Can create a custom list using SharePoint Designer or SharePoint site.
Default views and forms are created to display and edit external data when the external list is created.	Default views and forms are created to display and edit list data when the custom list is created.
Can create custom actions and initiate workflows.	Can create custom actions and initiate workflows.
Can be used with SharePoint workspace or Outlook to display external data.	Can be used with SharePoint workspace or Outlook to display external data.
Customize forms using InfoPath.	Customize forms using InfoPath.
Does not allow management of non-external content types.	Allows management of content types.
Versioning is not supported.	Supports versioning on items.
Can't add additional columns unless the ECT is changed.	Can create columns or use existing site columns

The solution you created earlier using .NET code and deployed to SharePoint in this exercise is deployed globally and will add the BDC model to the BDC Service Application. This means any Web application in the farm can access this ECT, from which you can create an external list. You will see this ECT under SharePoint Designer as a .Net type. We will see how to create an external list from it.

Creating an ECT Using SharePoint Designer and .NET Type

As mentioned earlier, you can also access and use the ECT you created from the .Net assembly. Launch SharePoint Designer and use the Open Site option to open your SharePoint site. From the Site Objects window, click External Content Types. In the External Content Types window, you'll see the list of available ECTs, including the one you created earlier, as shown in Figure 4–32.

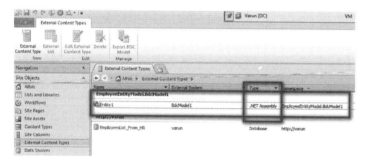

Figure 4–32. External Content Types in SharePoint Designer

Click on Entity1 to load the Entity1 external content type. From the Lists & Forms section on the ribbon, click the Create Lists & Form button as shown in Figure 4–33. Also note the operations available with the ECT in the External Content Type Operations section.

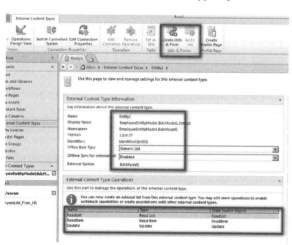

Figure 4–33. Creating an external list from an exisiting ECT using SharePoint Designer

In the Create Lists and Form for window (Figure 4–34), select Create New External List and enter a value for List Name. Leave the other default input values and click OK. If there are more than one model definitions available in the .NET assembly, you can choose one from the *System Instance* drop-down.

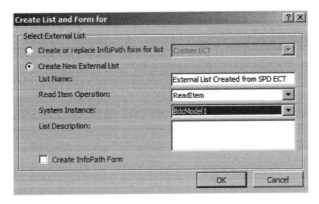

Figure 4–34. *Creating a new external list*

Return to your SharePoint site and find the list with the name (*External List Created from SPD ECT*) you provided in the previous step. Launch the external list and you'll see this new list with view and edit functionality; it is similar to the lists created using other techniques.

Again, even with Visual Studio and writing a custom .NET assembly connector, you haven't seen or edited any XML file so far, either while creating the model or when defining your entity. This I'd say is one of the biggest advantages when compared with the BDC in MOSS 2007.

Another important improvement of this version over the prior is in the runtime object model. There have been phenomenal changes and more capabilities added in the new version. Let's take a look at them.

BDC Runtime

Recall the question[10] I asked in the Introduction section of this chapter? I'd say the BDC runtime is one of the answers for it. With BDC runtime you now have the ability to represent the external system either using the server-side object model or the client-side. Both server-side and client-side object models are symmetrical; this means that what you can do with the server object model can also be done using the client object model and, in fact, the assembly is the same for both.

Using the BDC runtime, you can not only read but also write back to the external system. There's also a batch-read process by which you can send multiple inputs as a batch and get the corresponding results in a single request and response. This should improve performance and latency phenomenally.

There are many other improvements including streaming support, an extensibility mechanism with .NET assembly connectors, custom connectors, secure store providers, and so on. But what actually compels here is, whenever you develop a custom object using the BDC runtime against an ECT or external system deployed to your farm, it's a one-time deal. As long as the ECT isn't updated, your custom object need not be changed.

---

[10] Question - Why use BDC when the functionality can be achieved by writing custom code?

What this also means is if your data source changes but your ECTs are untouched, your application will not be affected. Great, isn't it? Let's perform a simple example to understand in more detail.

PROBLEM CASE

Using the BDC runtime, access the ReadList method from the previously deployed ECT Entity1 and retrieve the Employee LoginID and Title.

Solution:

First let's take a look at the ECT we previously developed and deployed using Visual Studio—Entity1. After deployment, you can locate Entity1 in CA ➤ Application Management ➤ Service Applications ➤ Manage service applications ➤ Business Data Connectivity Service (refer back to Figure 4–33).

Before you begin, you will need a few values from the ECT, as well as the code from which it has been deployed.

1. Note the Name of the ECT and the corresponding namespace as you'll be using them in the BDC runtime (Figure 4–35).

2. Next, since the goal is to access the Read List method, you need to obtain the exact method name from the code. If you followed previous example, you know it is named as ReadList.

3. Finally, you need the column names for the Login ID and title, which are *LoginID* and *Title*.

Figure 4–35. Entity1 in the BDC Service Application

Launch Visual Studio and from File ➤ New ➤ Project, select the Visual C# Console Application template and ensure that you have selected .NET Framework 3.5. Provide the Name, Location, and Solution Name, and click OK. Add references to the following assemblies:

1. C:\Program Files\Common Files\Microsoft Shared\Web Server Extensions\14\ISAPI\Microsoft.BusinessData.dll

2. C:\Program Files\Common Files\Microsoft Shared\Web Server Extensions\14\ISAPI\Microsoft.SharePoint.dll

3. C:\Windows\assembly\GAC_64\Microsoft.SharePoint.BusinessData.Administration.
    Client\14.0.0.0__71e9bce111e9429c\Microsoft.SharePoint.BusinessData.Adminis
    tration.Client.dll

4. System.Web

▓ **Tip** Notice that Microsoft.SharePoint.BusinessData.Administration.Client.dll assembly is in a 64–bit assembly folder.

Replace the code in Program.cs with that of Listing 4–8. Ensure that you change the SharePoint site URL correctly to your own. Also, if the method names, ECT name, or namespace are different, make sure to change them accordingly in the code.

Listing 4–8. Code for the BDC Runtime

```csharp
using System;
using System.Collections.Generic;
using System.Linq;
using System.Text;
using Microsoft.SharePoint;
using Microsoft.SharePoint.BusinessData.SharedService;
using Microsoft.SharePoint.BusinessData.MetadataModel;
using Microsoft.BusinessData.MetadataModel;
using Microsoft.BusinessData.Runtime;
namespace BCSRunTime // Set namespace according to your project
{
    class Program // Set class name as per your project
    {
        static void Main(string[] args)
        {
            ExecuteBcsEctMethods(@"http://yoursharepointsite/"); // set your site URL
        }
        static void ExecuteBcsEctMethods(string siteUrl)
        {
            using (SPSite site = new SPSite(siteUrl))
            {
                using (new SPServiceContextScope(SPServiceContext.GetContext(site)))
                {
                    BdcServiceApplicationProxy proxy =
(BdcServiceApplicationProxy)SPServiceContext.Current.GetDefaultProxy(typeof(BdcServiceAp
plicationProxy));
                    DatabaseBackedMetadataCatalog model =
proxy.GetDatabaseBackedMetadataCatalog();
                    IEntity entity = model.GetEntity("EmployeeEntityModel", "Entity1");
// Namespace, Entity name
                    ILobSystemInstance lobSystemInstance =
entity.GetLobSystem().GetLobSystemInstances()[0].Value;
                    IMethodInstance method = entity.GetMethodInstance("ReadList",
MethodInstanceType.Finder); // Finder method name
                    IView view = entity.GetFinderView(method.Name);

                    IFilterCollection filterCollection =
entity.GetDefaultFinderFilters();
```

```
                        IEntityInstanceEnumerator entityInstanceEnumerator =
        entity.FindFiltered(filterCollection, method.Name, lobSystemInstance,
        OperationMode.Online);
                        Console.WriteLine("Employee Login ID | Title");
                        while (entityInstanceEnumerator.MoveNext())
                        {

        Console.WriteLine(entityInstanceEnumerator.Current["LoginID"].ToString() + " - " +
        entityInstanceEnumerator.Current["Title"].ToString()); // Column names

                        }
                        Console.ReadLine();
                    }
                }
            }
        }
    }
```

Save the file, then build and run the code. You should see output similar to what's shown in Figure 4–36.

Figure 4–36. Accessing external system data through the ECT using the BDC runtime

What you achieved just now is this: you are able to execute a finder method in the ECT and retrieve the data from the external system. Similarly, you can execute any method that you define in the ECT, whether for updating the data in a default view or reading a specific item.

Note that the logic in the code is unaware of the external system. All it cares about is the ECT name, its finder method, and the namespace. As long as these don't change, your logic runs forever.

The BCS comes with many more features. You can use it not only with SharePoint but can integrate with other Office applications, and you can work offline using SharePoint workspace. In the next section we will discuss some of these capabilities.

Integration with Office Applications

You can integrate BCS with Office applications such as Outlook and Word. If you recall the Office client layer (refer back to Figure 4–7), that's what we'll be using now. We will demonstrate a simple example using Office Word; if you'd like to understand how BCS can be integrated with Outlook, we recommend you read Chapter 9 in Sahil Malik's *Microsoft SharePoint 2010 Building Solutions for SharePoint 2010* (Apress, 2010).

Integration with Office Word

Launch your SharePoint site and create a document library from Site Actions ➤ More Options ➤ Create. Once the document library is created, open the library settings and click on Create Column. Enter the column name and select External Data as the type of information (Figure 4–37).

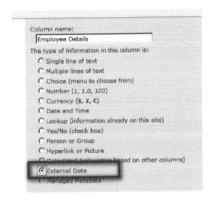

Figure 4–37. Creating an external data column

Under Additional Column Settings, select the external content type you created earlier in this chapter. Select all fields or only those you wish (Figure 4–38) and click OK.

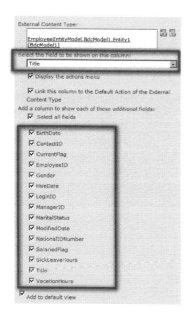

Figure 4–38. *Choosing fields for the external data column*

Return to the document library and upload a document by choosing the Add document link and clicking OK. Note that the document can't be empty. Also, before you save the document to the library, select data from External Items icon. Then enter text in the Title textbox and click the Save button as shown in Figure 4–39.

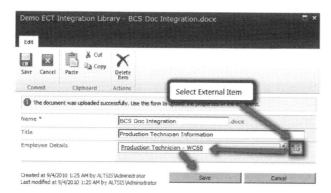

Figure 4–39. *Selecting an external item*

The selected data item is added as an entry to the document library with the columns you chose in previous step. From the document's ECB menu, click Check Out, then click OK in the pop-up window. Click on the document to launch the document in Office Word 2010.

Go to Word ➤ Insert ➤ Text ➤ Quick Parts, then choose Document Property and select Employee Details as shown in Figure 4–40.

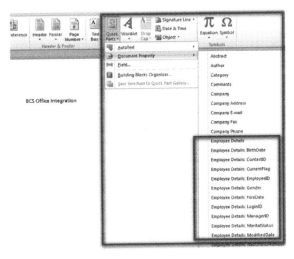

Figure 4–40. Choosing document properties under Quick Parts

After you choose the values you're interested in, the final document should look something like the one in Figure 4–41.

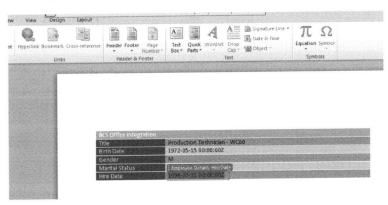

Figure 4–41. Document properties displaying data

You can now save the document, check it in, provide any version comments from the Backstage window of the ribbon, and then close the document.

Another important feature of BCS is its integration with SharePoint Workspace 2010. You can work in offline mode and sync back data to SharePoint lists and libraries using SharePoint Workspace.

Integration with SharePoint Workspace

SharePoint Workspace is the next generation of Office 2007 Groove. SharePoint Workspace is a client application that not only enables access to SharePoint Server 2010 and SharePoint Foundation 2010 document libraries and lists, but also can be used in offline mode. We won't cover it in detail here, but you can find more information at http://technet.microsoft.com/en-us/library/ee649102.aspx. Now we'll discuss how to integrate BCS external lists with SharePoint Workspace.

Launch SharePoint Workspace 2010 on your computer. The first time you start Workspace, the Account Configuration Wizard will launch, as shown in Figure 4–42.

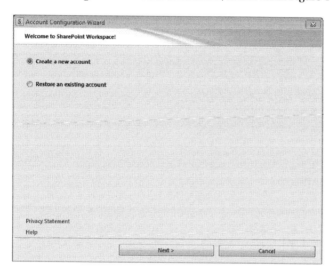

Figure 4–42. SharePoint Workspace Account Configuration Wizard

You can create a new account using an e-mail address or Account Configuration Code. Once the account is created, the Workspace client will launch. If you have an account file (.grv), you can also restore an existing account using the wizard. From the Workspaces section of the Home tab on the ribbon, select New SharePoint Workspace. In the New SharePoint Workspace window, enter your SharePoint site URL location as shown in Figure 4–43. You can choose and configure a library or list and add others later.

Figure 4–43. Setting up a new SharePoint Workspace

SharePoint Workspace will begin syncing your SharePoint site lists to your computer. You will be prompted with couple of approval (Figure 4–44) and information (Figure 4–45) screens. After successful completion, click the Open Workspace button.

Figure 4–44. Verifying the publisher

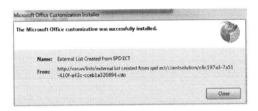

Figure 4–45. Microsoft Office Customization Installer

Once the synchronization (Figure 4–46) is successful, Workspace opens and displays the newly connected SharePoint site in the Workspaces list, as shown in Figure 4–47.

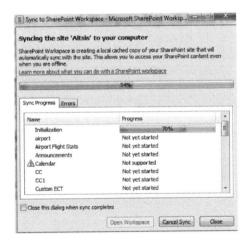

Figure 4–46. Synchronizing the SharePoint Workspace to the computer

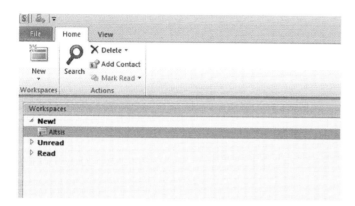

Figure 4–47. *The new SharePoint Workspace*

Double-click the name of your server under Workspaces to launch content from all available document libraries and lists (or the selected lists). In the External Lists section, click on the external list you created earlier in this chapter. This will retrieve and display list items as shown in Figure 4–48. If you like, you can choose to disconnect your workspace from the active connection to SharePoint and use the data in *offline* mode. You can perform all CRUD operations on the list and, when you are ready, you can sync data back to the SharePoint list. If you work in *online* mode and some changes happen on the server, you will be notified about the update and prompted to refresh the data.

You can search for an item in the list or double-click on a specific row item to edit it. In the Edit Item window (Figure 4–49), you can change values and then click the *Save & Close* button in the *List Item* section on the ribbon.

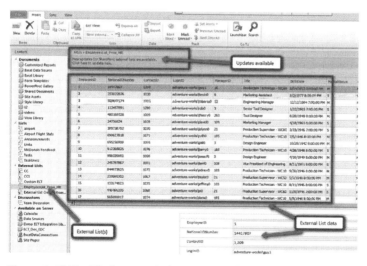

Figure 4–48. *The Workspace window connected to a SharePoint list and data*

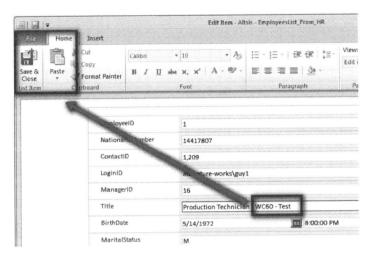

Figure 4–49. Editing a list item in Workspace

Here is an important factor to keep in mind. In both offline and online mode, if data for one item is changed both locally and externally, there will be a conflict between the local and external system values. The conflict will be displayed as an icon on the row column, and when you open the item, you'll see a Resolve option on the ribbon on the Error Tools menu. To proceed with any changes, you'll have to resolve the conflict by choosing to keep either the external system value or the local value, as shown in Figure 4–50.

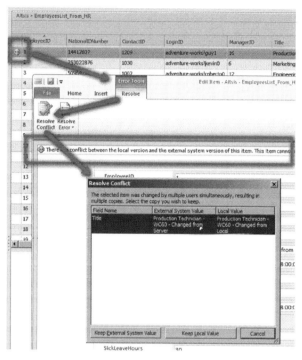

Figure 4–50. Data conflict between local and server versions

■ **Note** If you are accessing an external list with a data source that is configured with SSS, Workspace will prompt you to enter SSS credentials.

PowerShell Commands

Now that you've seen how useful the BCS can be, it's time to learn the Windows PowerShell cmd lets you can use to configure it. These commands are shown in Tables 4–2 through 4–8.

Table 4–2. Clear and Copy Operations

Command	Description
Clear-SPSiteSubscriptionBusinessDataCatalogConfig	Command to delete all the data from the BDC Metadata Store for a specific partition or site.
	Example: Clear-SPSiteSubscriptionBusinessDataCatalogConfig –ServiceContext http://yourservername
Copy-SPBusinessDataCatalogAclToChildren	Command to copy a set of permissions to child objects from the BDC Metadata Store object. You need to create the metadata object first using the Get-SPBusinessDataCatalogMetadataObject command.
	Example:
	$yourmetadataobject = Get-SPBusinessDataCatalogMetadataObject –BdcObjectType "LobSystem" –ServiceContext http://yoursharepointsite –Name "contentdatabase"
	Copy-SPBusinessDataCatalogAclToChildren –MetadataObject $<yourmetadataobject>

Table 4–3. Disable and Enable Operations

Command	Description
Disable-SPBusinessDataCatalogEntity	Command to disable an ECT in the BDC Metadata Store. You need to create the metadata object first using the Get-SPBusinessDataCatalogMetadataObject command.
	Example: Disable-SPBusinessDataCatalogEntity –Identity $<yourmetadataobject>
Enable-SPBusinessDataCatalogEntity	Command to enable an ECT in the BDC Metadata Store. You need to retrieve entity details from metadata object first using the Get-SPBusinessDataCatalogMetadataObject command.
	Example: Enable-SPBusinessDataCatalogEntity –Identity $<yourentity>

Table 4–4. Export and Import Operations

Command	Description
Export-SPBusinessDataCatalogModel	Command to export a BDC Model. You need to retrieve model details from the metadata object first using the Get-SPBusinessDataCatalogMetadataObject command.
	Example: Export-SPBusinessDataCatalogModel –Identity $<yourmodel> –Path "<path\file.dcm>"
Export-SPSiteSubscriptionBusinessDataCatalogConfig	Command to export data from BDC Metadata Store associated with a partition or site.
	Example: Export-SPSiteSubscriptionBusinessDataCatalogConfig –ServiceContext http://yoursite –Path "path\file.xml"
Import-SPBusinessDataCatalogDotNetAssembly	Command to import a .NET assembly.
	Example: Import-SPBusinessDataCatalogDotNetAssembly –LobSystem $<your db> -Path "filename"
Import-SPBusinessDataCatalogModel	Command to import a BDC model. You need to retrieve Metadata Store details from the metadata object first using the Get-SPBusinessDataCatalogMetadataObject command.
	Example: Import-SPBusinessDataCatalogModel –Path "path\file.bdcm" –Identity $MetadataStore
Import-SPSiteSubscriptionBusinessDataCatalogConfig	Command to import data from an exported file containing all data for the BDC Metadata Store for a given partition or site.
	Example: Import-SPSiteSubscriptionBusinessDataCatalogConfig –Path "<filepath>" –ServiceContext http://yoursharepointsite

Table 4–5. Get and Set Operations

Command	Description
Get-SPBusinessDataCatalogMetadataObject	Command to retrieve BDC Metadata Store metadata object.
	Example: Get-SPBusinessDataCatalogMetadataObject –BdcObjectType "Model" –Name "yourmodel" –ServiceContext http://yoursharepointsite
Get-SPBusinessDataCatalogThrottleConfig	Command to retrieve BDC service application throttling configuration.
	Example: Get-SPBusinessDataBCatalogThrottleConfig –Scope Database –ThrottleTypeItems –ServiceAppicationProxy $proxy
Set-SPBusinessDataCatalogMetadataObject	Command to set BDC Metadata Store metadata object property or attribute value. You need to retrieve identity object details from the metadata object first using Get-SPBusinessDataCatalogMetadataObject command.
	Example: Set-SPBusinessDataCatalogMetadataObject –Identity $<identityobject> -PropertyName <propertyname> -PropertyValue <value>
Set-SPBusinessDataCatalogServiceApplication	Command to set BDC service application global properties.
	Example: Set-SPBusinessDataCatalogServiceApplication –Identity $<serviceapplication> -FailoverDatabaseServer <servername>
Set-SPBusinessDataCatalogThrottleConfig	Command to set BDC application throttling configuration.
	Example: Set-SPBusinessDataCatalogThrottleConfig –Maximum <value> -Default <value>

Table 4–6. Grant and Revoke Operations

Command	Description
Grant-SPBusinessDataCatalogMetadataObject	Command to grant permissions to a principal for a specified BDC metadata object. You need to retrieve model details from meta data object first using Get-SPBusinessDataCatalogMetadataObject command and claim details from New-SPClaimObject command.
	Example:
	$yourclaim = New-SPClaimObject –User "domain\username" –Type windowssamaccountname
	$yourmodel = Get-SPBusinessDataCatalogMetadataObject –BdcObjectType "Model" –ServiceContext http://yoursharepointsite –Name "yourmodel"
	Grant-SPBusinessDataCatalogMetadataObject –Identity $<yourmodel> –Principal $<yourclaim> –Right <right>
Revoke-SPBusinessDataCatalogMetadataObject	Command to revoke rights for user in BDC Metadata Store metadata object. You need to retrieve model details from the metadata object first using the Get-SPBusinessDataCatalogMetadataObject command and claim details from New-SPClaimObject command.
	Example: Revoke-SPBusinessDataCatalogMetadataObject –Identity $<metadataobject> -Principal $<claims> -Right <right>

Table 4–7. New Operations

Command	Description
New-SPBusinessDataCatalogServiceApplication	Command to create a new BDC service application in the farm.
	Example: New-SPBusinessDataCatalogServiceApplication –ApplicationPool "<AppPool>" –DatabaseName "<dbname>" –DatabaseServer "<DBServer Name>" –Name "<BDCServiceAppName>"
New-SPBusinessDataCatalogServiceApplicationProxy	Command to create a new BDC service application proxy in the farm.
	Example: New-SPBusinessDataCatalogServiceApplicationProxy –Name "proxyname" –ServiceApplication $<serviceapplication>

Table 4–8. Remove Operations

Command	Description
Remove-SPBusinessDataCatalogModel	Command to delete the BDC model. You need to retrieve model details from the metadata object first using Get-SPBusinessDataCatalogMetadataObject command.
	Example: Remove-SPBusinessDataCatalogModel –-Identity $yourmodel
Remove-SPSiteSubscriptionBusinessDataCatalogConfig	Command to remove the BDC Metadata Store for a partition or site.
	Example: Remove-SPSiteSubscriptionBusinessDataCatalogConfig –-ServiceContext http://yoursharepointsite

Summary

Figure 4–51 highlights what you've learned in this chapter, which includes

- BCS terminology
- BCS setup and administration
- Differences between BCS features across SharePoint editions

- BCS architecture

- Authoring ECTs using SharePoint Designer

- Creating ECTs with Visual Studio

- Using a .NET assembly connector

- BDC runtime

- BDC integration with Office client applications

- Using PowerShell commands for administration

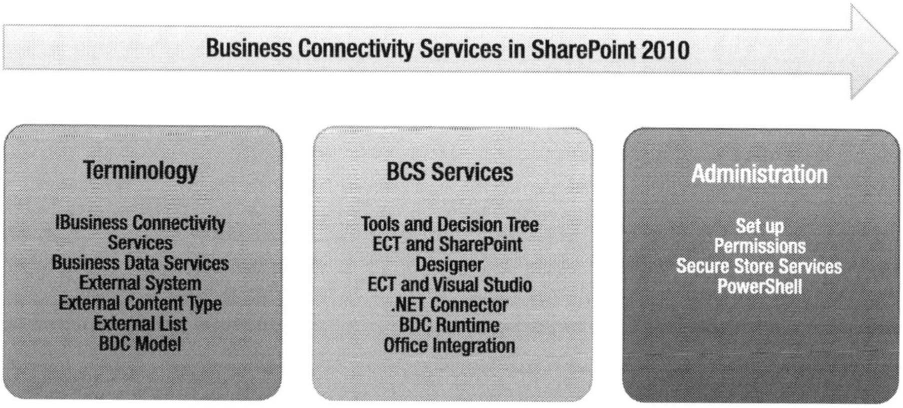

Business Connectivity Services in SharePoint 2010

Terminology

IBusiness Connectivity
Services
Business Data Services
External System
External Content Type
External List
BDC Model

BCS Services

Tools and Decision Tree
ECT and SharePoint
Designer
ECT and Visual Studio
.NET Connector
BDC Runtime
Office Integration

Administration

Set up
Permissions
Secure Store Services
PowerShell

Fig 4–51. Business Connectivity Services road map

What's Next?

In the next chapter, you will learn about Excel Services, in particular about the improvements in the new version. After an introduction, we will walk you through setting up Excel Services, show you what's new, and show you how to author and publish Excel to SharePoint 2010. You will also learn how to consume Excel Services through SOAP, the REST-based API, and the JavaScript Object Model. Lastly, we will introduce you to PowerPivot and its capabilities.

■ ■ ■

CHAPTER 5

Excel Services

During my presentations, I always ask, "How many of you use Excel?" and "How many of you use Excel with SharePoint?" And the answers are always the same. A lot of people use Excel. And many of them use Excel with SharePoint by collaborating on workbooks. But there's lots more you can do, using Excel Services. Of all the SharePoint facilities, Excel Services offers you perhaps the greatest "bang for the buck" value. Let's start exploring Excel Services.

What Will You Learn in This Chapter?

As we delve into Excel Services, we'll be covering a lot of ground, as you can see from the following list of topics.

- Introduction to Excel Services

- Setting up Excel Services

- Authoring and publishing Excel to SharePoint 2010

- What's new in Excel Services 2010

- Consuming Excel Services through SOAP interface

- Connecting Excel and SSAS

- Excel and PowerPivot

- Connecting through REST based API

- ECMAScript (JavaScript Object Model) and Excel Services

- Managing Excel Services

Software Prerequisites

To get the most out of this chapter, you'll need the following software:

- SharePoint Server 2010 Enterprise Edition

- Office Excel 2010 x86 or x64 (though the 64-bit version is required when you want to handle large datasets).

- SQL Server 2008 R2 x64 or SQL Server 2008 x64

- Adventure Works Database (SQL Server 2008 or R2), downloadable at `msftdbprodsamples.codeplex.com/`.

- SQL Server 2008 R2 Client Tools, downloadable at `technet.microsoft.com/en-us/library/ms143219.aspx`.

- PowerPivot Add-In for Excel 2010, downloadable at `http://www.powerpivot.com/download.aspx`,

Introduction

Excel is a great tool for many reasons. You can use it to perform basic mathematics, compute complex calculations, and even as a database. It is also used as a statistical tool, or rather a business intelligence tool. Excel makes it simple to transform data from one format to another. For instance, importing a CSV file into Excel is a very common task that you've probably done at least once in some scenario. We could go on and on—Excel offers an almost endless variety of possibilities and functions useful in almost every organization.

Due to the rich features of the Excel client, it is very heavily used in the real world. Excel has so many built-in functions and formulas that users can easily write their own macros to meet specific needs. And they do. So here, what we'll discuss is not how to use Excel, but how to share it.

What does this mean, practically speaking? It means a business user who is Excel savvy, can craft complex Excel sheets with lots of embedded logic and intelligence, then publish the worksheets to the server right through the Excel client. And by doing so, the entire calculation logic will be exposed on the server for many clients to consume. Moreover, business users need to be able to secure the data and formulas on the calculated columns, and prevent others from reauthoring the sheets.

To sum up, we need a server (preferably a web server) where

1. The Excel calculation engine is available.

2. Workbooks can run just as they run on your Excel client.

3. Workbooks can be shared.

4. Data and formulas are secure to prevent reauthoring.

Excel Services in SharePoint Server 2010 renders workbooks that are authored using the Excel thick client in a read-only and optionally parameterized format in the web browser. The worksheets that are published on SharePoint present the Excel calculation engine, and also have the ability to connect with various data sources. And they can enhance Excel's calculation abilities through the use of custom user-defined functions (UDFs).

Now that we know where we're going, let's take a look at the Excel Services architecture.

Architecture

Excel Services architecture consists of a number of components that can be grouped as follows:

- *Front-end or web front-end server:* REST API service, ECMAScript (the JavaScript Object Model or JSOM), Excel Web Access (EWA) and Excel Web Services (EWS).

- *Application Server:* User-defined functions (UDF) and Excel Calculation Services (ECS).

- *Data Sources:* All other data sources.

Of course, you can scale the infrastructure to meet your organization's needs. While the components are logically separated as shown in Figure 5–1, they can all be installed one server if you like.

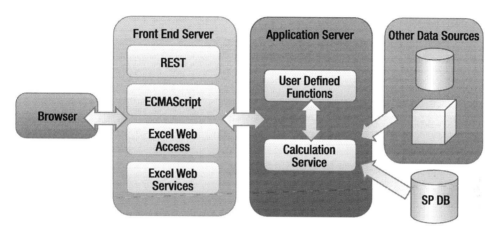

Figure 5–1. *Excel Services 2010 architecture*

■ **Note** Excel Web Services and the Excel Web Access web part are not the same. The Excel Web Access web part is the UI element that renders the workbooks as HTML output, while Excel Web Services provide access to web services by which you can programmatically set, calculate, and retrieve values from workbooks.

Before going any further, let's set up the basic infrastructure for using Excel Services.

Setting up Excel Services

Excel Services are installed by default with the SharePoint Server 2010 Enterprise version; you don't need to install anything else. But you do need to configure it. First, on your SharePoint site, ensure that the SharePoint Server Enterprise Site Collection Features feature is activated under the Site Collection Features.

Excel Services in MOSS 2007 are managed via the Shared Service Provider (SSP). In SharePoint 2010, however, the Shared Service Provider is no longer available; it has been replaced with Service Applications, which allow better management, control, and deployment. You can access them from Central Administration ➤ Application Management ➤ Service Applications ➤ Manage Service Applications. You can create a new service application, manage an existing service application instance, or connect to a service application on a different server.

To create a new Excel Services application, click the New button on the Service Applications menu and choose Excel Services Application (Figure 5–2). In the Create New Excel Services Application pop-up window, fill in the values for Name and Application Pool and choose whether the service application should be added to farm's default proxy list.

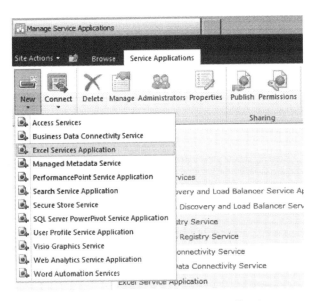

***Figure 5–2.** Creating a new Excel Services Application*

To edit and configure an existing Excel Service application instance, click on the Excel Service Application link from the list of available Service Applications (see Figure 5–3). You can also select the row and click the Manage button.

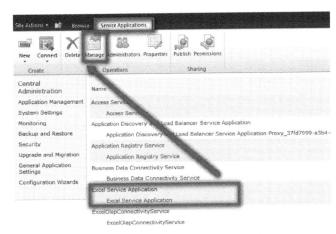

***Figure 5–3.** Managing an existing Excel Service Application instance*

The Manage Excel Services Application page (Figure 5–4) shows the various settings that can be configured.

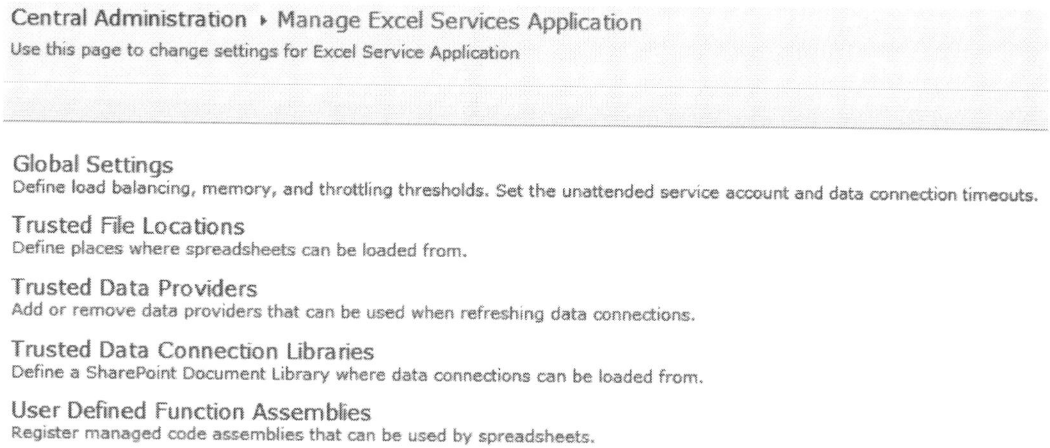

Central Administration ▸ Manage Excel Services Application

Use this page to change settings for Excel Service Application

Global Settings
Define load balancing, memory, and throttling thresholds. Set the unattended service account and data connection timeouts.

Trusted File Locations
Define places where spreadsheets can be loaded from.

Trusted Data Providers
Add or remove data providers that can be used when refreshing data connections.

Trusted Data Connection Libraries
Define a SharePoint Document Library where data connections can be loaded from.

User Defined Function Assemblies
Register managed code assemblies that can be used by spreadsheets.

Figure 5–4. The Excel Services Application configuration page

While most of the settings can be left to the default values, some need to be configured to address specific requirements.

Global Settings

Use global settings to configure the security model, session management, load balancing of ECS sessions, and memory utilization (Figure 5–5).

Security

File Access Method: Set the authentication method either to impersonate or to use the process account that ECS will use for all non-SharePoint trusted file locations. Use impersonation when you want ECS to *authorize users* when they try to access workbooks stored in UNC and HTTP locations. Impersonation also allows a thread to run in a different security context from the context in which the process that owns the thread runs. (Note that this setting doesn't have any impact on the workbooks that are stored in a SharePoint Server 2010 database.) Use a process account when users can't be impersonated and the ECS application server opens UNC shares or HTTP web sites. A process account is technically a local Windows account that has permissions on the shared folder where the workbook files are stored.

▓ **Note** The use of a process account in combination with anonymous access to SharePoint Foundation presents the risk that information may be disclosed. For more information on best practices, follow the recommendations at msdn.microsoft.com/en-us/library/ms545631.aspx.

Connection Encryption: Choose whether or not to encrypt the communication between the client and the front-end components of the Excel Services Application. The default setting is *not required,* so change the setting to *Required* to enable encryption. When you choose to encrypt communication, ECS transmits data over an SSL connection that you need to configure manually.

Allow Cross Domain Access: Select this option if a page in one HTTP domain needs to display files from a different HTTP domain.

Load Balancing

Load-Balancing Scheme: If your infrastructure has multiple application servers, Excel Services handles the load by distributing requests across ECS occurrences on the application servers in the farm. For the scheme, you can choose among Workbook URL, Round Robin with Health Check, and Local in order to load-balance sessions across ECS processes. With Workbook URL, a URL specified in the workbook is used to indicate which ECS process should run the workbook. This way, requests are always routed to the same ECS session. When *Round Robin with Health Check* is used, the ECS process is selected using the round-robin load-balancing mechanism to open a selected workbook. Finally, local should be used when the ECS process and workbook are on the local computer. If a local ECS process is not available, the round-robin scheme will be assigned to the ECS process.

Session Management

Maximum Sessions Per User: Set the maximum sessions allowed per user with the ECS. Any positive integer is a valid value. If the maximum number of sessions is reached, a new session will take the place of the oldest session. Set the value to -1 to enable unlimited sessions per user. Note that the higher the value, the greater the resource consumption for these concurrent ECS sessions. So, keep this value low for better performance.

Memory Utilization

Maximum Private Bytes: Set the maximum number of private bytes (in MB) that ECS processes can use. Valid values are any positive integer or -1. If the value is -1, the limit is set to 50 percent of the physical memory of the machine hosting the ECS process.

Memory Cache Threshold: Set the memory cache threshold (as a percent) for inactive objects. Valid values are 0 through 95. Caching of inactive objects is disabled if the value is set to zero. Unused cached objects are released when the maximum value is exceeded.

Maximum Unused Object Age: Set the value (in minutes) that inactive objects can remain in the memory cache. Valid values are from 1 through 34560 (24 days maximum). Set the value to -1 for unlimited utilization of the memory.

Workbook Cache

Workbook Cache Location: Set the location of the file system hosting the ECS server where workbook files are cached. If the location isn't set, the subdirectory under system temporary directory will be used.

Maximum Size of Workbook Cache: Set the maximum workbook cache (in MB) that ECS can use on the disk. This value also counts for recently used files that are currently not opened. Valid values are any positive integers.

Caching of Unused files: If you need to cache files that are unused in any session by ECS, check the *Caching Enabled* box.

External Data

Connection Lifetime: Set the external data connection lifetime. Valid values are -1 and 0 through 2073600 (24 days). In the event of new queries, older, expired connections are reopened. If no connections are to be closed or reopened, set the value to -1. It is highly recommended you limit this value to reduce the risk of a denial-of-service attack.

Unattended Service Account and Application ID: Set the Unattended Service Account ID for single sign-on using the Secure Store Service application. The Application ID must be preconfigured in the Secure Store Services application. You'll learn how to configure Secure Store Services shortly in the "Excel Services and SSAS" section.

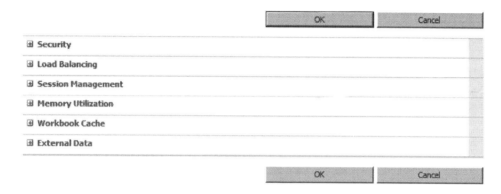

Figure 5–5. *Excel Services Global Settings*

Trusted File Locations

Remember how you used SSP in MOSS 2007 to make an Excel file location trusted? In SharePoint 2010, by default all SharePoint (Microsoft SharePoint Foundation) locations are trusted. However, administrators can set rules to protect or unprotect specific file locations. Click on Add Trusted File Location (Figure 5–6) to add and configure trusted file locations.

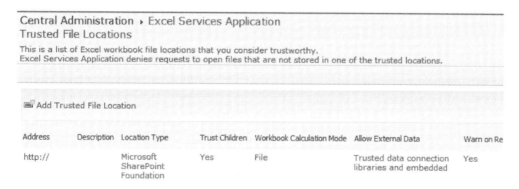

Figure 5–6. *Excel Services Trusted File Locations*

Location

Address: Set the trusted location from which workbooks should be loaded. These can be any Microsoft SharePoint Foundation or network file share or a web folder address.

Location Type: Choose the storage location type based on the address you set. If the address is a SharePoint document library, select Microsoft SharePoint Foundation. If the address is a network share, choose UNC Path. And for a web folder address, select http web site.

Trust Children: Choose whether or not directories or child libraries can be trusted.

Session Management

When a user requests a workbook from server, the server creates a new session and opens the latest version of the workbook. Note that there may be different users accessing the same workbook and hence you may have multiple sessions opened for the same workbook. It's important to control the resource consumption as well as duration of any concurrently open ECS sessions. With the help of the following settings, you can manage resource availability and sessions, which can improve the performance of ECS.

Session Timeout: Set the maximum timeout value (in seconds) for an ECS session to open and remain inactive before shut down. This value is measured from the end of *each open* request. Valid values are -1 through 2073600 (24 days). If the value is set to zero, the session expires by end of each single request. Set the value to -1 for no time out.

Short Session Timeout: Set the maximum timeout value (in seconds) for an Excel Web Access session to open and remain inactive *without any user interaction* before shutting down. This value is measured from the end of *original open* request. Valid values are -1 through 2073600 (24 days). If the value is set to zero, the session expires by the end of each single request. Set value to -1 in order to disable short session timeout.

New Workbook Session Timeout: Set the maximum timeout value (in seconds) for an ECS session to open a new workbook and remain inactive before shutting down. This value is measured from the *end of each* request. Valid values are -1 through 2073600 (24 days). If the value is set to zero, the session expires by the end of each single request. Set the value to -1 for no time out.

Maximum Request Duration: Set the maximum duration (in seconds) of a single request in a session. Valid values are -1 through 2073600 (24 days). For no limit, set the value to -1.

Maximum Chart Render Duration:- Set the maximum duration (in seconds) to render a single chart. Valid values are -1 through 2073600 (24 days). For no limit, set the value to -1.

Workbook Properties

Maximum Workbook Size: Set the maximum size (in MB) for a workbook that can be opened by ECS. Valid values range from 1 to 2000 MB.

Maximum Chart or Image Size: Set the maximum size (in MB) of chart or image that ECS can open. Valid values are any positive integers.

These values impact the performance and resources of the server. The bigger the workbook size or the chart or image size, the greater the resource consumption and, thus, the worse performance.

Calculation Behavior

Volatile Function Cache Lifetime: The maximum time a volatile function is cached in order to compute values for automatic recalculations of sheets containing volatile information. Volatile functions, such as RAND(), TODAY(), and NOW(), are those that are always calculated. Valid values range -1 to 2073600 (24 days). If set to -1, calculations are loaded once while opening. Set to zero in order to always calculate.

Workbook Calculation Mode: Set the value to

- *File* to load calculations specified in a file.

- *Manual* to recalculate only when a request is received.

- *Automatic* to recalculate on any change to a value that all other values are dependent on,

- *Automatic except data tables* to recalculate on any change to a value that all other values are dependent on as long as the values are not in a data table.

External Data

Allow External Data: To allow ECS to process external data connections, set to

- *None* to disable all external data connections.

- *Trusted data connection libraries only* to allow data connections that are saved to a trusted data connection library and ignore those embedded in the worksheet.

- *Trusted data connection libraries and embedded* to allow data connections to data sources that are saved to a trusted data connection library. If the connection fails, the server will enable connections embedded in the worksheet.

- *Warn on Refresh:* Choose this option to display a warning message before refreshing the external data for files in this location.

- *Display Granular External Data Errors:* Choose to display error messages when files in the location have data failures.

- *Stop when Refresh on Open Fails:* Choose to stop opening a file when the user does not have permissions to open the workbook.

- *External Data Cache Lifetime:* Set the maximum time that external data query results can be used by the system. Set the maximum refresh time value in seconds for either automatically or manually refreshing external query results the system can use. Valid values range from 0 to 2073600 (24 days). Set to -1 to prevent data refresh after initial query.

- *Maximum Concurrent Queries Per Session:* Set the maximum number of data queries that can run simultaneously in a single session. Valid values are positive integers.

- *Allow External Data Using REST:* Choose to enable the data refresh from REST APIs. However, if the Allow External Data is set to *none*, this wouldn't be in effect.

User-Defined Functions

User-defined functions allowed': Set this if user-defined functions in ECS for workbooks under the trusted file locations are allowed.

Trusted Data Providers

ECS uses data providers that are trusted to access data from external data sources for use in Excel workbooks. There are many data providers that are trusted natively. However, when you have to retrieve external data using custom data provider information in the connection, you need to manually define the provider as trusted. Click on Add Trusted Data Provider and furnish Provider ID, Type (OLE DB, ODBC, or ODBC DSN), and Description values (Figure 5–7). After adding the trusted data provider, use the Provider ID in the connection string.

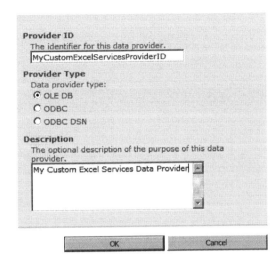

Figure 5–7. Trusted Data Provider settings

Trusted Data Connection Libraries

You can set a SharePoint document library as trusted. Data connection files (*.odc) hosted in this document library will be loaded by ECS for connecting to databases. To create a Trusted Data Connection Library click on the Add Trusted Data Connection Library link. Type the document library Address where files will be saved and fill in the Description as shown in Figure 5–8.

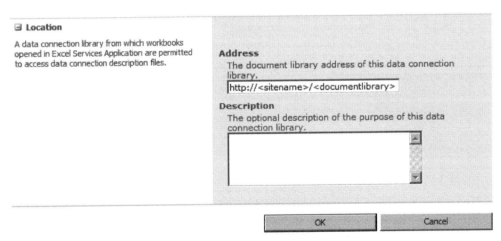

Figure 5–8. Trusted Data Connection Library settings

User-Defined Function Assemblies

Click on *Add User-Defined Function Assembly* to set and enable .NET assemblies containing user-defined functions that extend ECS capabilities. The assembly details are shown in Figure 5–9.
Assembly: Type the assembly path, either the full path or the strong name of the assembly.
Assembly Location: Choose between GAC or the file path for the assembly location.
Enable Assembly: If checked, ECS will load and use the assembly. Unchecking this option disables the assembly without deleting the assembly from the entry list.
Description: Optional text describing the user-defined function assembly.

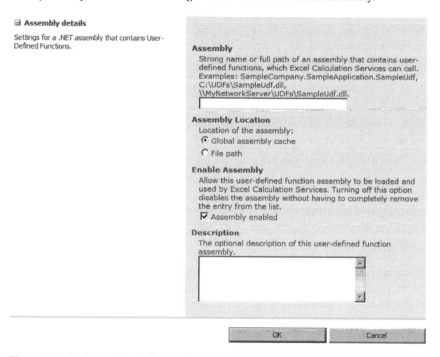

Figure 5–9. Setting up UDFs for Excel Services

■ **Note** For more information on what UDFs are and how to create your own, visit

blog.srinisistla.com/Lists/Posts/Post.aspx?ID=207.

Now that we've have set up Excel Services, let's author a simple Excel file and publish it to Excel Services.

Authoring Your First Excel Sheet and Publishing it to Excel Services

One fine morning my program manager came to me and said, "Hey, why not take the tasks from Team Foundation Server (TFS), export them to Excel, and display status charts based on those tasks on our intranet web site?" Well, that's a great idea—and it can serve as a dashboard for our project status. So we exported tasks for all work items from TFS and saved the file to one of our local drives as TeamTasks.xlsx, as shown in Figure 5–10.

ID	Work It	Rank	State	Assigned	Title	Discipline	Des	Estimate	Complet	Start Data	Finish da
					Project Tasks						
1	Task	1	Closed	SM	Excel Services Architecture Design	Architecture	Excel S	32	30	4/1/2010	4/4/2010
2	Task	1	Closed	JH	Prepare 64-bit Server infrastructure	Architecture	Prepar	40	32	4/1/2010	4/5/2010
3	Task	1	Closed	SM	Setup Excel Services	Architecture	Setup	24	16	4/8/2010	4/10/2010
4	Task	1	Closed	SM	Setup Secure Store Services	Architecture	Setup	16	12	4/11/2010	4/12/2010
5	Task	1	Closed	SR	Setup users on SP Farm	Development	Setup	8	4	4/13/2010	4/13/2010
6	Task	1	Closed	SR	Prepare 64-bit developer machine	Development	Prepar	16	12	4/14/2010	4/15/2010
7	Task	1	Closed	JB	Design Requirement Documents	Project Management	Design	40	30	3/24/2010	3/31/2010
8	Task	1	Closed	JB	Create Project Charter	Project Management	Create	16	14	4/1/2010	4/2/2010
9	Task	1	Closed	JH	Assign Project Task	Project Management	Assign	8	8	4/3/2010	4/3/2010
10	Task	1	Active	SR	Database design	Development	Databa	40	24	4/16/2010	4/20/2010
11	Task	1	Active	SR	Excel Sample	Development	Excel S	10	2	4/21/2010	4/22/2010

Figure 5–10. Sample data exported from TFS into Excel

■ **Note** We recommend you create an Excel file with the data as shown in Figure 5–10 since we'll be using it in most of the examples in this chapter.

Since the idea is to have this information on our intranet SharePoint site, we created a document library named Excel Library to act as a container for the TeamTasks.xlsx file. We then followed these steps to publish TeamTasks.xlsx to Excel Library.

1. Selected Save to SharePoint from the Backstage View[1] of Excel.

2. Clicked the Save As button under Locations.

3. In the *Save As* dialog, provided the URL and the document library name and clicked on Save.

■ **Tip** To do this in a Windows Server 2008 R2 environment, follow the instructions at blog.srinisistla.com/Lists/Posts/Post.aspx?ID=209. You may not have any issues with Windows 7 or Windows Vista.

---

[1] Backstage View, introduced in Office 2010, has an interface you can view when you click it on the File tab. This view has features that are not available as part of the ribbon.

■ **Note** To open an Excel file in your browser, you'll have to perform a preliminary step. On the ribbon, click Library Tools ➤ Library tab ➤ Settings and then click the Library Settings button. Then, under General Settings, click on Advanced Settings and in the Opening Documents in the Browser section, ensure that the default behavior of opening browser-enabled documents is set to Use the server default (Open in the browser).

4. Opened our intranet SharePoint site and accessed the Excel Library document library.

5. From the context menu on the *TeamTasks.xlsx* item under the *Name* column, selected the *View in Browser* option (Figure 5–11).

6. The file was rendered in the browser as shown in Figure 5–12.

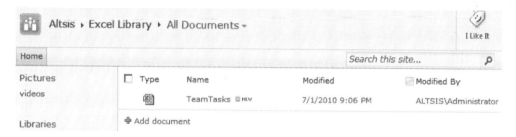

Altsis ▸ Excel Library ▸ All Documents ▾

I Like It

Home			Search this site...	🔍
Pictures	☐ Type	Name	Modified	☐ Modified By
videos	📲	TeamTasks ☀ NEW	7/1/2010 9:06 PM	ALTSIS\Administrator
Libraries	✚ Add document			

Figure 5–11. Published Excel Workbook in SharePoint document library

Altsis ▸ Excel Library ▸ TeamTasks.xlsx

File | 🗷 Open in Excel | 🗐 Data ▾ | 🔍 Find

ID	Work It	Rank	State	Assigned	Title	Discipline	Des	Estimate	Complet	Start Data	Finish da
1	Task	1	Closed	SM	Excel Services Architecture Design	Architecture	Excel S	32	30	4/1/2010	4/4/2010
2	Task	1	Closed	JH	Prepare 64-bit Server infrastructure	Architecture	Prepar	40	32	4/1/2010	4/5/2010
3	Task	1	Closed	SM	Setup Excel Services	Architecture	Setup	24	16	4/8/2010	4/10/2010
4	Task	1	Closed	SM	Setup Secure Store Services	Architecture	Setup	16	12	4/11/2010	4/12/2010
5	Task	1	Closed	SR	Setup users on SP Farm	Development	Setup	8	4	4/13/2010	4/13/2010
6	Task	1	Closed	SR	Prepare 64-bit developer machine	Development	Prepar	16	12	4/14/2010	4/15/2010
7	Task	1	Closed	JB	Design Requirement Documents	Project Management	Desigr	40	30	3/24/2010	3/31/2010
8	Task	1	Closed	JB	Create Project Charter	Project Management	Create	16	14	4/1/2010	4/2/2010
9	Task	1	Closed	JH	Assign Project Task	Project Management	Assign	8	8	4/3/2010	4/3/2010
10	Task	1	Active	SR	Database design	Development	Databa	40	24	4/16/2010	4/20/2010
11	Task	1	Active	SR	Excel Sample	Development	Excel S	10	2	4/21/2010	4/22/2010

Figure 5–12. SharePoint 2010 Excel Viewer rendering the Excel file in a browser

That was pretty simple. Well, you can add a lot of other functionality to the file. But first, let's discuss some of the highlights of Excel Services, which

- renders Excel workbooks in a browser

- exposes and distributes Excel using a Excel Web Access web part

- accesses workbook content using either the REST API or the JavaScript Object Model (JSOM)

- aggregates data using multiple data sources

- hosts the Excel Calculation Engine

Note An Excel workbook accessed via the Excel viewer or Excel Web Access web part cannot be edited.

Using Excel as the client and SharePoint 2010 with Excel Services as the platform is the perfect blend for Business Intelligence. Excel Services 2010 includes a number of new enhancements, as we'll see.

What's New in Excel Services 2010

- *Security using Unattended Service Account:* use a low-privilege unattended service account to authenticate and retrieve data from various data sources using Secure Store Services.

- *Windows PowerShell Capabilities:* use PowerShell commands to administer Excel Services. Perform operations such as retrieving or setting trusted locations, user-defined functions, etc.

- *Manage Service Application:* Manage any Excel Services you have permissions to administer using the Service Application.

- *Trusted Locations:* except UNC path(s), all SharePoint library locations are by default trusted. Additional manual configuration is required for UNC paths.

- *Delegate Service permissions:* You can delegate specific permissions to a user to handle service applications.

- *Client Fidelity:* Workbooks are rendered with high visual fidelity and maintain compatibility of content and formulas between the Excel rich client and the Excel web app. Most browsers are supported.

- *Multi-user collaboration:* multiple users can simultaneously edit workbooks. Updates are applied based on the sequence of changes: the most recent change overwrites the rest.

- *PowerPivot:* PowerPivot[2] is an add-on to Excel and SharePoint that provides a platform for performing end-to-end solutions and BI analysis.

---

[2] PowerPivot is explained in more detail in the "PowerPivot and Excel" section.

- *New APIs (REST[3] and JSOM[4]):* These two new functionalities have been added to this version.

- *Slicers:* You can filter data based on a member using *Slicer* window under Pivot Charts and Tables.

- *Sparklines:* Add Sparklines or miniature charts on columns based on data.

- *Workbook interactions:* You can turn on interactivity on the *Excel Web Access* web part to interact with data on the Excel workbook.

So far we've experienced Excel Services from the UI. Now we'll take a look at some alternative mechanisms for configuring Excel Services settings.

PowerShell Commands

The functionalities we'll discuss now are the same ones we looked at earlier in the "Setting up Excel Services" section, but now we'll use PowerShell commands.

These commands can be classified into four basic groups: *Create* (new) operations, *Set* operations, *Get* operations, and *Delete* (remove) operations, as described in Tables 5–1 through 5–4. You will notice that these commands use the Excel Service Application name to get the identity. Make sure you are using the correct name. Again, these commands use other commands to get references, so we recommend you go through all the commands first and then use them according to your needs.

▨ **Tip** To get help with PowerShell commands, use the following from the PowerShell command window to obtain full details and examples:

`Get-Help <PS Cmdlet>` for details and `Get-Help <PS Cmdlet>` `-examples` for samples

---

[3] REST is explained in more detail in the "Collaboration with REST API" section.

[4] JSOM is explained in more detail in "Excel Services and ECMAScript" section.

Table 5–1. Create / New Operations

Command	Description
New-SPExcelBlockedFileType	Block a specified file type during loading.
	Example: Get-SPExcelServiceApplication –identity "Excel Services Application"	New-SPExcelBlockedExcelFileType –FileType XLSX
New-SPExceldataConnectionLibrary	Add a data connection library to trusted location.
	Example: Get-SPExcelServiceApplication –Identity "Excel Services Application"	New-SPExcelDataConnectionLibrary –address "http://yoursite/doclib" –description "some description"
New-SPExcelDataProvider	Add a new safe data provider to Excel Services application.
	Example: Get-SPExcelServiceApplication –identity "Excel Services Application"	New-SPExcelDataProvider –providerID "provider ID Name" –ProviderType OleDb –description "some description"
New-SPExcelFileLocation	Add a new trusted file location to Excel service application.
	Example: Get-SPExcelServiceApplication -identity "Excel Services Application"	New-SPExce lFileLocation -address "http://yoursite/" -locationType SharePoint -description "some description"
New-SPExcelServiceApplication	Create a new Excel service application.
	Example: New-SPExcelServiceApplication –Name "New Excel Service" –ApplicationPool "your application pool" –SessionsPerUserMax 10
New-SPExcelUserDefinedFuntion	Add a new user-defined function to an Excel service application.
	Example: New-SPExcelUserDefinedFunction –ExcelServiceApplication "yourexcelserviceapplication" –Assembly "yourassembly" –AssemblyLocation GAC

Table 5–2. Set Operations

Command	Description
Set-SPExcelDataConnectionLibrary	Set properties of the data connection library for an Excel service application.
	Example: Get-SPExcelServiceApplication –Identity "Excel Services Application"	Get-SPExcelDataConnectionLibrary	where {$_.address –eq "http://yoursite" }	Set-SPExcelDataConnectionLibrary –Address "http://yoursite/doclib"
Set-SPExcelDataProvider	Set properties of a safe data provider for an Excel Services application.
	Example: Gct-SPExcelServiceApplication -Identity "Excel Services Application"	Get-SPExcelDataProvider	where {$_.providerID -eq "SQLOLEDB" }	Set-SPExcelDataProvider -Description "some description"
Set-SPExcelFileLocation	Set a trusted file location for an Excel Services application.
	Example 1: Get-SPExcelFileLocation -ExcelServiceApplication "yourexcelserviceapplication"	where { $_.externaldataallowed -eq "DclAndEmbedded"}	Set-SPExcelFileLocation -ExternalDataAllowed Dcl
	Example 2: Get-SPExcelServiceApplication	Get-SPExcelFileLocation	where {$_.Address –eq http://}	Set-SPExcelFileLocation –Description "some_description"
Set-SPExcelServiceApplication	Set the global properties of an Excel Services application.
	Example: Set-SPExcelServiceApplication ExcelServiceApplication –sessionsperusermax 10
Set-SPExcelUserDefinedFunction	Set the properties for a user-defined function in an Excel Services application.
	Example: Set-SPExcelUserDefinedFunction -ExcelServiceApplication "ExcelService" -Identity "yourassemblydetails" -Description "some_description"

Table 5–3. Get Operations

Command	Description
Get-SPExcelBlockedFileType	Get file type(s) that are blocked from loading.
	Example: Get-SPExcelServiceApplication -Identity "Excel Services Application" | Get-SPExcelBlockedFileType | format-table
Get-SPExcelDataConnectionLibrary	Get a list of trusted data connection libraries.
	Example: Get-SPExcelserviceapplication -Identity "Excel Services Application" | Get-SPExcelDataConnectionLibrary
Get-SPExcelDataProvider	Get a list of safe data provider(s).
	Example: Get-SPExcelServiceApplication -Identity "Excel Services Application" | Get-SPExcelDataProvider | where {$_.ProviderID -eq "SQLOLEDB"}
Get-SPExcelFileLocation	Get a list of trusted file location(s).
	Example: Get-SPExcelServiceApplication -Identity "Excel Services Application" | Get-SPExcelFileLocation
Get-SPExcelServiceApplication	Get the Excel Service Application object.
	Example: Get-SPExcelServiceApplication "ExcelService"
Get-SPExcelUserDefinedFunction	Get user-defined function(s).
	Example: Get-SPExcelServiceApplication -Identity "Excel Services Application" | Get-SPExcelUserDefinedFunction -Identity "yourUDFfunction"

Table 5–4. Delete / Remove Operations

Command	Description
Remove-SPExcelBlockedFileType	Remove an entry from a list of blocked file types.
	Example: Get-SPExcelServiceApplication -Identity "Excel Services Application" | Remove-SPExcelBlockedExcelFileType -FileType XLSX
Remove-SPExcelDataConnectionLibrary	Remove a data connection library from an Excel Services application.
	Example: Get-SPExcelServiceApplication -Identity "Excel Services Application" | Remove-SPExcelDataConnectionLibrary -Identity "http://yoursite/doclib"
Remove-SPExcelDataProvider	Remove data providers from an Excel Services application.
	Example: Get-SPExcelServiceApplication -Identity "Excel Services Application" | Get-SPExcelDataProvider | where {$_.providerID -eq "SQLOLEDB" } | Remove-SPExcelDataProvider
Remove-SPExcelFileLocation	Remove a trusted file location from an Excel Services application.
	Example: Remove-SPExcelFileLocation -ExcelServiceApplication "Excel Services Application" -Identity http://yoursite/
Remove-SPExcelUserDefinedFunction	Remove user-defined function(s) from an Excel Services application.
	Example: Remove-SPExcelUserDefinedFunction -ExcelServiceApplication "Excel Services Application" -Identity "yourUDFfunction"

Backup and Recovery Operation

Excel Services support backup and restore operations with a few exceptions that are mentioned below. You will have to manually take care of backing up these files and settings unless you are doing a content database backup and restore.

- Trusted data provider binaries
- User-defined function assemblies
- Excel Web Access web part properties

- Office data connection files and workbook files

As we've seen, Excel 2010 has a lot of new features. Let's implement some of them with an example and then publish the workbook to Excel Services.

Authoring and Publishing

We will use some of the new features to add more functionality to the TeamTask.xlsx file we created earlier.

PROBLEM CASE

Author and publish the *TeamTasks.xlsx* file to SharePoint Excel Services, and use an Excel Web Access web part to view the workbook.

Solution:

1. Open the *TeamTask.xlsx* file you created earlier. Create a new calculated column to compute the difference between Estimated Hours and Completed Hours. Name this column heading Remaining Work (hours).

2. Select all the other rows in the Remaining Work column and click on the Conditional Formatting button on the Home tab of the ribbon, then select Data Bars ➤ Gradient Fill, then choose the red data bar as shown in Figure 5–13.

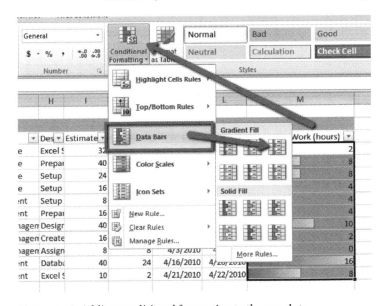

Figure 5–13. Adding conditional formatting to the row data

3. Select all rows under the Title and the Remaining Work columns. From the Insert tab, click on Pie and select 3-D Pie, as shown in Figure 5–14. Choose one of the Chart Styles available from Chart Tools ➤ Design tab.

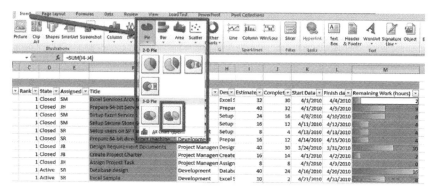

Figure 5–14. Adding a chart to workbook sheet

4. Once the Chart is rendered, set Chart Layouts to display the legend and slice details (Layout 1 in this example). From Chart Tools ➤ Layout, set the Chart Name[5] to Task Status (for this example), as shown in Figure 5–15.

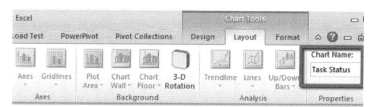

Figure 5–15. Setting the Chart Name

5. Create another calculated column of data for computing Task Allocation estimated hours per assignee. To compute the sum of task allocation estimated hours per assignee, you can create a pivot table from the Excel data. From the Insert tab, select Pivot Table. In the Create PivotTable window, choose the range to extend from the Assigned To column to the Estimated Work (hours) column, then choose to place the PivotTable in a New Worksheet and click OK. A new sheet will be created and you'll see a PivotTable added to the sheet. From the PivotTable Field List, select the Assigned To and Estimated work (hours) items and see how that data is added to the PivotTable as shown in Figure 5–16.

---

[5] We'll use the Chart Name to access the chart when we examine the REST API later in this chapter.

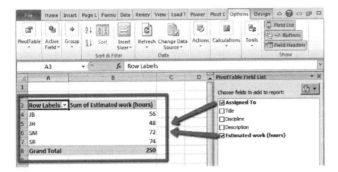

Figure 5–16. Using a pivot table to sum data in an Excel workbook

6. Return to Sheet1 and insert another 3-D Pie chart, then select the previously created pivot table as the data range for this chart. Set the chart layout (Layout 1) to display percentage of task allocation.

7. Your Excel worksheet should now look similar to the one in Figure 5–17.

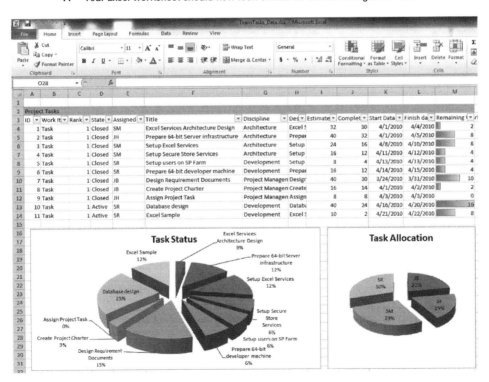

Figure 5–17. Excel workbook loaded with data and graphs, and with conditional formatting

8. From the Backstage View, click on *Save & Send*. Choose *Save to SharePoint* and save the worksheet to the SharePoint document library you created. Overwrite or provide a new file name if a file already exist with the same name.

9. Open the SharePoint site, and go to the document library where you saved the Excel file.

10. Click the Excel file. It should render in the browser as shown in Figure 5–18.

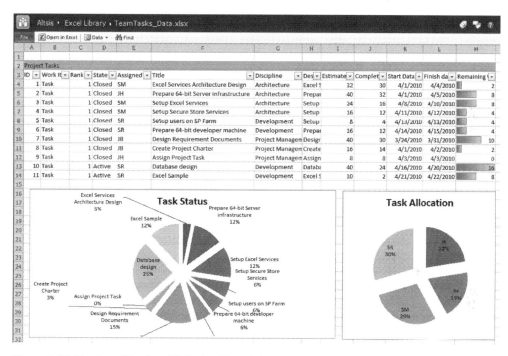

Figure 5–18. *Excel workbook published to SharePoint 2010*

Amazing, isn't it? All the calculation, conditional formatting, and charts are rendered very much as in the Excel client.

■ **Note** The Excel viewer supports 3-D charts by converting them to 2-D charts. Graphic effects such as Shadow, Glow, Soft Edges, Bevel, 3-D Rotation will be converted to their respective 2-D counterparts.

Now we've seen how a published Excel file renders in a browser. It can also be loaded using an Excel Web Access (EWA) web part, which has the same rendering behavior—but EWA comes with more functionality that we will discuss now.

Using an Excel Web Access Web Part (EWA)

1. Using the Copy Shortcut link from the context menu, retrieve the URL of *TeamTasks.xlsx*.

2. Create a page under Site Pages library called Excel Demo.

3. Open and edit the page. Choose Web Part item from the Editing Tools ➤ Insert tab. Under Business Data Category, select the Excel Web Access web part and click the Add button to add a web part to the page.

4. Edit the EWA web part or choose to open the tool pane. From the configuration window, enter the TeamTasks.xlsx URL path under the workbook input box. You can also use the text box's pick URL icon.

5. Leave all other entries with the default settings and click OK.

6. *TeamTasks.xlsx* will render in the EWA web part, as shown in Figure 5–19.

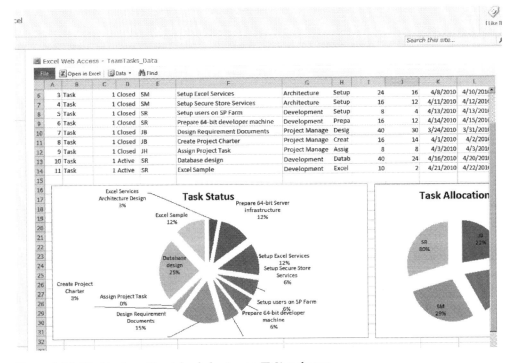

Figure 5–19. The Excel workbook loaded using an EWA web part

■ **Note** *Excel Services vs. Excel Web Apps.* Note that *Excel Services* in SharePoint is a platform for hosting Excel client files on a server using the Excel calculation engine. *Excel Web Apps*, on the other hand, is an online version of Office Excel. For more information, read the article "Excel Service and Excel Web Apps common/different features" at `blogs.technet.com/b/tothesharepoint/archive/2010/07/21/Excel-services-and-Excel-web-apps-common-different-features.aspx`.

Now let's see how easy it is to extract content from this Excel sheet—including the charts—and use it in a Word application. To do this, we'll use the REST-based API.

Excel Services REST API

As mentioned earlier, the REST API was introduced in Excel Services in SharePoint 2010. It enables simple yet flexible and secure access to Excel workbook content via a URL. You can either manually or programmatically access resources such as ranges, charts, tables, PivotTables, and Atom feeds over HTTP.

A URL through which you can access workbook content consists of three parts:

- URI: the Excel REST page

- Location of workbook: the relative path to the workbook, including the file name

- Location of resource: the path of the resource for the workbook

Here is a sample URL that contains all three elements.

```
http://<site>/_vti_bin/ExcelRest.aspx/<exceldocumentlibraryname>/<excelfilename>/<resoucelocat
ion>
```

In the this example,
`http://<site>/_vti_bin/ExcelRest.aspx` is the URI;
`/<exceldocumentlibraryname>/<excelfilename>` is the location of the workbook; and
`<resourcelocation>` is the location of the resource.

■ **Note** For more information on accessing the resource location using the REST API, read "Resources URI for Excel Services REST API" at `msdn.microsoft.com/en-us/library/ff394530.aspx`.

Let's use the TeamTasks.xlsx file and retrieve the embedded chart using the REST API. But first let's generate an Atom feed from the Excel workbook using the *discovery user interface* in the Excel Services REST API. This mechanism enables us to explore the elements that exist in the workbook. Copy the shortcut to the Excel file from the document library. Construct a URL like the following that generates output as shown in Figure 5–20.

```
http://<yourServerName>/_vti_bin/excelrest.aspx/<Excel lib>/<Excel file>.xlsx/model
```

If www.sharepointsite.com is your SharePoint site, Excel Library is the document library where your Excel file is published, and TeamTasks_data.xlsx is your Excel file, the URL to obtain the feed would look like this:

```
http://www.sharepointsite.com/_vti_bin/excelrest.aspx/Excel%20Library/TeamTasks_data.xlsx/model
```

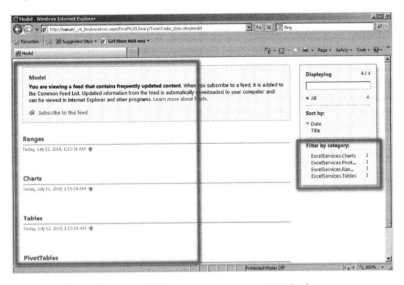

Figure 5–20. *Excel Services REST API delivering an Atom feed*

In order to access and retrieve the chart image from your Excel workbook using REST, you need to build the URL with a different resource location. Remember the Chart Name you provided in the previous exercise (Figure 5–15)? You'll have to use that chart name to retrieve the chart from your Excel workbook. Construct the URL as shown here and enter it in the address location of the browser to get the output.

```
http://<yourServerName>/_vti_bin/excelrest.aspx/<Excel lib>/<Excel
file>.xlsx/model/charts('<chart name>')?$format=image
```

Let's use the previously constructed URL to generate the chart image and embed it into a Word document. Open the Word 2010 client. From the Insert tab, choose Quick Parts, then Field. In the Field window, choose IncludePicture from Field names section, then paste the URL in the Filename or URL text box as shown in Figure 5–21.

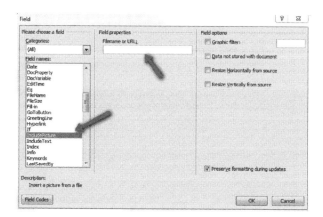

Figure 5–21. Configuring a Word document with the Excel Services REST API URL

In this example, if www.sharepointsite.com is your SharePoint site, Excel Library is the document library where your Excel file is published, TeamTasks_data.xlsx is your Excel file, and Task Status is the chart name, then the URL to obtain the chart as an image should look like this:

```
http://www.sharepointsite.com/_vti_bin/excelrest.aspx/Excel%20Library/TeamTasks_data.xlsx/mode
l/charts('Task%20Status')?$format=image
```

Leave other settings to the defaults and click the OK button. The chart embedded in the Excel workbook that is chosen using the *<chart name >* parameter in the URL will be rendered as an image in the document as shown in Figure 5–22. You can add a title to the chart and any additional information related to the chart as needed.

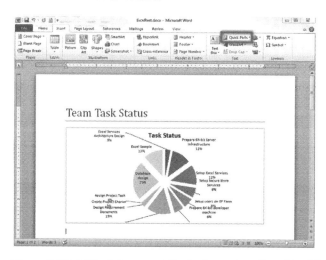

Figure 5–22. A Word document displaying a chart from Excel Services using REST API

■ **Tip** You can use this technique to display an object on a non-SharePoint web site or a SharePoint web site in another farm using the Content Editor web part.

What's so interesting about the chart image in Figure 5–22 is that it is real-time, live, and up-to-date. This embedded chart image will reflect changes immediately, as soon as data changes in the workbook and the field is updated in the Word document.

■ **Note** To retrieve external data using REST, ensure that the "Allow external data using REST" box is checked under Central Administration ➤ Application Management ➤ Service Applications ➤ Manage Service Applications ➤ Excel Services Application ➤ Trusted File Locations ➤ {Edit location} ➤ External Data. For analysis purposes, you can set the values in the workbook using the REST API and observe the changes in the charts.

That was easy, effective, and very useful. However, there are few features that are not supported in Excel Services REST API.

- *Floating charts:* If you request a range through REST that contains a chart, only the range will be returned, not the chart.

- *Sparklines and conditional formatting:* Sparklines on columns and conditional formatting are not supported.

- *Output not as pixel perfect as EWA:* HTML output generated by REST and EWA are similar. However, when CSS is used, the REST API can't access all the classes as the EWA does.

- *Tables:* All cells are treated without any distinction when accessed through the Atom feed. You can't differentiate among table, cell, header, or general data.

- *URL size*: If there are many subfolders or parameters, the URL may not be set properly as there's a limitation of approximately 2,000 characters.

- *Special characters:* characters such as ? or # are not supported.

Excel Services 2010 can now also use the Excel Services SOAP API. By using the SOAP API, you can not only read the workbook content but also edit and save the workbook programmatically. In the next section, we will demonstrate on how to use the Excel Services SOAP API with a simple example.

Excel Services SOAP API

Excel Web Services can now expose an Excel workbook and its sheets using the SOAP API. You can both read and write programmatically to the Excel worksheet while other users are editing the workbook, which allows multiuser collaboration. All you need is a simple reference to the SOAP API.

You can communicate with the Excel file securely either by impersonation or by using credentials while connecting to data. Let's see how to connect with TeamTasks.xlsx file using the SOAP API.

PROBLEM CASE

Connect to the TeamTasks Excel worksheet that we've published to our SharePoint environment, programmatically retrieve data, add tasks to the sheet, and then retrieve the updated data.

Solution:

We will use the Excel Services SOAP API to retrieve the Title information and the Remaining Work (hours) from TeamTasks.xlsx in this example.

1. Open Visual Studio 2010. From the File menu, select New and click on Project.

2. In the New Project window, choose Windows from the Installed Templates section under Visual C#.

3. Choose .NET Framework 3.5 and select Console Application.

4. Enter a proper Name, Location, and Solution Name, and click OK. After successful creation of the project, you'll see that the program.cs and app.config files are added by default to the project.

5. Right-click on References and choose Add Service Reference....

6. In the Address box in the Add Service Reference window, enter the URL `http://<servername>/_vti_bin/excelservice.asmx` and hit the Go button (see Figure 5–23).

7. This action will discover and display the ExcelService service in Services section.

8. Choose the ExcelService service and provide a valid name in the Namespace text box (Figure 5–23) and click OK.

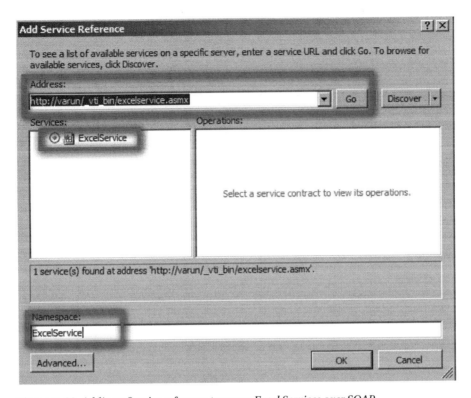

Figure 5–23. Adding a Service reference to access Excel Services over SOAP

9. Right-click on References. From the Add Reference window, on the .NET tab choose System.Web.Services Component.

10. Open the Program.cs file and add a reference to the namespaces as follows:

```
using ES_Soap.ExcelService; // ES_Soap is your console application project namespace
using System.Web.Services.Protocols;
```

11. Declare variables and set values under the program class:

```
static string sheet = "Sheet1";
static string excelFilePath = "http://<site>/<doc lib>/<excelfile>.xlsx";
```

12. Add a static method called GetData and copy and paste the following code in the method:

```
ExcelService.ExcelServiceSoapClient es = new ExcelService.ExcelServiceSoapClient();
es.ClientCredentials.Windows.AllowedImpersonationLevel =
System.Security.Principal.TokenImpersonationLevel.Impersonation;

        Status[] status;
        RangeCoordinates rangeCoordinates = new RangeCoordinates();
        try
```

```
        {
                string session = es.OpenWorkbook(excelFilePath, "en-US", "en-US", out
status);
                for (int i = 3; i <= 13; i++)
                {
                        Console.WriteLine("Remaining hours for the task " +
es.GetCell(session, sheet, i, 5, false, out status) + " is: " + es.GetCell(session,
sheet, i, 12, false, out status));
                }
                Console.Read();
        }
        catch (SoapException soapException)
        {
                Console.WriteLine(soapException.Message);
        }
```

13. Call the GetData method from the Main method:

```
[STAThread]
static void Main(string[] args)
{
    GetData();
}
```

14. Open the app.config file and modify the security section under basicHttpBinding, as shown here:

```
<security mode="TransportCredentialOnly">
    <transport clientCredentialType="Ntlm" proxyCredentialType="Ntlm"
                            realm="" />
    <message clientCredentialType="UserName" algorithmSuite="Default" />
</security>
```

15. Hit F5 to view the output of the application as shown in Figure 5–24.

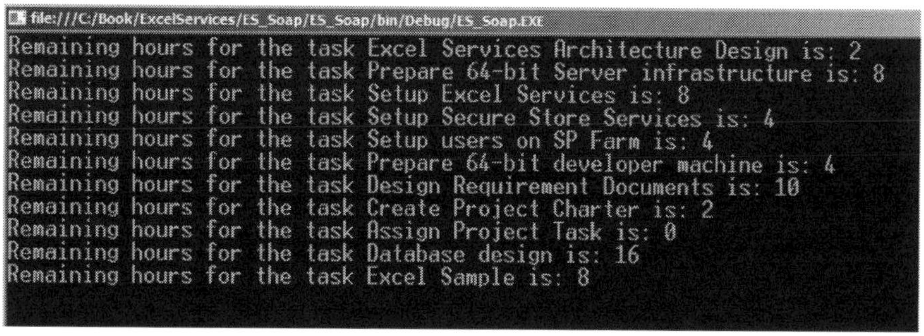

Figure 5–24. Displaying Excel workbook output using SOAP and Excel Services

As you've seen, this functionality is built to retrieve information from an Excel workbook. Let's now extend the functionality and write to this Excel file.

16. Copy and paste the following code toward the end of previously added code under the GetData method.

```
Console.WriteLine();
```

```
Console.WriteLine("----------- WRITE & READ NEW VALUES TO/FROM EXCEL WORKBOOK ----------
-");
es.SetCell(session, sheet, 14, 5, "New Task for Srini"); // Assign new task to Srini
es.SetCell(session, sheet, 14, 12, "8"); // Assign estimated hours as 8 for the task
Console.WriteLine("Remaining hours for the task " + es.GetCell(session, sheet, 14, 5,
false, out status) + " is: " + es.GetCell(session, sheet, 14, 12, false, out status));
```

17. Press F5. View the output and notice that the code first performs a read operation on the workbook, then a write operation. Finally the updated rows are retrieved and displayed as shown in Figure 5–25.

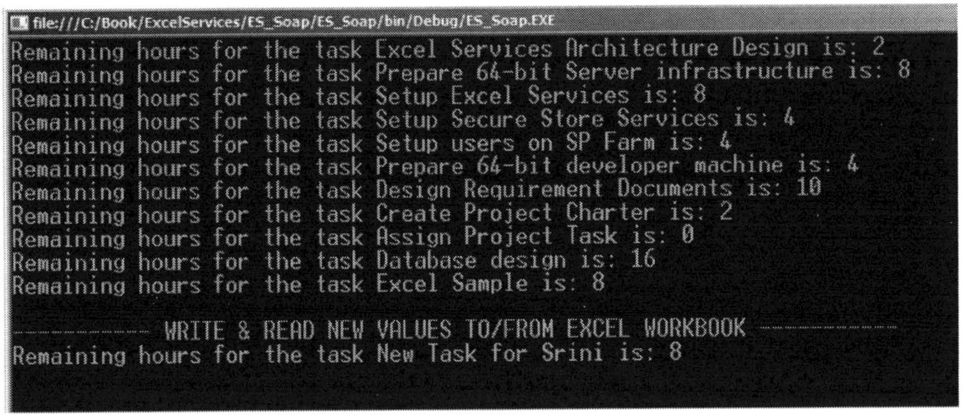

Figure 5–25. Displaying both read and write capabilities in Excel workbook output using SOAP and Excel Services

18. Instead of impersonating the user, you can also submit user credentials (Network) for authentication, like so:

```
es.ClientCredentials.Windows.ClientCredential = new
System.Net.NetworkCredential("UserName", "Password", "Domain");
```

The final logic looks like this:

```
using System;
using System.Collections.Generic;
using System.Linq;
using System.Text;
using ES_Soap.ExcelService;
using System.Web.Services.Protocols;
namespace ES_Soap
{
    class Program
    {
        static string sheet = "Sheet1";
        static string excelFilePath = "http://<site>/<doc lib>/<excelfile>.xlsx";
        [STAThread]
        static void Main(string[] args)
        {
            GetData();
        }
```

```
        static void GetData()
        {
            ExcelService.ExcelServiceSoapClient es = new
ExcelService.ExcelServiceSoapClient();
            es.ClientCredentials.Windows.AllowedImpersonationLevel =
System.Security.Principal.TokenImpersonationLevel.Impersonation;
            //es.ClientCredentials.Windows.ClientCredential = new
System.Net.NetworkCredential("UserName", "Password", "Domain");
            Status[] status;
            RangeCoordinates rangeCoordinates = new RangeCoordinates();
            try
            {
                string session = es.OpenWorkbook(excelFilePath, "en-US", "en-US", out
status);
                for (int i = 3; i <= 13; i++)
                {
                    Console.WriteLine("Remaining hours for the task " +
es.GetCell(session, sheet, i, 5, false, out status) + " is: " + es.GetCell(session,
sheet, i, 12, false, out status));
                }
                Console.WriteLine();
                Console.WriteLine("----------- WRITE & READ NEW VALUES TO/FROM EXCEL
WORKBOOK -----------");
                es.SetCell(session, sheet, 14, 5, "New Task for Srini"); // Assign new
task to Srini
                es.SetCell(session, sheet, 14, 12, "8"); // Assign estimated hours as 8
for the task
                Console.WriteLine("Remaining hours for the task " + es.GetCell(session,
sheet, 14, 5, false, out status) + " is: " + es.GetCell(session, sheet, 14, 12, false,
out status));
                Console.Read();
            }
            catch (SoapException soapException)
            {
                Console.WriteLine(soapException.Message);
            }
        }
    }
}
```

So far the data we've been using has been quite simple. However, with Excel you can connect and integrate with huge data sources such as OLAP databases. You can even use cube data in Excel with very little configuration and the default settings. Let's see how to connect with multidimensional data sources and gain some insights into using Excel Services.

Excel Services and SSAS

SQL Server Analysis Services (SSAS) and Excel together—now that's a great combination for those who would like to analyze and slice and dice cube data. To do this, we will use the AdventureWorks DW database and demonstrate how to configure and connect to SSAS.

As a prerequisite, Secure Store Services need to be configured to authenticate with SSAS. This is similar to what you've done in previous chapters, but we will run through the exercise once again.

Configuring Secure Store Services

From Central Administration ➤ Application Management ➤ Manage Service Applications choose Secure Store Service. Click the New button and enter the Target Application Settings as shown in Figure 5–26. Choose Group for the Target Application Type, which ensures that access is granted to the entire group rather than an individual. Click Next to continue.

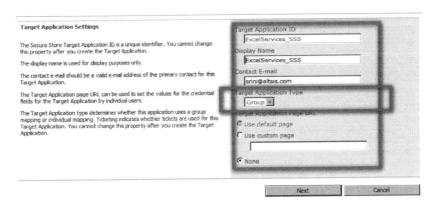

Figure 5–26. *Setting up a new SSS Application ID for Excel Services*

In the credentials fields, choose Windows User Name and Windows Password as shown Figure 5–27 and click Next.

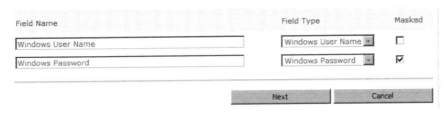

Figure 5–27. *Setting up credentials for the SSS Application ID*

Enter user(s) who can manage the application as Target Application Administrators, and users who are Members who are allowed to use the application (Figure 5–28) and click OK.

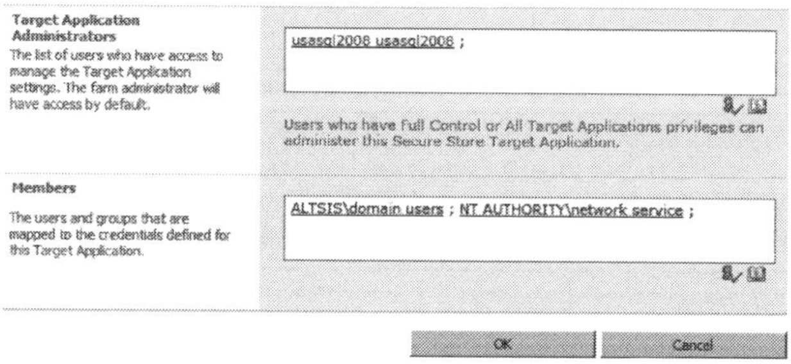

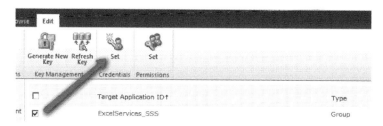

Figure 5–28. *Setting up Target Application Administrators and Members for SSS*

After returning to the SSS home screen, choose the Application from the store you just created and set the credentials by clicking on the *Set* button as shown in Figure 5–29.

Figure 5–29 *Set credentials for Target Application ID in SSS*

Enter values in the credential fields for the Target Application that has access to the SSAS database as shown in Figure 5–30.

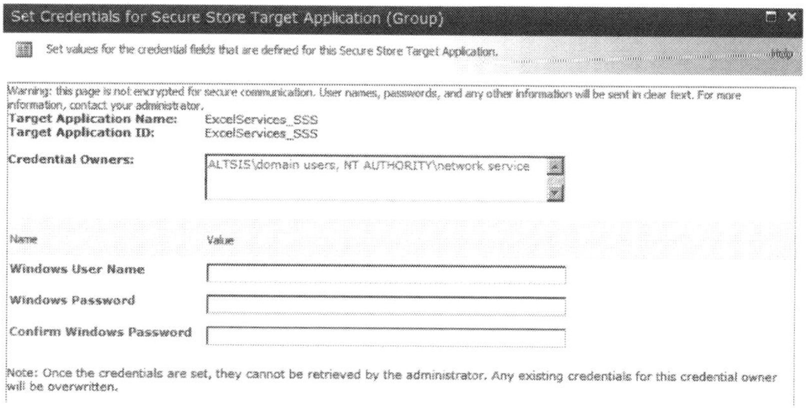

Figure 5–30. *Setting credentials for the SSS Target Application group*

Now that your credential cache is ready, let's see how to connect Excel with SSAS using the Secure Store Service Application ID.

PROBLEM CASE

Connect Excel with the multidimensional cube and analyze the Internet Sales information from Adventure Works DW database

Solution:

1. Open the Excel 2010 client. On the Data tab, choose From Analysis Services, as shown in Figure 5–31.

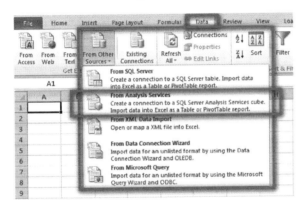

Figure 5–31. Choose the SSAS data source for the Excel workbook

2. In the Data Connection Wizard, enter a Server name and choose the Log-on credentials. Use Windows Authentication for impersonation or enter a User Name and Password to use specific credentials. Click the Next button.

3. On the Select Database and Table screen, choose the Adventure Works DW 2008 database as shown in Figure 5–32.

4. Under Connect to a specific cube or table, select the Adventure Works cube as shown in Figure 5–32. Click Next to continue.

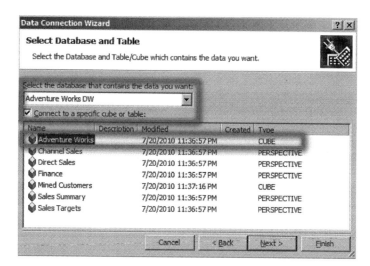

Figure 5–32. Choose the Adventure Works database and its cube

5. In the Save Data Connection File and Finish window (Figure 5–33), enter a valid file name and choose a location to save the data connection file (*.odc).

6. Enter a logical description and a friendly name.

7. Make sure to check the Always attempt to use this file to refresh data box.

8. Click the Authentication Settings button to choose the type of authentication that will be used for the data.

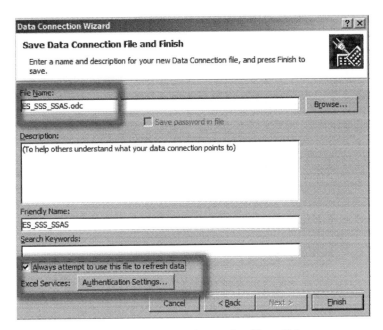

Figure 5–33. Saving the Office Data Connection file to disk

9. In the Excel Services Authentication Settings window (Figure 5–34), choose SSS – SSS ID and provide the Application ID you created in earlier section (ExcelServices_SSS), then click OK. After returning to the Save Data Connection File and Finish window, click Finish to complete the Data Connection Wizard.

Figure 5–34. Setting up the SSS Application ID for ODC

10. In the Import Data window, choose PivotChart and PivotTable Report and for the existing worksheet leave the default selection (=Sheet1!A1) as shown in Figure 5–35. Click on the Properties button to view and alter connection settings, then click OK to close the window.

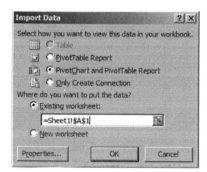

Figure 5–35. Import Data wizard window

■ **Note** If you choose only PivotTable Report, only the Pivot Table wizard is displayed. If you need both PivotTable and PivotChart, choose the PivotChart and PivotTable Report.

The Excel sheet will prepopulate the PivotTable and Pivot Chart, as shown in Figure 5–36. The worksheet includes the PivotTable, PivotChart, and PivotTable Field List. You use the PivotTable field list to select the fields for the PivotTable and the PivotChart.

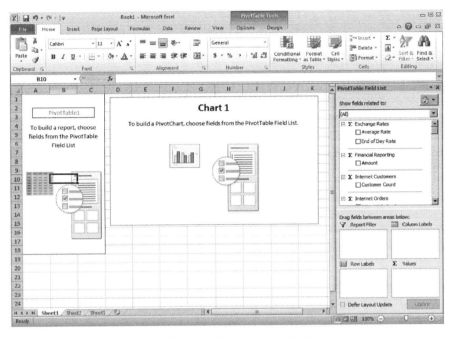

Figure 5–36. *Excel workbook with pivot table, chart, and fields*

11. From the PivotTable Field List, choose Sales Amount from the Sales Summary.

12. From Date ➤ Fiscal, choose Fiscal Year.

13. From Product, choose Product Categories.

Choosing these three fields adds a pivot table with data and the chart to the worksheet. Now let's now add a little more functionality to the sheet. We will create some trends based on the data using *sparklines*.

14. Select cells ranging from B3 through F7 and from the *Insert* tab choose Sparklines, then choose Line.

15. In the Create Sparklines window with the data range selected, enter the location range where you want to display the Sparklines (in this case, use G3:G7) and click OK. Sparklines will be created in the selected range as shown in Figure 5–37.

16. Choose a specific design format for the sparklines from Sparkline Tools ➤ Design ➤ Style. Under the Show section, select High Point, Low Point, First Point, and Last Point (Figure 5–37). Add a header title for the column, such as FY2004 ~ FY2002.

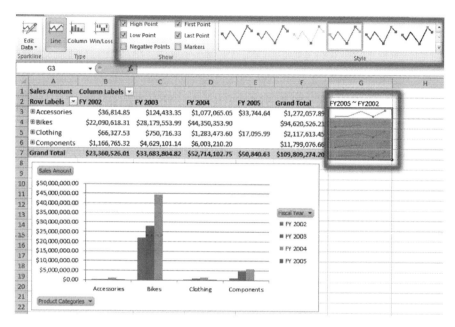

Figure 5–37. *Excel sparklines and conditional formatting*

Let's add a trend to this sheet, a rather simple one. Let's get trends on the difference in Sales Amount from FY 2004 and FY 2002. Note that if you're using the Adventure Works DW 2008R2 database, you'll have data for FY2006 through FY2009.

17. Place the difference formula between D3 and B3 and choose column H to display the results. Repeat the step for the range D4:D7 and B4:B7.

18. Select all the calculated columns (H3:H7). From the Styles section on the Home tab, click on Conditional Formatting, then on Data Bars. Select the green data bar and then Gradient Fill.

Note There are many other conditional formats, designs, and layouts you can use. We recommend you try other options for styling the sparklines and charts.

After you add sparklines and conditional formatting to the sheet, it should look similar to what's shown in Figure 5–38.

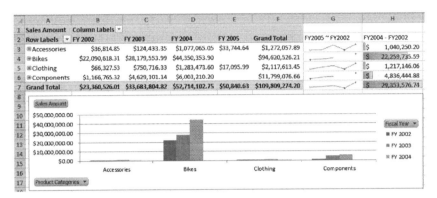

Figure 5–38. *Sparklines, conditional formatting and graphs in Excel*

What would be more interesting is if you could add an intuitive mechanism to the sheet for analyzing data. And you can—the Slicer is another utility available in Excel that you can use to filter data, and slice and dice it.

19. From the Filter section on the Insert tab, click on Slicer. If you have more than one connection file related to this Excel workbook, you'll be prompted to choose the Existing Data Connections. Select the previously created data source connection and click the Open button. Otherwise, skip this step.

20. From the Insert Slicers window, choose Fiscal Year from the Date section and Product from the Product Categories section and click on OK. This adds two slicers, Fiscal Year and Product, as shown in Figure 5–39.

21. Place the slicers below the graph and from Slicer Tools Options buttons, change the value in the Columns input. Increase the value to fit the columns in single row.

The final sheet should look like the one in Figure 5–39.

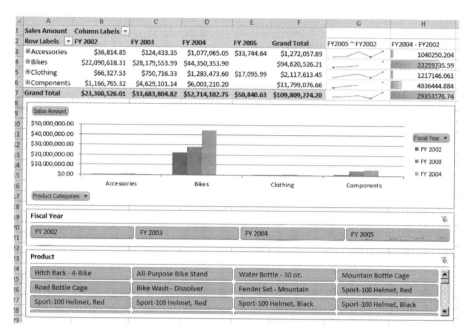

Figure 5–39. Slicers in Excel

22. Click on any of the Slicer filters and see how the data gets filtered on the PivotTable and Chart.

You saw earlier how to publish an Excel workbook to a SharePoint library. Figure 5–40 shows the final Excel workbook sheet after publishing to SharePoint. On the Product slicer, click on Hitch Rack-4-Bike and view the output as shown Figure 5–40.

287

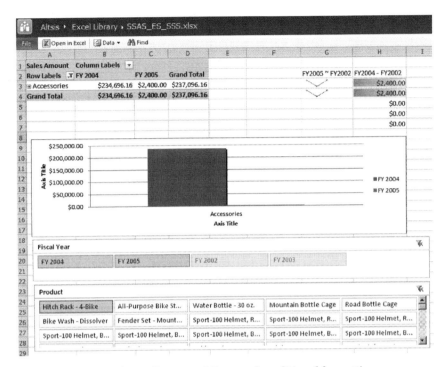

Figure 5–40. All together—slicers, sparklines, and conditional formatting

Important: Let's understand an important step in the previous exercise: precisely, step #5. You've saved the data connection file (.odc) to the local file system. As you are aware, this will definitely not be the scenario in a production environment. You will have to save the file to a location that is trusted. To accomplish this, you'll have to upload the .odc file to the Data Connection Library (DCL) on your SharePoint site.

To create a DCL, go to your SharePoint site, then to Site Actions ➤ View All Site Content. Choose Data Connection Library from the Library Filter, provide a valid Name, and click on Create. On successful creation of the library, upload the .odc file as shown in Figure 5–41. By default, the location of the .odc file will be in c:\users\<UserName>\Documents\My Data Source\ unless you've chosen a different location. Make sure to "Approve" the file.

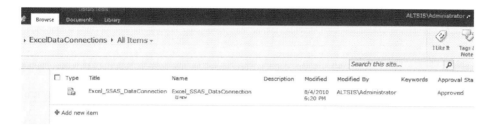

Figure 5–41. Adding an .odc file to a Data Connection Library

After approving the file, click on it. This opens a new Excel workbook using the Excel client on your local machine, which will be readily connected to the data source embedded the .odc file.

The Excel workbook will be prepopulated with the PivotTable. However, to add a PivotChart, select a chart from the Charts section of the Insert tab. Following steps 8 through 16 in the previous exercise would produce the results shown in the Figure 5–40.

Important: Since SQL Server Analysis Server uses an Active Directory account, be sure to do the following:

- Monitor errors in the %program files%/common files/Microsoft shared/web server extensions/14/logs folder.

- Ensure that the logged-in user or the unattended account under Secure Store Services has the required level of access permissions for SQL Server Analysis Services.

- Make sure that Windows Firewall between the SharePoint server and the SSAS server allows SSAS ports for operations (the defaults are 2382 and 2383).

- Ensure that the firewall is not blocking SQL Server Analysis Services or Excel Services.

Be aware that if SSS is not configured properly, you might end up with the error shown in Figure 5–42 when refreshing or filtering the data in the Excel workbook. In such situations, verify that the unattended service account credentials are accurate and have sufficient privileges. Also ensure that in the Trusted File Locations (Excel Service Application on Central Administration) ➤ External Data section, you have correctly configured all the settings values.

Figure 5–42. Data connection authentication error

So far we've seen how to consume data from data sources small and large in Excel and how to publish Excel workbooks to SharePoint. However, an even bigger question is whether Excel is capable of doing complex calculations and processing lots of information in a short time. Let's see how some of these challenges can be addressed in the next section.

PowerPivot for Excel

As it becomes increasingly important to support large amounts of data, the need for additional infrastructure that can support Excel also becomes significant. The PowerPivot add-in helps support such requirements. Here's a summary of PowerPivot features and capabilities.

- Handle larger data sets

- Process large amounts of data much more quickly

- Access various data sources including databases, feeds, text files, reporting services etc.

- Rich-client interface running over the PowerPivot engine

- Integrate with existing Excel features such as Slicers, PivotCharts and Tables.

- Excellent BI and data management capabilities, such as the PowerPivot Management Dashboard.

- Run analytics on data and calculations faster; uses powerful capabilities such as Data Analysis Expressions (DAX). To learn more about DAX, go to http://technet.microsoft.com/en-us/library/ee835613.aspx.

- Enhanced Security.

The major components involved are the Excel 2010 client, the PowerPivot Excel add-in, and PowerPivot for SharePoint. Excel workbooks with PowerPivot data can be published to SharePoint Server 2010 with Excel Services. You can open workbooks with PowerPivot data using Excel 2007 in read-only and non-interactive mode. However, to use all the features of PowerPivot, you need Excel 2010.

Download and install PowerPivot for Excel from `www.powerpivot.com/download.aspx`. For instructions related to PowerPivot for SharePoint 2010, visit `msdn.microsoft.com/en-us/library/ee210654(SQL.105).aspx`. And for hardware and software requirements, go to `msdn.microsoft.com/en-us/library/ee210640.aspx`.

■ **Note** SharePoint standalone installations as well as a developer edition that runs on Windows 7 are supported for PowerPivot. You need a SharePoint server farm with Excel Services, Secure Store Services, and Claims to Windows Token Services running on the same application server where you plan to set up PowerPivot.

After installing PowerPivot on compatible hardware (x86 or x64), the Excel client will include a new PowerPivot menu, as shown in Figure 5–43. It is highly recommended to use the 64-bit edition of Excel 2010 as well as a 64-bit operating system.

Figure 5–43. The PowerPivot tab in Excel

Launching PowerPivot opens a new design window. With PowerPivot, you can simply copy and paste a large chunk of data into the Excel sheet and perform analysis on the data. You can also connect to other data sources and perform the same operations as you can perform with Excel.

Figure 5–44 shows various data sources that can be connected to PowerPivot. You can access the list of data sources from Get External Data ➤ From Other Sources.

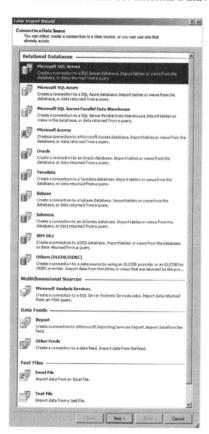

Figure 5–44. Data sources available with PowerPivot

Setting Up PowerPivot

Before you begin to use PowerPivot, you do need to perform a few manual steps. After installing PowerPivot for SharePoint Server 2010, two solutions are deployed at the farm level, namely powerpivotfarm.wsp and powerpivotwebapp.wsp. You can view them under Central Administration ➤ System Settings ➤ Farm Management ➤ Manage Farm Solutions,. The resulting screen is shown in Figure 5–45.

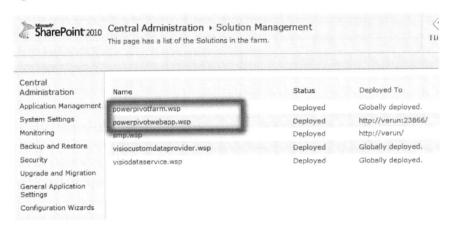

Figure 5–45. PowerPivot solution files under Central Administration

After the initial setup, *powerpivotwebapp.wsp* will only be deployed to a Central Administration web application. Click on the *.wsp* link to open the properties window (Figure 5–46).

Deploy Solution	Retract Solution	Back to Solutions

Name:	powerpivotwebapp.wsp
Type:	Core Solution
Contains Web Application Resource:	Yes
Contains Global Assembly:	No
Contains Code Access Security Policy:	No
Deployment Server Type:	Front-end Web server
Deployment Status:	Deployed
Deployed To:	http://varun:23866/
Last Operation Result:	The solution was successfully deployed.
Last Operation Details:	VARUN : http://varun:23866/ : The solution was successfully deployed.
Last Operation Time:	5/25/2010 12:09 AM

Figure 5–46. PowerPivot solution deployment status

Click Deploy Solution to deploy the solution to the required web application as shown in Figure 5–47.

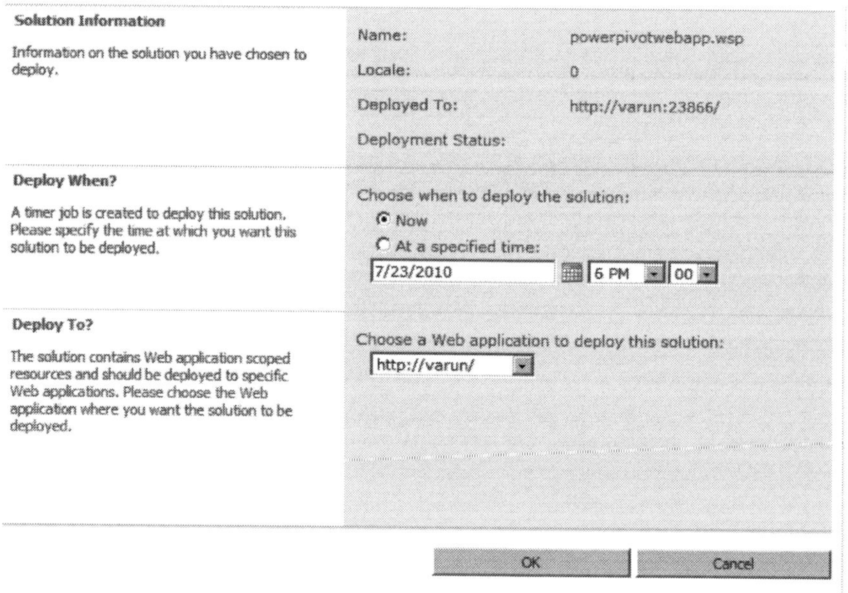

Solution Information

Information on the solution you have chosen to deploy.

Name: powerpivotwebapp.wsp

Locale: 0

Deployed To: http://varun:23866/

Deployment Status:

Deploy When?

A timer job is created to deploy this solution. Please specify the time at which you want this solution to be deployed.

Choose when to deploy the solution:

○ Now

○ At a specified time:

7/23/2010   6 PM   00

Deploy To?

The solution contains Web application scoped resources and should be deployed to specific Web applications. Please choose the Web application where you want the solution to be deployed.

Choose a Web application to deploy this solution:

http://varun/

OK   Cancel

Figure 5–47. PowerPivot solution deployment to web application

After successful deployment, make sure that PowerPivot Feature Integration for Site Collection is activated in the Site Collection Features of your SharePoint site (Figure 5–48).

Figure 5–48. Activating PowerPivot Feature Integration for Site Collections

You are now ready and can fully utilize the capabilities of PowerPivot in your SharePoint site. Let's do a simple exercise and see what PowerPivot brings to the table.

PROBLEM CASE

Connect the Sales data cube and use PowerPivot to retrieve data and populate charts.

Solution:

PowerPivot for SharePoint Server 2010 brings with it a special document library called the PowerPivot Gallery. To create a PowerPivot Gallery, go to your SharePoint site and from Site Actions ➤ View All Site Content, click the Create button. Then choose PowerPivot Gallery (Figure 5–49) under the Library section (use Filter By). Enter a valid name and click Create.

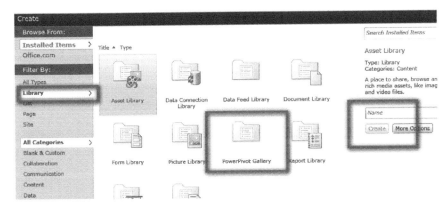

Figure 5–49. *Creating PowerPivot Gallery*

Once the PowerPivot Gallery library is created, go to Library Tools ➤ Library ➤ Library Settings ➤ Advanced Settings and set the Allow management of content type? value to Yes.

Open the PowerPivot Library. From Library Tools ➤ Documents ➤ New ➤ New Document, choose PowerPivot Gallery Document. This opens the Excel workbook client. From the PowerPivot tab, launch PowerPivot.

1. In the PowerPivot window, in Get External Data ➤ From Database, choose From Analysis Services or PowerPivot (Figure 5–50).

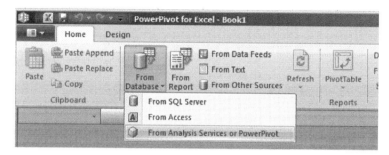

Figure 5–50. Choosing SSAS or PowerPivot as database

2. In the Table Import Wizard, provide a friendly connection name, a server to connect, and the log-on credentials.

3. For the database, choose either Adventure Works DW or Adventure Works DW 2008R2, whichever you selected earlier. Click on Test Connection to ensure the success of the connection.

4. Click on the Advanced button to view the connection properties. After successful verification, you can click either OK or Test Connection.

5. Click Next to configure the MDX query. Provide a valid Friendly Query Name and click on Design to open the Table Import Wizard.

6. The Table Import Wizard lets you select dimensions and measures from the available cube in the Adventure Works database.

7. In the Measure Group pane, expand the Measures. Select and expand Internet Sales and choose Internet Sales Amount. Drag and drop to the pane on the right.

8. From the Dimensions, choose Date ➤ Fiscal ➤ Date.Fiscal Year. Drag and drop Fiscal Year onto the Dimensions window. In the Filter Expression column, select All Periods and click OK.

9. Drag and drop the attribute Date Fiscal to the section on the right.

10. Repeat step 9 for the Dimension – Product. Choose Category and drag and drop Category on to section on the right.

11. Add Subcategory in the case of Adventure Works DW (or Sub-Categories in case of Adventure Works DW 2008 R2) to the section on the right.

Your final window, before you click OK, should look like the one in Figure 5–51. Once you verify, click OK.

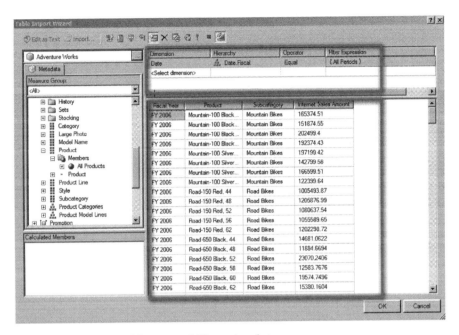

Figure 5–51. Importing Measure and Dimension data

12. The window returns to the Specify a MDX Query screen and the MDX Statement is now populated with the MDX query as shown in Figure 5–52. Click the Validate button to ensure the generated query is correct. Once it's been validated, click the Finish button.

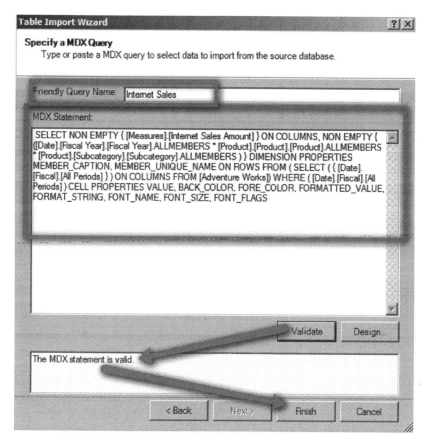

Figure 5–52. Generate and Validate MDX query

■ **Note** If you already know how to build a MDX query, you can create and paste it in the MDX Statement window and avoid the design step.

When you click the Finish button, the wizard imports the data and displays a success or failure notification. You can close the window on successful confirmation. PowerPivot will display the data from the MDX query. Change the column header names (titles) to make them more logical; for instance, change MeasureInternet Sales Amount to Internet Sales Amount.

13. Select the column Internet Sales Amount and from the Formatting section, select the Data Type and choose Currency.

14. After formatting the data and changing the column names, the final PowerPivot data should look like what's shown in Figure 5–53.

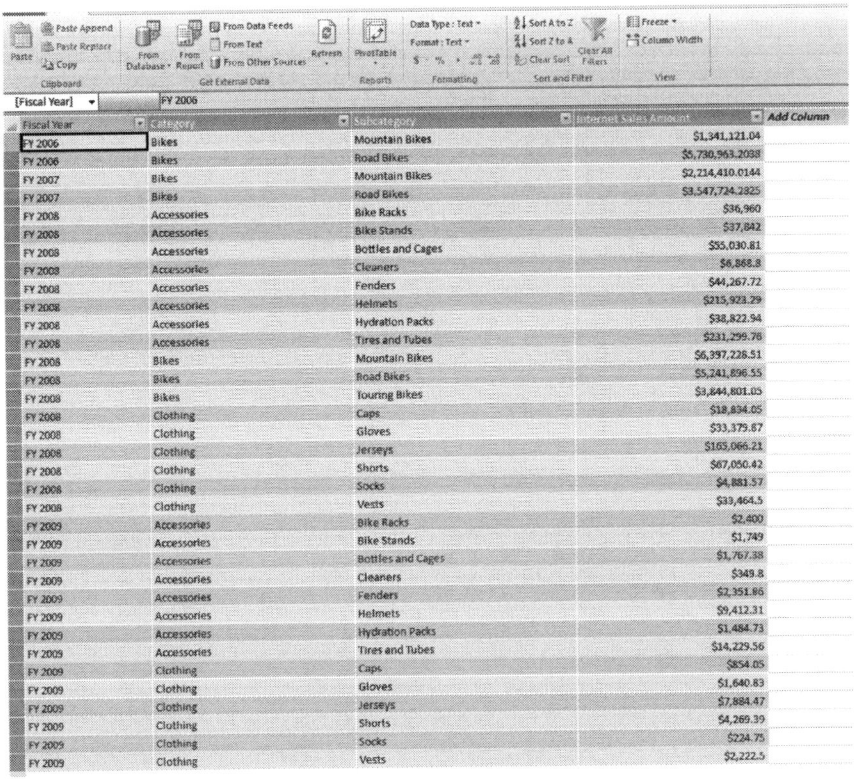

Fiscal Year	Category	Subcategory	Internet Sales Amount
FY 2006	Bikes	Mountain Bikes	$1,341,121.04
FY 2006	Bikes	Road Bikes	$5,730,963.2038
FY 2007	Bikes	Mountain Bikes	$2,214,410.0144
FY 2007	Bikes	Road Bikes	$3,547,724.2325
FY 2008	Accessories	Bike Racks	$36,960
FY 2008	Accessories	Bike Stands	$37,842
FY 2008	Accessories	Bottles and Cages	$55,030.81
FY 2008	Accessories	Cleaners	$6,868.8
FY 2008	Accessories	Fenders	$44,267.72
FY 2008	Accessories	Helmets	$215,923.29
FY 2008	Accessories	Hydration Packs	$38,822.94
FY 2008	Accessories	Tires and Tubes	$231,299.76
FY 2008	Bikes	Mountain Bikes	$6,397,226.51
FY 2008	Bikes	Road Bikes	$5,241,896.55
FY 2008	Bikes	Touring Bikes	$3,844,801.05
FY 2008	Clothing	Caps	$18,834.05
FY 2008	Clothing	Gloves	$33,379.87
FY 2008	Clothing	Jerseys	$165,066.21
FY 2008	Clothing	Shorts	$67,050.42
FY 2008	Clothing	Socks	$4,881.57
FY 2008	Clothing	Vests	$33,464.5
FY 2009	Accessories	Bike Racks	$2,400
FY 2009	Accessories	Bike Stands	$1,749
FY 2009	Accessories	Bottles and Cages	$1,767.38
FY 2009	Accessories	Cleaners	$349.8
FY 2009	Accessories	Fenders	$2,351.86
FY 2009	Accessories	Helmets	$9,412.31
FY 2009	Accessories	Hydration Packs	$1,484.73
FY 2009	Accessories	Tires and Tubes	$14,229.56
FY 2009	Clothing	Caps	$854.05
FY 2009	Clothing	Gloves	$1,640.83
FY 2009	Clothing	Jerseys	$7,884.47
FY 2009	Clothing	Shorts	$4,269.39
FY 2009	Clothing	Socks	$224.75
FY 2009	Clothing	Vests	$2,222.5

Figure 5–53. Data retrieved from the MDX query displayed in the PowerPivot window

15. From the *Reports* section, choose PivotTable (or Chart and Table) from the PivotTable drop-down menu. In the Create PivotChart and PivotTable window, select New Worksheet and click OK.
16. From the PowerPivot Field List, drag and drop Internet Sales Amount to the Values section of the configuration window
17. Drag and drop Fiscal Year to the Row Labels section of the configuration window
18. Drag and drop Product and Subcategory to the Slicers Vertical section of the configuration window
19. Click on Chart and configure it in the same way as the previous steps. Drag and drop Internet Sales Amount to Values section of the configuration window.
20. Drag and drop Fiscal Year to the Axis Fields section of the configuration window.

21. Drag and drop Category to the Axis Fields section of the configuration window. Rename the sheet to an appropriate name and save the file.

22. You can save the file by using the Save & Send option from the Backstage and saving it directly to the SharePoint library (PowerPivot Library), or you can first save the file manually to the file system and later upload it to SharePoint PowerPivot library.

Your final Excel workbook with the PowerPivot data will look like the one in Figure 5–54.

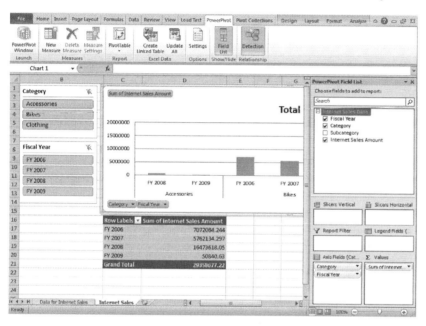

Figure 5-54. PowerPivot window after setting up the data source

23. In the Connections section of the Data tab, click on Properties. In the Connection Properties window, select the Definition tab and click on the Authentication Settings button. Select SSS – SSS ID and provide the SSS Application ID you set earlier to connect to the SSAS database. Click OK as needed to close all the open windows. Finally, save the Excel sheet to your local disk.

24. Open the SharePoint site and go to the PowerPivot Library. From the ribbon, choose Upload Document to upload your saved Excel file. Enter the Name and Title and save the file. Your PowerPivot library will now display the document as shown in Figure 5–55, using a Silverlight control.

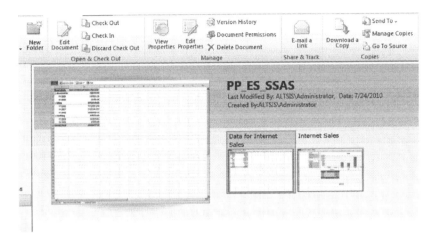

Figure 5–55. PowerPivot library on the SharePoint site

■ **Tip** Save the data connection file (.odc) to the data connection library as we discussed in the earlier examples and then perform the steps in this section.

---

25. Click on the Internet Sales sheet to load the Excel worksheet in the browser as shown in Figure 5–56.

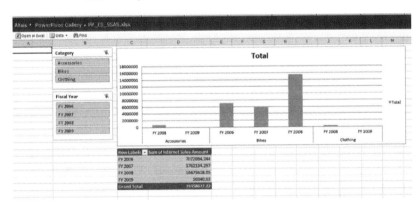

Figure 5–56. Excel Viewer displaying Excel with PowerPivot and data on SharePoint

26. You can now click on the slicer (filter) to analyze the filtered data.

■ **Tip** There is much more to this Excel data. You can use the path of the published Excel file as a data source and connect using SQL Server Analysis Services. You can also load the data while using SQL Server Reporting Services.

Silverlight PivotViewer is a powerful web control that can be used for Business Intelligence. You can download Silverlight PivotViewer and get more information at `www.silverlight.net/learn/pivotviewer/`.

You've already seen how to use Excel Services with the REST-based API. Another API introduced in SharePoint 2010 is the JavaScript Object Model (JSOM) for Excel Services. With JSOM you can handle events on user actions and connect with one or more EWA web parts on the page.

Excel Services and ECMAScript

You can use JSOM to retrieve data from sheets, tables, PivotTables, chart, and cells or a range of cells. You can subscribe to many events in order to handle various user actions, such as active selection changed or cell value editing.

■ **Tip** You'll find a full object model diagram at

`blogs.msdn.com/blogfiles/Excel/WindowsLiveWriter/IntroducingtheJavaScriptObjectModelforEx_1231`
`E/image_2.png`.

JSOM is very simple to use. All you need is to write some JavaScript and add it to the page either directly or by using Content Editor web part. The JSOM classes and members are available in the EwaMoss.js file located in the **%ProgramFiles%\Common Files\Microsoft Shared\Web server extensions\14\template\layouts** directory.

■ **Note** Reference to EwaMoss.js is by default available in the default master page. You need to refer the file when custom master pages are designed.

Let's now see how to use JSOM to retrieve data from an Excel workbook that is published to SharePoint 2010.

PROBLEM CASE

Retrieve a selected range of cell values and display them on the page using the JavaScript Object Model. Use the Excel workbook you created using SSAS data earlier in this chapter.

Solution:

You've already performed a similar kind of exercise earlier in Chapter 2, Visio Services to retrieve the data. We will follow the same methodology to retrieve data from the Excel workbook in this case. The major steps involved in this exercise are:

1. First, add the page-load event handler

```
window.attachEvent("onload", Page_Load);
```

2. On page load, create a delegate method for application ready. As soon as the Excel Services JavaScript Object Model is ready, this delegate method will be called.

```
Ewa.EwaControl.add_applicationReady(GetEwaWebpart);
```

3. When the delegate method is called, get the instance of the Excel web part on the page. In the code, index 0 is used with the expectation that only one instance of the EWA web part is available.

```
ewaWebPart = Ewa.EwaControl.getInstances().getItem(0);
```

4. Verify if the instance of EWA is available and add the `ActiveSelectionChanged` event handler to the Excel Web Access web part instance.

```
ewaWebPart.add_activeSelectionChanged(activeSelectionChangedHandler);
```

5. With the `activeSelectionChangedHandler`, when a user changes a selection on the EWA web part, you need to capture the selection sheet and the range of the selection.

```
var selection = rangeArgs.getRange();
    var selectedSheet = selection.getSheet().getName();
```

6. Retrieve the values of the selected range.

```
var selectedValues = rangeArgs.getFormattedValues();
```

7. Assign the value retrieved in previous step to Div text.

```
document.getElementById('ewaText').firstChild.data = selectedValues;
```

All of this together becomes the final code as follows:

```
<script type="text/javascript">
var ewaWebPart = null;
if(window.attachEvent)
{
    window.attachEvent("onload", Page_Load);
}
function Page_Load()
{
    Ewa.EwaControl.add_applicationReady(GetEwaWebpart);
}
```

```
function GetEwaWebpart()
{
    ewaWebPart = Ewa.EwaControl.getInstances().getItem(0);
    if(ewaWebPart)
    {
        ewaWebPart.add_activeSelectionChanged(activeSelectionChangedHandler);
    }
}
function activeSelectionChangedHandler(rangeArgs)
{

    var selection = rangeArgs.getRange();
    var selectedSheet = selection.getSheet().getName();
    var selectedValues = rangeArgs.getFormattedValues();
    if(selectedSheet = "Sheet1")
    {
        document.getElementById('ewaText').firstChild.data = selectedValues;
    }
}
</script>
<div id="ewaText" style="font-family: Verdana; font-style: bold; font-size:14pt;
color:red;"> </div>
```

8. Copy this code to a file and save it as a *propername*.html file.

9. Open your SharePoint site. Create a document library to host the script file. Upload the file to this document library and copy the file's shortcut URL.

10. Edit the page where you previously added the Excel Web Access web part and add the Content Editor web part that is available in the Media and Content category.

11. Edit the Content Editor web part and under the Content Link, add the .html file path from step 9 and click OK.

12. Exit Edit mode or click Stop Editing.

13. Select some range of cells on the EWA web part and the Content Editor web part will display the selected values as shown in Figure 5–57.

■ **Tip** If you have security concerns about using JavaScript in the Content Editor web part, you can add the above code directly on the page and avoid steps 8 through 12.

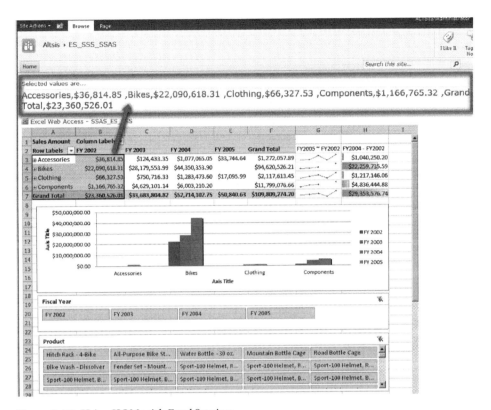

Figure 5–57. Using JSOM with Excel Services

Now that you have seen some working examples, you need to be aware of best practices, as well as some of the known issues and tips for Excel Services 2010.

Plan and Know Excel Services

It's not just enough to use what is available. You need to plan very well before implementing them. You'll find guidelines from Microsoft for Mitigating Threats, Setting up of UDFs, and other general topics at msdn.microsoft.com/en-us/library/ms545631.aspx.

You can read about some of the known issues and tips for Excel Services at msdn.microsoft.com/en-us/library/ms501525.aspx.

And, finally, here are the Error Codes generated by Excel Services during various errors msdn.microsoft.com/en-us/library/ms575980.aspx.

Summary

As shown in Figure 5–58, in this chapter we have looked at the following:

- Capabilities and new features of Excel Services in SharePoint 2010
- The Excel client and its new features
- Setting up Excel Services (Administration)
- Integrating Excel with SharePoint using EWA
- Extracting Excel graphs using the REST API
- SOAP, SSAS, and ECMAScript support in Excel
- PowerPivot for Excel

Excel Services in SharePoint 2010

Excel Client	Integration with SPS	Administration
Sparklines Slicers PowerPivot Conditional Formatting External Data	EWA web part Web part connections SOAP, SSAS REST, ECMAScript, PowerPivot	Set up Excel Services Features Secure Store Services Performance

Figure 5–58. Excel and Excel Services

What's Next?

In the next chapter, you will learn about PerformancePoint Services and its BI capabilities. This is the platform where everything comes together. We will walk you through installation and setting up of PerformancePoint Services, as well as administration and migration. We will also demonstrate authoring KPIs and scorecards, and integrating dashboards with various other services.

■ ■ ■

CHAPTER 6

PerformancePoint Services

Throughout this book, we have explored how the SharePoint platform can be used to provide a user interface for business intelligence and data analysis. Up to now, we have examined individual technologies such as Excel Services, Visio Services, and SQL Server Reporting Services as isolated solutions for specific needs. In this chapter, we will discover how PerformancePoint Services allows us to build integrated business intelligence solutions that bring these capabilities together into powerful interactive dashboards.

What Will You Learn in This Chapter?

- Introduction to PerformancePoint Services

- The architecture of PerformancePoint Services

- Setting up PerformancePoint Services

- Authoring and publishing PerformancePoint solutions in SharePoint 2010

- Integrating PerformancePoint dashboards with Visio and Excel Services

- Managing PerformancePoint using PowerShell

Software Prerequisites

- SharePoint Server 2010 Enterprise Edition

- Office Excel 2010 x64

- Office Visio 2010 x64

- SQL Server 2008 R2 x64 / SQL Server 2008 x64

- AdventureWorks Database (SQL Server 2008 R2) downloadable at http://msftdbprodsamples.codeplex.com/

- SQL Server 2008 R2 Client Tools – downloadable at http://technet.microsoft.com/en-us/library/ms143219.aspx

Introduction

Though PerformancePoint Services is a new feature in SharePoint Server 2010, it is far from being a new product. Like many Microsoft products, including SharePoint itself, PerformancePoint has a long, and sometimes inglorious, history.

In the early years of this century, the "scorecard" became a popular business metaphor for bringing together related pieces of information from throughout the enterprise to provide decision makers with a high-level view of the business. Special-purpose scorecards like the "Balanced Scorecard" became popular but there were no good tools available to deliver them. After a few attempts at getting Excel and web-based templates deployed, Microsoft published the Office Business Scorecard Manager 2005.

In 2006, Microsoft purchased ProClarity Corporation, thereby acquiring one of the premiere business intelligence software companies. Microsoft immediately began integrating features of ProClarity's rich server- and client-based data analysis tools into its products.

When MS PerformancePoint Server was released in 2007, it contained two major modules: monitoring & analysis (M&A) and planning. The M&A component combined the features of the Business Scorecard Manager product with new capabilities brought in from ProClarity and saw good adoption. Use of the planning module, however, was sparse and in 2009, Microsoft dropped it due to lack of market interest. What remained of PerformancePoint was then rolled into the enterprise license of Microsoft Office SharePoint Server (MOSS) 2007. In fact, at that point, the MS PerformancePoint Server 2007 product could be loaded onto a MOSS server farm (with Enterprise Client Access Licenses, or CALs) without additional licensing.

Now, with the release of SharePoint Server 2010, PerformancePoint has become a fully integrated service within the SharePoint environment. You get all of SharePoint's administration and content management tools along with the analytic abilities of PerformancePoint.

PerformancePoint Services Architecture

PerformancePoint Services is implemented using the new service application framework introduced in SharePoint Server 2010. In the same way that Excel Services and Visio Services run as separate service processes, so does PerformancePoint.

Service Components and Interfaces

Figure 6–1 shows the primary components that cooperate to provide the business intelligence experience PerformancePoint Services makes possible.

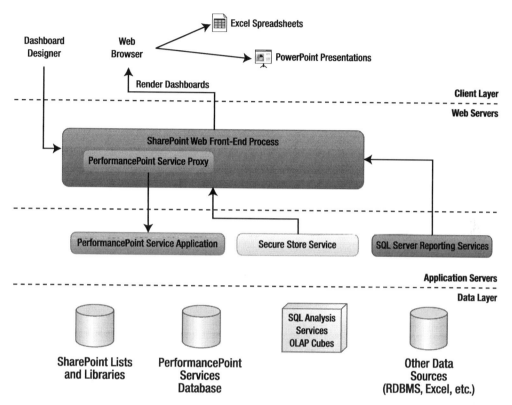

Figure 6–1. PerformancePoint services and related components

The PerformancePoint end-user experience is designed to be very simple. A PerformancePoint dashboard is deployed as nothing more than a folder containing one or more web pages within a SharePoint library. These pages contain all of the user interface elements necessary to perform complex business analysis on the underlying business data. This user interface is designed to require very little specialized training. With some experience, most users find the scorecards, charts, and reports very easy to interpret and manipulate. All of this content is delivered via a web browser, of course, but there are also many opportunities to take data offline into office applications such as Excel for deeper ad hoc analysis.

In order to deliver this sophisticated user interface, the KPIs, scorecards, dashboards, and other BI components must first be defined and deployed to SharePoint. The tool for accomplishing this is the Dashboard Designer, a Windows application for defining BI components and deploying them to SharePoint. This tool does not need to be separately downloaded and installed. It is automatically installed as a "one-click" application when needed. See "Authoring and Publishing PerformancePoint Solutions" later in this chapter for a tour of this tool. Note that this is a development tool and is not designed for use by most end users.

At the application layer, PerformancePoint conforms to the typical design of a SharePoint service. It is made up of a service process and a proxy component. The proxy component provides code running within the IIS application pool process with access to the functionality of the PerformancePoint service application. The service runs as an independent process in the operating system and is often deployed on a separate tier of application servers that sits between the web front-end server and the database servers, as shown in Figure 6–1.

Other application-level services commonly employed as part of a PerformancePoint solution include the Secure Store Service (SSS) and SQL Server Reporting Services (SSRS). SSS provides a location for logon credentials to be securely stored within the SharePoint environment. For more details on the purpose and configuration of the Secure Store Service, see Chapter 5. While not part of SharePoint Server, the SSRS component of SQL Server is frequently leveraged in conjunction with PerformancePoint solutions due to the ease with which it allows complex reports to be created and delivered.

On the database layer of the architecture, there are several data sources you'll have to become familiar with.

SharePoint Content Lists and Libraries

As you are probably aware, SharePoint stores its web site contents in content databases. These databases contain the site collections, sites, lists, libraries, and pages that make up the sites served by SharePoint. In the context of PerformancePoint, most of the business intelligence objects, including the dashboards themselves, are also stored in lists and libraries within SharePoint's content databases.

PerformancePoint Service Databases

Like the other service applications in SharePoint Server 2010, PerformancePoint Services needs to store data that does not fit well into the usual format of lists and libraries in SharePoint. This data is stored in a separate database that's created when a new instance of the PerformancePoint service application is created. The tables in this database, like all SharePoint databases, should never be manipulated directly but only through PerformancePoint Services. These tables contain various parameters used by PPS, as well as dashboard annotations and comments entered by users.

SQL Server Analysis Services (SSAS) Cubes

Because of the types of analysis normally performed with PerformancePoint Services, perhaps the most common data source for Key Performance Indicators (KPIs), scorecards, and dashboards is SQL Server Analysis Services (SSAS). The cubes stored in SSAS contain the raw business information that PPS will "slice and dice" to perform the analysis required by the user. For a full description of using SSAS cubes to store and manipulate multidimensional data, see Chapter 1.

Other Reporting Data Sources

While SQL Analysis Services is the most common source of information for PPS dashboards, it is far from the only option. Any data store from which you can read data is a potential data source for PerformancePoint. Additional data sources supported out of the box include SQL Server relational tables, Excel spreadsheets (either file-based or via Excel Services), and SharePoint lists.

With a little more effort, you can expand the available data sources to include any ODBC-compliant relational database and even data accessed via custom code written and deployed by the user's organization. For details on creating custom data source providers for PerformancePoint Services, see msdn.microsoft.com/en-us/library/bb836514.aspx. To access other non-Microsoft databases, you can use either Business Connectivity Services (see Chapter 4) to expose the data as a SharePoint list or a SQL linked server to expose the data as a SQL Server table (msdn.microsoft.com/en-us/library/ms188279.aspx).

Securing PerformancePoint Solutions

Much of the security for a PerformancePoint solution is handled by the SharePoint Foundation component. The dashboards exposed by PerformancePoint Services are stored as ASPX pages in a folder within a SharePoint document library. The permissions associated with the libraries, folders, and dashboard pages will control who is allowed to access which pages.

However, the page itself is not usually what is most important. It is the data that we want to protect. Security can become problematic when we have to access data sources outside of SharePoint. PerformancePoint Services provides three authentication methods for accessing backend data sources: per-user identity, an unattended service account (USA), and a custom connection string for SQL Server Analysis Services.

Per-user identity allows a PPS dashboard to impersonate the user's credentials when accessing backend data. This is a very secure way to access data because it provides a second check before allowing the user to access not just the dashboard, but the data underlying the dashboard. However, this form of authentication requires Kerberos delegation to be in place between the PerformancePoint server and the data source, so it's not always possible to use this type of authentication. See "Planning Considerations for Services that Access External Data Sources" at technet.microsoft.com/en-us/library/cc560988.aspx#ConsiderationsForAccessingExternalData.

The most commonly used form of authentication with PerformancePoint services is the unattended service account. This is an account that is configured in the Secure Store Service and used to access a backend data source. The data source will see only the service account's credentials, so it will not be able to filter the data it returns based on the identity of the user accessing the dashboard. The service account must be given access to all necessary data within all data sources in order for PerformancePoint to function properly. It is a best practice to use a service account with the least permissions that will allow it to access the needed data.

The last option, called "Custom Data," uses the unattended account but also includes the user's login name on the connection string. This option works only with SQL Server Analysis Services 2006 or later. In SSAS, this is known as "Dynamic Security." The idea is to allow the SSAS server to filter the query results when full Kerberos delegation is not possible. The user's login can be used in MDX queries and SSAS role assignments to limit the data returned by the cube.

The most important thing to note when choosing among these authentication options is that the choice can now be made for each data source that is configured. In PerformancePoint Server 2007, it was necessary to configure a single authentication mode for the entire server application. It was not possible to configure one data source using per-user identity and another to use an unattended service account. In SharePoint 2010, if multiple types of authentication are required, you don't need to configure multiple PerformancePoint service application instances. Creating separate data sources is sufficient. However, the unattended account is configured for a PPS application instance so all data sources running against the USA in that instance will use the same account. See "Setting up PerformancePoint Services" and "Creating a Data Source" later in this chapter for details.

Business Intelligence Solution Components

A PerformancePoint solution is built by creating a set of business intelligence components that work together to control how business data is aggregated and displayed. This section will introduce the concepts behind these components and how they are deployed to a PerformancePoint service environment. For a step-by-step guide to creating a real-world PPS solution, see "Authoring and Publishing PerformancePoint Solutions" later in this chapter.

BI Component Types

The components that go into a PerformancePoint solution are described at a conceptual level in this section. Later we'll describe how these components are represented and stored in SharePoint.

Dashboards

A *dashboard* is a set of web pages displayed by SharePoint to allow the user to view and analyze data. Figure 6–2 shows a sample dashboard.

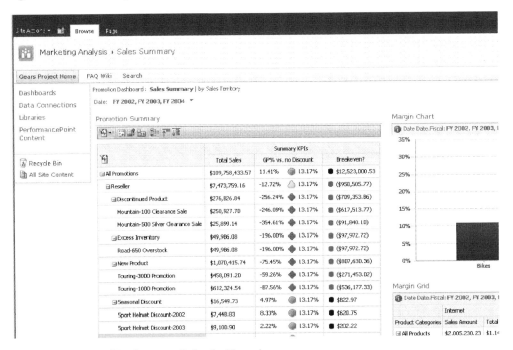

Figure 6–2 . A typical PerformancePoint dashboard

A dashboard page consists of several parts. Typically, a page contains a navigation area at the top of the page, as shown in Figure 6–3. In this case, the pages of the dashboard, "Sales Summary" and "by Sales Territory," are presented as links in the header of the page. Clicking on an active link takes the user to a new page in the dashboard while preserving the filters used on the current page. This allows multiple pages to act as a single dashboard.

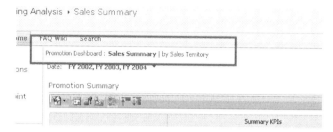

Figure 6–3. *Dashboard navigation links*

The rest of the page is separated into *zones*, similar to the web part zones used in SharePoint pages. The difference is that dashboard zones can be added, modified, and removed from a dashboard page after it is created. These zones allow dashboard components, including filters, scorecards, and reports, to be stacked and connected in the same way web parts can be manipulated on a web part page. Figure 6–4 highlights the zones and direction (vertical vs. horizontal) of the default dashboard page layout.

Figure 6–4. *Default dashboard zones*

The BI components that make up the page are assembled, arranged, and connected using the Dashboard Designer. When the dashboard is deployed to SharePoint, the various object definitions control the page's behavior. A common pattern, as shown in Figure 6–4, is to place visible filters in the header zone of the page and then to fill the other zones with scorecards and reports as needed.

The connections created between components allow them to act together. For example, when the user changes the Date filter on the sample dashboard, each of the scorecards and reports on the page are updated to reflect data only from those periods. When a row is selected in the scorecard shown on the left, the data on the reports in the right column are filtered to match. We will be creating this dashboard and its connections later in this chapter.

Indicators and Key Performance Indicators

A *Key Performance Indicator* is a definition of business-relevant measurements (or "metrics") used to display easy-to-understand conditions as shown in Figure 6–5.

Figure 6–5. A key performance indicator

KPIs are defined in PerformancePoint as a set of metrics that are either "actual" or "target" metrics. Actual metrics are the values that are calculated from the underlying business data. In the example in Figure 6–5, "Total Sales" is an actual metric. Target metrics, in contrast, define a desired goal for the actual metric, based on some condition or formula specified as part of the KPIs definition. The "GP% vs. no Discount" column is a target metric in this example. Target metrics can be displayed in several ways but include three basic components: the indicator and a value before and/or after the indicator. The meaning of these values can be defined wherever the KPI is displayed. In this case, the highlighted line shows an actual value of "-12.72%", a yellow triangle indicator, and a target value of "13.17%".

The definition of the KPI specifies where the actual and target values come from as well as what type of indicator to show. PerformancePoint comes with a large set of indicators to choose from, as Figure 6–6 shows. Through Dashboard Designer you can also create your own custom indicators using custom images.

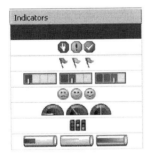

Figure 6–6. Some common indicator types

Data Sources

The first components to be created in a PerformancePoint solution are data sources. These define the locations and parameters to use when accessing the data that will be used by the dashboard. PerformancePoint supports two major categories of data sources: tabular and multidimensional.

Tabular data sources are those that provide PPS with a relational table of data to work with. The most commonly used data sources of this type are SQL Server tables. Other options include cells retrieved from Excel spreadsheets, either through Excel Services or directly from a file, or the items in a SharePoint list. It is also possible to use SharePoint's Business Connectivity Services (BCS) or SQL linked servers to pass data from other RDBMS or line-of-business applications into a PerformancePoint dashboard.

Multidimensional data sources are the most common type used in PerformancePoint solutions. They use SQL Server Analysis Services (SSAS) cubes to furnish and process data. Analysis Services is the only currently supported OLAP data source.

Filters

Filters are components that let users select parts of the data set to examine while excluding the rest. For example, you can use a filter to examine data only for certain time periods, as Figure 6–7 shows.

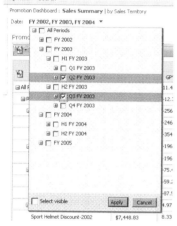

Figure 6–7. A multi-selectable member-selection filter

When creating a filter, there are two primary considerations: the type of filter and the display method to be used.

The types of filters available are:

- *Custom Table:* This filter connects to a tabular data source to retrieve a list of options from a table.

- *MDX Query:* This filter evaluates an MDX query against an OLAP data source to produce a set of members to serve as options in the filter control.

- *Member Selection:* This filter takes its options directly from a dimension in an OLAP data source, which can be either all members or a subset of the members in the dimension.

- *Named Set:* This filter uses an SSAS Named Set (i.e., an MDX expression) to evaluate which members to include. Note that SQL Server 2008 introduced the concept of "dynamic" named sets that are context-aware, which can make them very powerful in this context. For more information on SSAS Named Sets, see msdn.microsoft.com/en-us/library/ms166594.aspx.

- *Time Intelligence:* This filter uses time dimensions in a way that lets users make time-based selections such as "year-to-date," "last six months," or "last year". The developer specifies formulas that select a subset of the time dimension's members to include in the calculation.

- *Time Intelligence (Connection Formula):* This variation on the Time Intelligence filter allows the user to select a single "current date." When connected to a dashboard, this date is evaluated against a date formula to create a dynamic time period based on that date. The user can therefore specify, for example, "5/11/2010" and generate a report on the six months of data prior to that date.

Once the type of filter has been selected, it can be displayed in three different ways.

- *List:* The filter options are presented in a drop-down list control as a flat list from which only one item can be selected.

- *Tree:* This form displays a hierarchical tree of members from which one option can be selected.

- *Multi-Select Tree:* This control, shown in Figure 6–7, also displays a tree but allows the user to select an arbitrary set of members from the tree.

When a filter is placed on a dashboard, it is not just a user interface control that controls the data displayed on that page. The selections made are written to PerformancePoint's database for later use. If the user returns to that page days later, that selection will still exist. The number of days the selection is retained can be configured in SharePoint Central Administration. See "Setting up PerformancePoint Services" later in this chapter. Because the filter is part of the dashboard, not just the page, that same filter selection will also be transferred to any other page that is part of the same dashboard. Therefore, if a selection is made on one page and then the user navigates to another page on the same dashboard, all of the filter selections made on the previous page apply to the new page as well.

Scorecards

A PerformancePoint scorecard, shown in Figure 6–8, is used to display a set of key performance indicator metrics. You can configure the KPIs to display differently depending on what you need the scorecard to reflect. For example, the designer may choose to use a background color for a KPI cell instead of displaying the indicator image.

Promotion Summary

	Summary KPIs		
	Total Sales	GP% vs. no Discount	Breakeven?
All Promotions	$109,758,433.57	11.41%　　13.17%	● $12,523,000.53
Reseller	$7,473,759.16	-12.72%　　13.17%	($950,505.77)
Discontinued Product	$276,826.84	-256.24%　◆ 13.17%	($709,353.86)
Mountain-100 Clearance Sale	$250,927.70	-246.09%　◆ 13.17%	($617,513.77)
Mountain-500 Silver Clearance Sale	$25,899.14	-354.61%　◆ 13.17%	($91,840.10)
Excess Inventory	$49,986.08	-196.00%　◆ 13.17%	($97,972.72)
Road-650 Overstock	$49,986.08	-196.00%　◆ 13.17%	($97,972.72)
New Product	$1,070,415.74	-75.45%　◆ 13.17%	($807,630.36)
Touring-3000 Promotion	$458,091.20	-59.26%　◆ 13.17%	($271,453.02)
Touring-1000 Promotion	$612,324.54	-87.56%　◆ 13.17%	($536,177.33)
Seasonal Discount	$16,549.73	4.97%　　 13.17%	● $822.97
Sport Helmet Discount-2002	$7,448.83	8.33%　　 13.17%	● $620.75
Sport Helmet Discount-2003	$9,100.90	2.22%　　 13.17%	● $202.22
Volume Discount	$6,059,980.77	10.95%　　13.17%	● $663,628.20
Volume Discount 11 to 14	$4,896,451.91	16.22%　　13.17%	◆ $794,013.51
Volume Discount 15 to 24	$1,037,643.33	-10.53%　　13.17%	($109,260.96)
Volume Discount 25 to 40	$124,148.53	-16.99%　◆ 13.17%	($21,098.59)
Volume Discount 41 to 60	$1,736.99	-1.48%　◆ 13.17%	($25.76)

Figure 6–8. A PerformancePoint scorecard

In addition to the KPI metrics, scorecards generally also include one or more sets of dimension attributes that are used to drill down or roll up the KPIs.

Reports

A report in PerformancePoint refers to a component that displays business data other than KPIs. Reports are authored separately and then connected to the filters and scorecards on a dashboard to filter the data returned in the report. Our sample dashboard contains two of the most common reports used in PerformancePoint server: the analytic chart and the analytic graph (Figure 6–9).

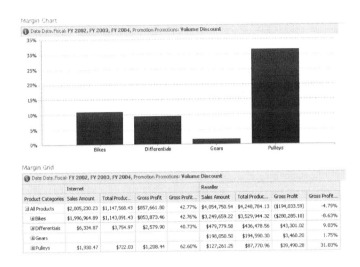

Figure 6–9. *Analytic chart and graph reports*

PerformancePoint generates some reports entirely within itself but some reports are created in cooperation with other technologies. Here are the report templates supported:

- *Analytic Grid:* As shown in Figure 6–9, this type of report displays figures as a set of rows and columns. This control is very similar in look and feel to the PivotTable report used in previous versions of PerformancePoint.

- *Analytic Chart:* As shown in Figure 6–9, this report displays an interactive chart of the specified data. The user can drill into and roll up the data on this type of chart just as with an Analytic Grid.

- *Excel Services:* An Excel spreadsheet published using Excel Services can be referenced and used to display its data as an integrated part of a dashboard. See Chapter 5 for a full description Excel Services' capabilities.

- *KPI Details:* This simple report displays all of the properties of a selected KPI metric on a scorecard. This report must be connected to a scorecard in order to display any data.

- *ProClarity Analytics Server Page:* To support backward compatibility with ProClarity's installed server base, this report will bring in a page defined in that product running separately from the SharePoint server farm.

- *Reporting Services:* An SSRS report can be connected to a dashboard for rich report rendering.

- *Strategy Map:* This type of report uses a Visio diagram as a template for displaying KPIs in a graphical format. A typical use of a strategy map report is to display a map color-coded by a KPI's indicators. It is also possible to display numeric and text data on the map.

- *Web Page:* An ordinary web page can also be used to display data on a dashboard. While this may be as simple as displaying an Internet site within your dashboard, the real purpose of this report type is to act as a jack-of-all-trades for PerformancePoint reporting. When dashboard components, like reports, are connected to other components, like filters and scorecards, the parameters selected in those connections are passed to the connected component in the "Request.Params" collection. This allows a custom ASPX page to be deployed that accepts filter and selection values to display arbitrary data in HTML format.

Each of these reports is rendered on the dashboard page using a web part that manages the connection with other parts of the dashboard.

PerformancePoint SharePoint Components

Now that we're familiar with the basic concepts of a business intelligence solution, let's take a look at how these pieces are put together in a SharePoint site.

PPS Content Types

A content type in SharePoint defines all of the metadata about how a particular type of list item or library document will be handled by SharePoint. This includes a list of the fields associated with the object and any custom actions it may support. In the case of PerformancePoint, the following content types are defined to enable its functionality.

- PerformancePoint Dashboard

- PerformancePoint Data Source

- PerformancePoint Filter

- PerformancePoint Indicator

- PerformancePoint KPI

- PerformancePoint Report

- PerformancePoint Scorecard

With the exception of data sources, all of these content types define items in a SharePoint list. Data sources are stored as documents in a library because they are stored as Office or Universal Data Connection (UDC) files or as PerformancePoint data source files. Bear in mind that these items represent the definition of the object, not an end-user-viewable object. These items can be edited using the Dashboard Designer but don't display any content on their own. Only when a dashboard is "deployed" is it compiled into a set of ASPX pages that can be viewed by users.

A major advantage of PerformancePoint Services over PerformancePoint Server 2007 is the use of content types. With content types, all of the functionality of SharePoint is now available for use with PerformancePoint artifacts. This includes participating in workflows, using information rights management policies, and including PPS objects in any list or library where the PPS features and content types are active. You are no longer constrained to using a special site definition with a predefined structure for your PPS solutions.

List and Library Templates

PerformancePoint defines list and library templates designed to store PerformancePoint artifacts.
List Templates:

- PerformancePoint Content List – Lists based on this template are used to store all of the PPS components listed in "Content Types" above except for Data Sources.

Library Templates:

- Data Connections Library for PerformancePoint – This template is used to store data sources defined by Dashboard Designer or as ODC or UDC files.

- Dashboards Library – This template is designed to store deployed PerformancePoint dashboards. Each dashboard is stored as a set of ASPX pages within a folder.

Web Parts

Dashboard pages are created as ordinary web part pages. The various components of a page are created as connected web parts. The web parts used by PerformancePoint are:

- The Filter Web Part, which displays the list or tree control for a filter component.

- The Scorecard Web Part, which displays the grid associated with a scorecard component.

- The Report View Web Part, which displays a PPS report. Depending on the type of report, this web part may link to other sites or applications.

- The Stack Web Part, which is used as a container for the web parts associated with a zone on a dashboard page.

Business Intelligence Center Site Template

PerformancePoint defines a sample site template to help designers begin using the service (Figure 6–10). This template is nothing more than an ordinary site with some prepopulated content to introduce the user to PerformancePoint features. The content is contained in a Content Editor Web Part and can be deleted when no longer needed. You can also add the PPS lists, libraries, and content types to any existing site instead of using the template. All that's required is for the PPS features to be activated.

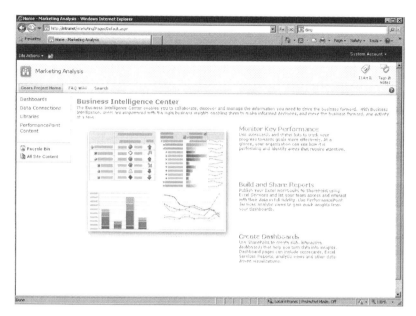

Figure 6–10. *The Business Intelligence Center Home Page*

In addition to this home page, the site template contains an instance of each of the lists and libraries described in "List and Library Templates" above. This makes the site a good location for one or more complete solutions to be stored. Additional content can be added to the site as needed.

Features

PerformancePoint Services is part of the Enterprise Client Access License (ECAL) for SharePoint Server 2010. In order to use any such features, your SharePoint site collection must have the SharePoint Server Enterprise Site Collection Features feature activated under the Site Collection Features.

The PerformancePoint functionality is enabled using two additional features. The first is the PerformancePoint Services Site Collection Features feature. This feature can also be found under Site Collection Features. The second feature is activated at the site level and is named PerformancePoint Services Site Features. See "Deploy the Business Intelligence Center" later in this chapter for step-by-step instructions for enabling these features.

Setting Up PerformancePoint Services

Like the other services we have examined in this book, PerformancePoint Services are configured using Central Administration or PowerShell commands (cmdlets). Let's take a look at the settings for PerformancePoint Services, along with the procedures for setting up a PPS instance.

The default, wizard-based installation of SharePoint Server 2010 includes an instance of the PerformancePoint Services application, so creating a new instance is not normally necessary. If you do need to create one, however, this can be easily accomplished through SharePoint Central Administration.

1. Open the Central Administration web site using the SharePoint 2010 Central Administration link available in the server's Start menu.

2. Navigate to the Central Administration ➤ Application Management ➤ Service Applications ➤ Manage Service Applications page. Note the default instance of PPS highlighted in Figure 6–11.

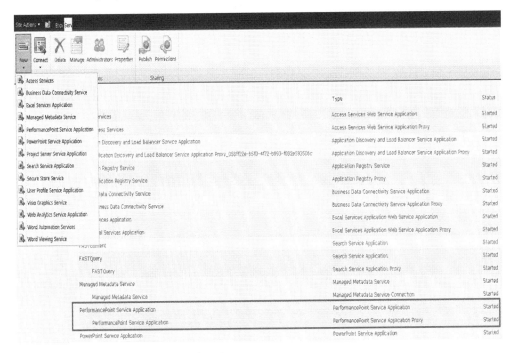

Figure 6–11. *The Manage Service Applications page*

3. To create a new PPS instance, select PerformancePoint Service Application from the New section of the ribbon, as shown in Figure 6–11. This brings up the New PerformancePoint Service Application dialog (Figure 6–12).

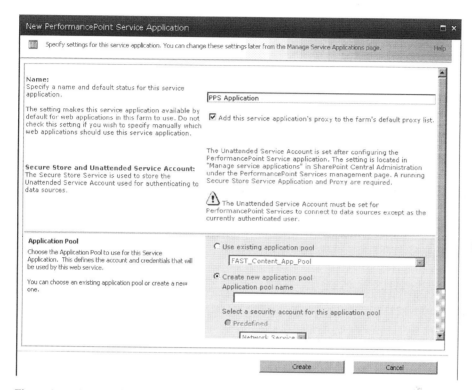

Figure 6–12. New PerformancePoint Service Application dialog

4. Set the name and application pool for the new PPS application instance or select an existing one. Use a new application pool when you wish to isolate PPS processing from other components within IIS.

5. Click Create.

After a few moments, the Manage Service Applications page will reappear with the new PPS application listed. It is now time to configure the application. If you are working with the default PPS instance, you should review the default settings, paying particular attention to the unattended service account, which should have the minimum privileges. See "Security PerformancePoint Solutions" earlier in this chapter to review why the USA is important.

To begin configuring the service application, click on the name of the service (PPS Application in our case) to be taken to the Manage PerformancePoint Services page as shown in Figure 6–13.

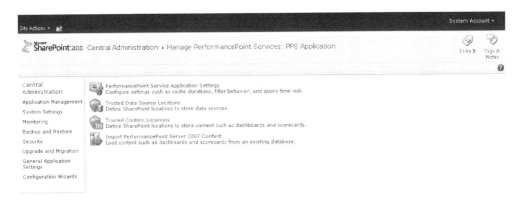

***Figure 6–13.** Manage PerformancePoint Services page*

On the Manage PerformancePoint Service page, there are various settings to configure, which we'll discuss now. While most of the settings can be left to their default values, some need to be configured in order to address specific requirements.

Application Settings

The PerformancePoint Server Application Settings page (Figure 6–14) contains a variety of settings that control the performance and behavior of PPS. These settings apply only to sites associated with this instance of PerformancePoint Services.

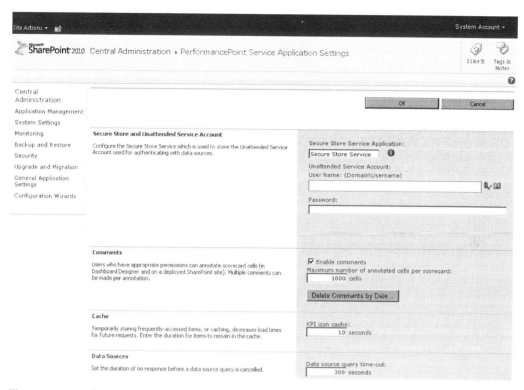

Figure 6–14 . PerformancePoint Services Application Settings page

Secure Store and Unattended Service Account

The purpose of this section is to configure the unattended service account. Recall that this is the Active Directory domain account that will be used when accessing data sources without using the user's own identity (Kerberos). The credentials for this account are stored in the Secure Store Service. See "Securing PerformancePoint Solutions" earlier in this chapter.

This section of the page has three entry boxes. The first textbox is used to identify the SSS application to be used for the account's credentials. The second and third boxes allow for the entry of the user name and password of the account, respectively. Remember that this account should have minimal permissions but provide access to all necessary data.

Comments

Each dashboard user can be given permission to add comments to the cells in a PPS scorecard. These comments are then available to other users when they view that scorecard. The comment functionality also uses the term *annotation*. Technically, a scorecard cell can have one annotation and each annotation can have multiple comments.

325

This section of the page contains a checkbox that can be used to enable the annotation feature within the PPS instance. There is also a setting that limits the number of annotations that can exist on a single scorecard. The default is 1,000 annotations per scorecard.

There is also a Delete Comments by Date... button that displays the dialog shown in Figure 6–15. This dialog can be used to start a background job that will clean up comments older than a given date, which can use useful if it becomes necessary to reclaim space in the SQL database associated with this PPS instance. The name of this database is based on the name of the PPS application and a unique GUID, like "PPS Application_d6430dcfa6de4086a84dcb1b0c39f78e".

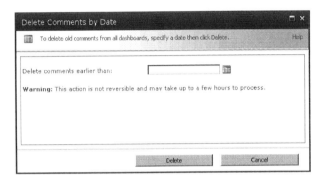

Figure 6–15. *The Delete Comments by Date dialog*

Cache

The cache section of the page contains a single entry that sets how long (in seconds) the images associated with KPIs should remain in memory before the memory is reclaimed. The default is 10 seconds, which should allow the image to be reused several times during the rendering of a single page. If your site makes heavy use of only a few unique indicators, it may make sense to extend this value to keep from frequently reloading them from disk.

Data Sources

This section allows the administrator to set a standard timeout on a data source, preventing pages from becoming unresponsive when a data source becomes slow or unavailable. The default is 300 seconds, which should be sufficient in most cases. If data access is consistently over 5 minutes, either the data source is not responding properly or the queries being used to access the data should be reconsidered. When data access for a dashboard page takes a very long time, two major problems result.

First, system resources are consumed processing and returning large amounts of data that will, most likely, never be used. The thread, table, memory, and I/O locking and contention created by executing very large queries can quickly drain system performance for all users.

Second, users are not going to wait for several minutes each time they interact with the dashboard. A user viewing a dashboard is trying to avoid information overload, so loading 1,000 or more records defeats this purpose. Long wait times degrade the user experience and lead to dashboards that aren't used.

Filters

Filters are used on dashboards to set how the data is "sliced." PerformancePoint dashboards have the ability to remember the last filter values used by each user. This is valuable when moving from one dashboard page to another or when returning to a dashboard on a future visit.

To avoid storing this data forever, this configuration section allows the administrator to set a time out (in days) for how long to retain unused filter values.

The maximum number of members that can be loaded into a filter tree (see Figure 6–16) is configured here as well. Each time you use a filter, you are selecting a set of values to apply with the filter. For example, if you select the year 2010 at the Months level of the date hierarchy, you are selecting 12 values that must be stored for the filter. If you are selecting at the Day level, there are 365 values that must be stored. Each of these values is called a *member* of the filter. This setting prevents very large selection lists from slowing down the server for all users.

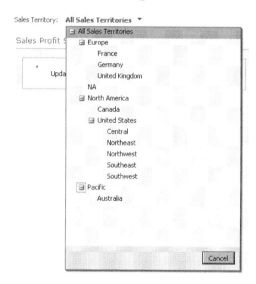

Figure 6–16. Sample filter tree control

Select Measure Control

This setting is similar to the Filters section except that it applies to the selection of measures on a dashboard.

Show Details

The Show Details feature allows an end-user to drill into a value that is derived from Analysis Services. The functionality of the drill-through is controlled by Analysis Services but it is rendered by PerformancePoint Services (see Figure 6–17). These settings limit the performance impact that this feature can have on the server hosting the PPS application.

Reseller Sales Amount	Reseller Order Quantity	Reseller Extended Amount	Reseller Tax Amount	Reseller Freight Cost	Discount Amount	Reseller Unit Price	Unit Price Discount Percent
164.4279	1	234.897	13.1542	4.1107	70.4691	234.897	0.3
1973.1348	12	2818.764	157.8508	49.3284	845.6292	234.897	0.3
164.4279	1	234.897	13.1542	4.1107	70.4691	234.897	0.3
780.8182	1	780.8182	62.4655	19.5205	0	780.8182	0
28.8404	1	28.8404	2.3072	0.721	0	28.8404	0
780.8182	1	780.8182	62.4655	19.5205	0	780.8182	0
35.994	1	35.994	2.8795	0.8999	0	35.994	0
40.373	2	40.373	3.2298	1.0093	0	20.1865	0
1242.8518	1	1242.8518	99.4281	31.0713	0	1242.8518	0
109.341	3	109.341	8.7473	2.7335	0	36.447	0
283.23	2	283.23	22.6584	7.0808	0	141.615	0
45.588	2	45.588	3.647	1.1397	0	22.794	0
2485.7036	2	2485.7036	198.8563	62.1426	0	1242.8518	0
182.352	8	182.352	14.5882	4.5588	0	22.794	0
224.97	5	224.97	17.9976	5.6243	0	44.994	0
20.1865	1	20.1865	1.6149	0.5047	0	20.1865	0
33.7745	1	33.7745	2.702	0.8444	0	33.7745	0
5.1865	1	5.1865	0.4149	0.1297	0	5.1865	0
60.5595	3	60.5595	4.8448	1.514	0	20.1865	0
22.794	1	22.794	1.8235	0.5699	0	22.794	0
105.294	2	105.294	8.4235	2.6324	0	52.647	0

Figure 6–17. Sample Show Details report

The "Initial retrieval limit" limits the number of rows that can be retrieved on the first page of the details report. The default of 1,000 is generally sufficient without creating too great a load on the server. The "Maximum retrieval limit" is used to prevent excessively large datasets from being returned on subsequent pages of the report. You can either choose a fixed number of rows or leave control of this setting with Analysis Services. To reduce page load times and unnecessary server traffic, consider reducing this value to one in line with the expected use of the report.

Decomposition Tree

The Decomposition Tree feature is a very powerful analytical tool, with an interface designed to be simple and intuitive to an untrained user (see Figure 6–18). The Decomposition Tree leverages the dimensions already built into the solution to drive the analysis. It allows users to do complex analysis without involving a developer.

However, because of the large number of members that a dimension might contain, it can become a performance drain on the system.

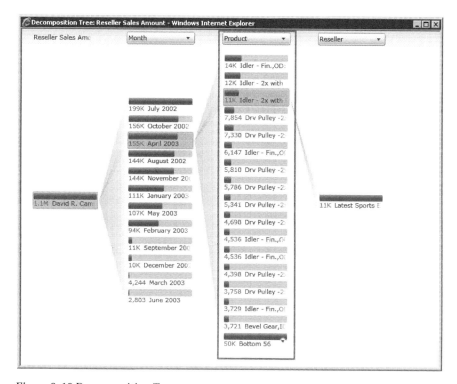

Figure 6–18 Decomposition Tree

Each item listed in a vertical column of the decomposition tree is counted against this limit. Note that this limit applies to only one column of items as highlighted in Figure 6–18. The total number of items in all columns may well exceed this value. This limit should not be set higher than is needed for the users to perform the analysis required.

Trusted Data Source Locations

PerformancePoint Services stores its metadata in SharePoint lists and libraries. These locations must be listed as "trusted" before PPS will consider them valid locations from which to read its objects. By default, all locations within SharePoint are automatically considered trusted, as Figure 6–19 shows.

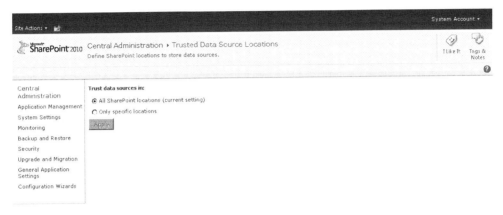

Figure 6–19. *Trusted data source locations (default setting)*

Note that just because the location is trusted by PerformancePoint, it is not necessarily accessible by any particular user. The SharePoint permissions on those items still control access to them. The fact that they are in a trusted location only allows PPS to use them if the user has access to them.

If there's a need to restrict the locations from which a PPS application can load data sources, switch this setting to "Only specific locations" and click Apply. This will enable a new set of options for adding specific locations, as shown in Figure 6–20.

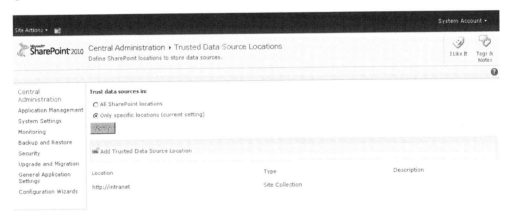

Figure 6–20. *Trusted data source locations (specific locations enabled)*

To add a location with this dialog box:

1. Click on Add Trusted Data Source Location. The dialog shown in Figure 6–21 will be displayed.

2. Enter the URL of a SharePoint-based site or document library. Only SharePoint locations can be used.

3. Click on the validation button to the right of the URL textbox. If the location is a valid one, the other controls will be enabled.

4. Select the Location Type option to use and enter a description for the trusted location.

5. Click OK to create the trusted location.

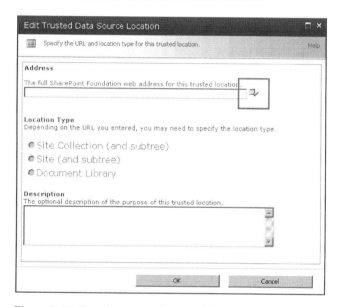

Figure 6–21. Creating a specific trusted data source location

Trusted Content Locations

Trusted Content Locations are configured in the same way as trusted data source locations with the following exception. PPS content items created by the Dashboard Designer application, such as KPIs, Scorecard, Reports, and so on are stored in SharePoint lists instead of in document libraries. Therefore, when selecting trusted locations, the options are Site, Site Collection, or List.

Import PerformancePoint Server 2007 Content

As mentioned in the introduction to this chapter, PerformancePoint was previously a stand-alone server product called Microsoft PerformancePoint Server 2007. The Monitoring module of that product supported many of the same types of objects (including scorecards and dashboards) that PerformancePoint Services now supports. The last option on the Manage PerformancePoint Services page is used to import objects from a PPS 2007 monitoring database into the SharePoint lists and libraries to be used with PerformancePoint Services. A wizard helps with the upgrade process.

The first page of the import wizard (Figure 6–22) contains general information about the import process. Before using the import wizard, you'll want to become familiar with both the PPS 2007 and SharePoint 2010 environments, including security and source and destination locations. Microsoft

provides guidance specifically for planning this process, which you'll find at
http://technet.microsoft.com/en-us/library/ee748616.aspx.

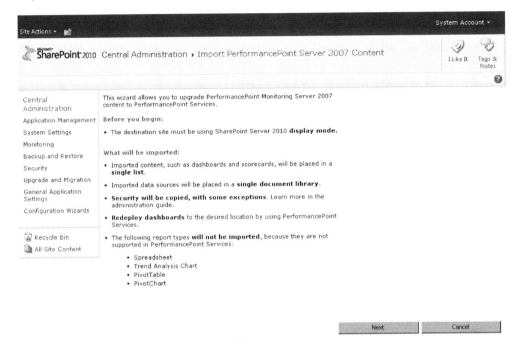

Figure 6–22. *The import wizard introduction page*

After you click Next on the introduction page, you'll see the page shown in Figure 6–23. This page
lets you identify the security mode used by the original PerformancePoint Server 2007 installation. Select
the correct mode and click Next.

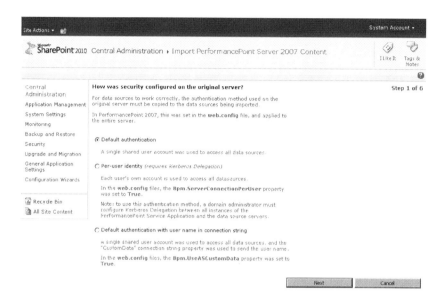

Figure 6–23. Step 1–Identifying the authentication mode

In step 2 of the wizard (Figure 6–24), you enter the database credentials to be used to connect to the PPS 2007 content database. This is the database where the dashboards were stored in the previous installation.

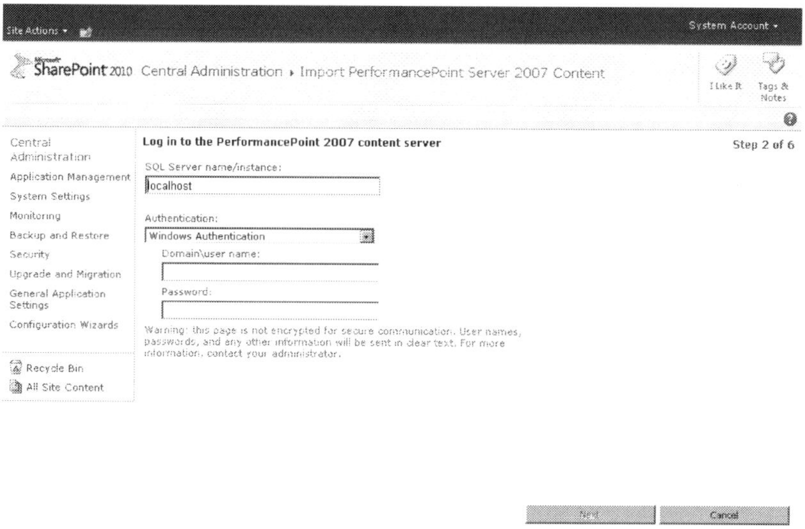

Figure 6–24. Step 2–Entering credentials

The credentials you enter can use either SQL or Windows authentication but they must have access to the PPS 2007 content to be migrated. Click Next when ready.

Step 3 (Figure 6–25) identifies the name of the content database to be accessed. Select the database and click Next.

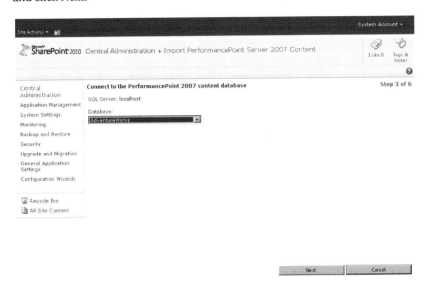

Figure 6–25. *Step 3 – Supplying the name of the content database*

In the remaining steps, you select the destination list and library that will receive the migrated content items. Once the migration starts, a bar will display showing its progress. When the migration is complete, be sure to review the objects and security permissions to resolve any inconsistencies between the old environment and the new. Remember, some PPS 2007 report types are not supported in SharePoint Server 2010, so it may be necessary to rework and redeploy some of your dashboards.

For a complete discussion of the options for upgrading PerformancePoint 2007 content to SharePoint 2010, take a look at the MSDN blog entry at `blogs.msdn.com/b/performancepoint/archive/2010/02/25/upgrading-performancepoint-server-2007-to-pps-2010.aspx`.

Managing PerformancePoint with PowerShell

The commands we'll discuss next are the same ones you used in "Setting up PerformancePoint Services," but now we'll use PowerShell commands. As you can see in Tables 6–1, 6–2, 6–3, and 6–4, there are four basic groups of commands: *New* operations, *Get* operations, *Set* operations and *Remove* (clear) operations.

■ **Tip** To obtain additional details and examples for each of these PowerShell commands, use the following commands from the PowerShell command line.

`Get-Help <PS Cmdlet>` for details and

`Get-Help <PS Cmdlet> -examples` for samples

Table 6–1. New Operations

PowerShell Command	Description
New-SPPerformancePointSericeApplication	Creates a new PerformancePoint Service application. Example: New-SPPerformancePointServiceApplication -Name "PPS Application" -ApplicationPool PPSAppPool2
New-SPPerformancePointSericeApplication Proxy	Creates a new proxy for an existing PPS application. Example: New-SPPerformancePointServiceApplicationProxy -Name "PPS Application Proxy" -ServiceApplication "PPS Application" -Default
New-SPPerformancePointSericeApplication TrustedLocation	Creates a new trusted location for data sources and/or PPS content types. Example: New-SPPerformancePointServiceApplication TrustedLocation -ServiceApplication "PPS Application" -url "http://intranet/central/dslib" -Type DocumentLibrary -TrustedLocationType DataSource

Table 6–2. Get Operations

PowerShell Command	Description
Get-SPPerformancePointSecureDataValues	Shows the values of the configuration parameters for the unattended service account. Example: Get-SPPerformancePointSecureDataValues –ServiceApplication "PPS Application"
Get-SPPerformancePointSericeApplication	Retrieves an instance of a PerformancePoint Service application. Example: Get-SPPerformancePointApplication –ServiceApplication "PPS Application"
Get-SPPerformancePointSericeApplication TrustedLocation	Retrieves one or more trusted data source and/or content locations for a PPS application. Example: Get-SPPerformancePointApplication TrustedLocation –ServiceApplication "PPS Application"

Table 6–3. Set Operations

PowerShell Command	Description
Set-SPPerformancePointSecureDataValues	Sets the values of the configuration parameters for the unattended service account. Example: Set-SPPerformancePointSecureDataValues -ServiceApplication "PPS Application" -DataSourceUnattendedServiceAccount (New-Object System.Management.Automation. PSCredential "CONTOSO\PPSService", (ConvertTo-SecureString "pass@word1" -AsPlainText -Force))
Set-SPPerformancePointSericeApplication	Sets top-level configuration parameters for an existing PPS instance. Example: Set-SPPerformancePointServiceApplication -Identity "PPS Application" -SelectMeasureMaximum 100

Table 6–4. Remove / Clear Operations

PowerShell Command	Description
Clear-SPPerformancePointSericeApplication TrustedLocation	Removes all of the configured trusted data source and/or content locations for a PPS instance.
	Example: Clear-SPPerformancePointServiceApplication TrustedLocation -ServiceApplication "PPS Application" -TrustedLocationType Content
Remove-SPPerformancePointSericeApplication	Removes an instance of the PerformancePoint Service application.
	Example: Remove-SPPerformancePointService Application -Identity "PPS Application"
Remove -SPPerformancePointSericeApplication Proxy	Removes a PPS application proxy object.
	Example: Remove-SPPerformancePointService ApplicationProxy -Identity "PPS Application Proxy"
Remove -SPPerformancePointSericeApplication TrustedLocation	Removes one trusted data source and/or content location.
	Example: Get-SPPerformancePointApplication TrustedLocation –ServiceApplication "PPS Application" 	Remove- SPPerformancePointServiceApplication TrustedLocation

Authoring and Publishing PerformancePoint Solutions

In this section, we will create all of the PerformancePoint content objects necessary to implement a typical business intelligence dashboard using data from the AdventureWorks sample database. Our solution will include the KPIs, scorecards, filters, reports, and dashboards necessary to provide the user with a rich data analysis environment. We will deploy this solution to SharePoint and explore the resulting user experience.

In the following section, "Advanced Report Types," we will then expand on this solution by adding reports to the dashboard based on Excel Services and Strategy Map report types.

> ■ **Note** This tutorial will make extensive use of the AdventureWorks SSAS solution. You can download the Adventure Works database from `http://msftdbprodsamples.codeplex.com/`. Take a look at Chapter 1 for details about deploying the solution as an SSAS database.

PROBLEM CASE

Author and publish a BI solution that allows a marketing manager at AdventureWorks to analyze the effectiveness of their marketing campaigns by product and sales channel.

Solution:

The solution for this case will be created in the following sequence.

1. Enable all necessary features in SharePoint and create a site using the Business Intelligence Center site template.

2. Create a Dashboard Designer workspace in which to create the solution components.

3. Create a data source from which to retrieve the business data.

4. Create a set of key performance indicators (KPIs) representing the data.

5. Create a scorecard to display the KPIs.

6. Create a set of filters to control how the data is sliced by the user.

7. Create a set of reports allowing the user to perform analysis on the underlying data.

8. Create a dashboard that integrates all of these components into an interactive analysis engine designed to help the user make decisions.

9. Deploy the solution to SharePoint and examine the user experience exposed by the dashboard.

Before attempting to follow this tutorial, you should already be familiar with basic BI and PPS concepts such as dimensions, measures, KPIs, scorecards, etc. If not, please refer to "Business Intelligence Solution Components" earlier in this chapter for PPS components and Chapter 1 for dimensional modeling concepts.

Deploying the Business Intelligence Center

We will create a work area for our solution by deploying the PerformancePoint Business Intelligence Center site template. First we must verify that the necessary features are activated at the site-collection level. You will need site collection administrator rights in order to enable features and create the site.

1. Open the root web site in the site collection to host the solution.

2. Select Site Settings from the Site Actions menu.

3. Select Site Collection Administration ➤ Site Collection Features.

4. Activate the SharePoint Server Enterprise Site Collection Features feature if it's not already active (Figure 6–26).

5. Activate the PerformancePoint Services Site Collection Features feature if it is not already active(Figure 6–26).

Figure 6–26. *Activating SharePoint and PerformancePoint site collection features*

6. Navigate to the site under which you want to create the BI Center. In the parent site, create the site using the Business Intelligence Center site template (Figure 6–27).

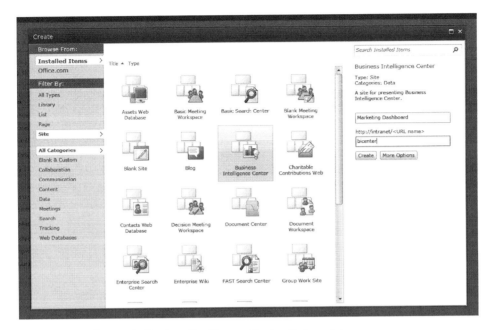

Figure 6–27. Selecting the Business Intelligence Center site template

The site created has all of the lists and libraries needed to deploy a complete PerformancePoint solution. It also contains informational content describing the site's purpose, which you can delete when you no longer need it.

Creating a Dashboard Designer Workspace

All of the objects we create for our solution will be stored in a Dashboard Designer Workspace file, which is stored on your local desktop with a DDWX file extension. This file acts as an offline store for these objects until you are ready to publish them to SharePoint. The workspace file is similar to a Visual Studio solution file in that it allows you to organize, edit, and manage all of the components of your solution in one place.

Because the Dashboard Designer is a one-click Windows application, there is no executable to download and install on the desktop. The easiest way to install it is simply to use it and then save a file. We will do this as part of the next section.

Creating a Data Source

Now let's create a data source from which to retrieve business data for our dashboard.

1. Navigate to the BI Center site and click on the Data Connections library link in the Quick menu to the left. This will take you to the data source library for the solution.

2. From the ribbon menu at the top of the page, select Library Tools ➤
   Documents ➤ New Document ➤ PerformancePoint Data Source (Figure 6–28).

Figure 6–28. *Adding a PerformancePoint data source*

This will launch the Dashboard Designer. If this is the first time you've used it, you'll see messages
and progress bars indicating that it's installing. The Web browser may ask you to authorize the
installation. Finally, the designer will be shown with an empty workspace and the Select a Data Source
Template dialog displayed, as shown in Figure 6–29.

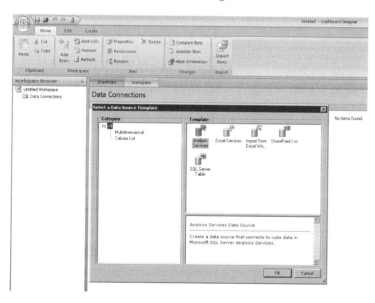

Figure 6–29. *Selecting a data source template*

3. Our data will come from the Adventure Works OLAP database, so select the Analysis Services template and click OK, and you'll see the dialog shown in Figure 6–30.

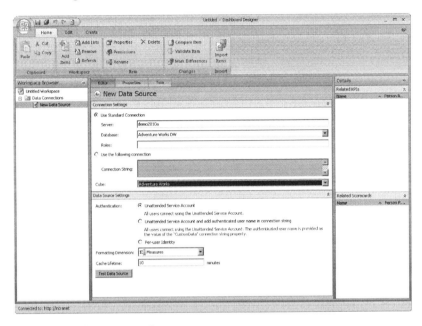

Figure 6–30. The New Data Source screen

Take a moment to find your way around the Dashboard Designer application—you'll spend a lot of time here! At the top is a ribbon menu system that works like any Office 2010 application. The options that appear in the ribbon will change as the context of the central window changes.

On the left side of the window is the Workspace Browser, which is a tree listing the contents of the workspace. Currently, this list shows one workspace file called Untitled Workspace, one SharePoint list called Data Connections, and one item within that list—a data source currently named New Data Source.

The editor for the item selected in the left-hand list is displayed in the center window where changes can be made. This window will have a set of tabs across the top based on the type of object being edited. The Properties tab is common to all objects and is used to name and organize objects within the workspace.

To the right of the center window are panels that list the objects within the workspace that are related to the current item.

4. In the center window, under New Data Source ➤ Connection Settings ➤ Use Standard Connection, enter the name of the SSAS server instance containing the AdventureWorks OLAP cubes in the Server textbox.

5. Select the "Adventure Works DW" SSAS database from the Database list.

6. At the bottom of Connection Settings, select the Adventure Works cube from the Cube list.

7. Note the defaults for the Data Source Settings panel but don't make any changes.

8. Switch to the Properties tab in the center window.

9. Enter "Adventure Works" for the name of the data source.

10. Switch to the Time tab, where you can specify the cube's primary time dimension (Figure 6–31).

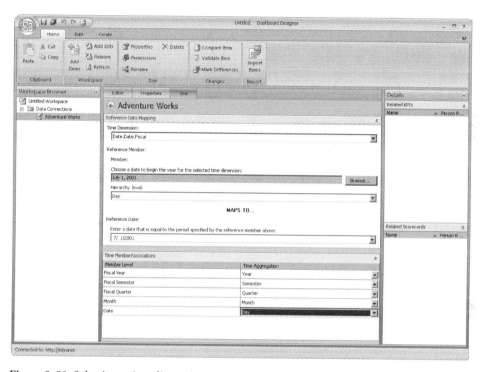

***Figure 6–31.** Selecting a time dimension*

11. The Time Dimension drop-down will list all of the hierarchies available in the cube. Select "Date.Date.Fiscal." This is a fiscal calendar that begins on the first of July of each year.

12. Under Reference Member, select a member from the dimension that represents the first day of the fiscal year, such as July 1, 2001.

13. For the Reference Date, enter the same date in your regional format. This allows PerformancePoint to understand how years are structured in the date dimension.

■ **Note** Depending on when you downloaded the AdventureWorks sample databases, the actual dates available in your cube may be different from those shown. The sample database used here has data from FY 2002 to FY 2005.

14. Under Time Member Associations, select the time dimension hierarchy levels as shown in Figure 6–32.

Time MemberAssociations		☆
Member Level △	Time Aggregation	
Fiscal Year	Year	▼
Fiscal Semester	Semester	▼
Fiscal Quarter	Quarter	▼
Month	Month	▼
Date	Day	▼

Figure 6–32. The time dimension hierarchy

At first glance, it may seem strange to enter all of this information about the time dimension in the editor you're using to create a data source. The reason for doing this is that it allows the use of Time Intelligence filters. These very powerful tools will help when it comes time to present data to the user. See "Creating Filters" later in this chapter for details. Now that the data source is set up, let's go back and finish setting up the workspace itself.

15. Select Untitled Workspace on the Workspace Browser.

16. Click the Save icon at the top of the window. This will cause the file save dialog to be displayed (Figure 6–33).

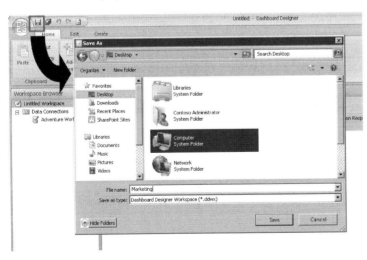

Figure 6–33. Saving the workplace

344

If you go back to the Data Connections library in your BI Center site, you'll see that there's one data source there. Why is it called New Data Source? The answer is that we haven't yet published the data source we created to SharePoint. We've only saved it to the workspace file.

■ **Hint:** You can tell that an item hasn't been published because there is a pencil superimposed on its icon in the Workspace Browser.

---

17. Select the Adventure Works data source in the Workspace Browser.

18. Click the Save icon again. The pencil icon will disappear from the item and the data source should appear correctly in the Data Connections Library (Figure 6–34).

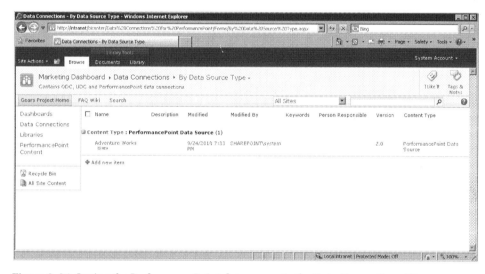

Figure 6–34. *Saving the PerformancePoint data source to the Data Connections Library*

Now that we have set up our data source and started our workspace file, let's get ready to retrieve data for analysis.

Creating Key Performance Indicators

Our dashboard will contain one set of KPIs. We will create a set of actual and target metrics that will allow the marketing department to track the effectiveness of their promotions in terms of their effect on Gross Profit Margin.

Our workspace is currently connected to the Data Connections library, but that area can only be used to store data sources. To create the KPI, we need to connect our workspace to the PerformancePoint Content list in the BI Center site.

1. Open the workspace file Marketing.ddwx that you created in the previous section.

2. In the Dashboard Designer's ribbon menu, select Home ➤ Workspace ➤ Add Lists.

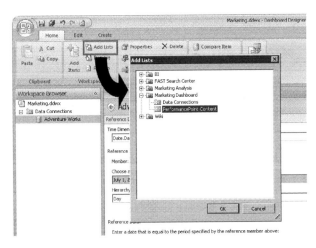

Figure 6–35. Selecting the PerformancePoint content

3. Select PerformancePoint Content from the BI Center site you created earlier and click OK (see Figure 6–35). The PerformancePoint Content list now appears in the Workspace Browser.

4. Right-click on the PerformancePoint Content list in the Workspace Browser and select New ➤ KPI (Figure 6–36).

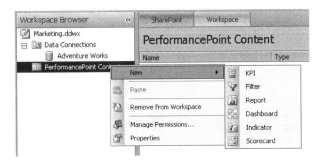

Figure 6–36. Creating a new KPI

5. Select Blank KPI from the Select a KPI Template dialog (Figure 6–37)and click OK.

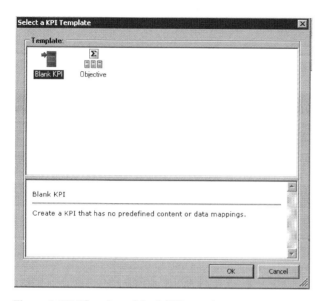

Figure 6–37. Choosing a blank KPI template

6. The KPI will be created with the name selected in the Workspace Browser, so you can immediately type a name for the KPI. Enter "Profit Margin KPI" and press Enter.

7. Select the Properties tab and set the Display Folder to "KPIs" (Figure 6–38).

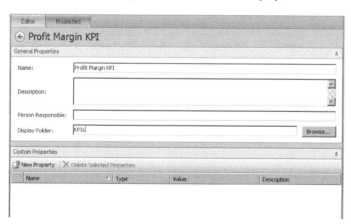

Figure 6–38. Setting the Display Folder;

8. Note that the KPI now appears inside a folder in the Workspace Browser (Figure 6–39).

Figure 6–39. The Profit Margin KPI in the Workspace Browser

▓ **Note** The use of display folders within the Dashboard Designer is entirely optional. Their purpose is only to help keep the solution organized. They have no effect on anything other than how items are displayed in the Workspace Browser. Workspace folders do not get reflected in the folder structure of the content list in PerformancePoint or anywhere else outside of Dashboard Designer. Typically, they are used to separate items by type (KPIs, Filters, Dashboards, etc.) or functionally by the part of the solution with which they are associated. Folders can be nested as needed by separating folder names with a backslash (\) character. For the rest of this chapter, items will be placed into such folders but the directions won't mention it each time from here on out.

---

9. Switch to the Editor tab (Figure 6–40), which displays the actual and target metrics for the KPI along with their various settings. We will customize the two metrics that were created by default and then add some or our own.

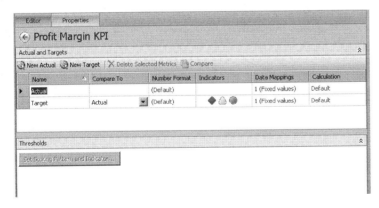

Figure 6–40. Editing the KPI

10. Select the Name cell, which currently contains "Actual," and change the name to "Gross Profit."

11. Click on the cell for the same row under Data Mappings to launch the data mapping dialog. Currently, it is set to return a fixed value of 1. Click the Change Source... button to bring up the Select a Data Source dialog (Figure 6–41).

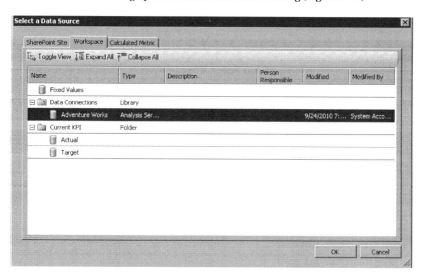

Figure 6–41. *Changing the data source*

12. This dialog allows us to select the data source from which we will retrieve the value of the metric we are creating. In this case, the Gross Profit will come from the cube we've configured as a data source. Select "Adventure Works" and click OK. The Dimensional Data Source Mapping dialog is displayed (Figure 6–42).

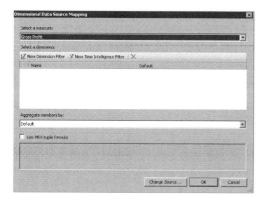

Figure 6–42. *Selecting a measure*

13. This dialog allows the designer to select a measure from the cube and, optionally, perform filtering on it or enter an MDX query expression to retrieve the value. Select "Gross Profit" from the Select a measure drop-down and click OK. The result is shown in Figure 6–43.

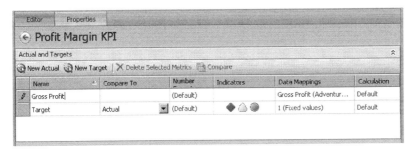

Figure 6–43. Mapping to the Gross Profit measure

14. Now we will create a target that indicates that we want to break even (GP >= $0) on each promotion. Set the name of the target metric to "Breakeven." Then, change the data mapping value to "0" instead of the default of "1". Notice that the Compare To field points to the Gross Profit actual metric. This indicates that the target value, 0, will be compared to the actual value, which is the Gross Profit measure returned from the cube (Figure 6–44).

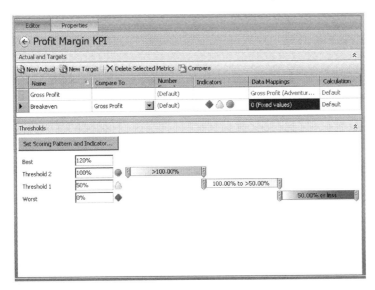

Figure 6–44. Creating a breakeven metric for Gross Profit

15. Now that the actual and target values are set, the Thresholds area at the bottom of the window is activated. The indicator type shown by default is not really appropriate so we will customize it. Click on the Set Scoring Pattern and Indicator… button in the Thresholds panel. This displays a three-step wizard we'll use to configure the appearance of this target metric (Figure 6–45).

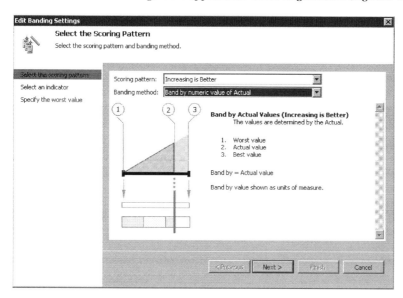

Figure 6–45. Selecting the scoring pattern

16. Select "Increasing is Better" and "Band by numeric value of Actual". Click Next.

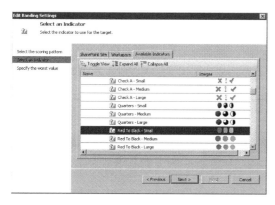

Figure 6–46. Choosing the indicator

17. Select "Red to Black – Small" under the Miscellaneous category (Figure 6–46). Click Next.

18. In this case, there is no selection to be made on the third step of the wizard, so click Finish.

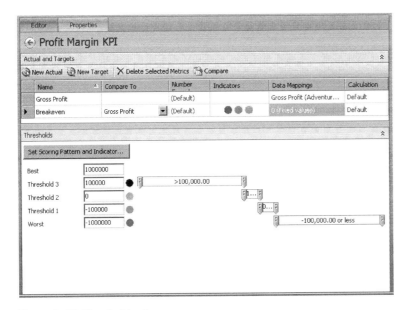

Figure 6–47. Threshold values

19. The indicator we selected has four possible statuses: black, grey, light red, and red (Figure 6–47). Thresholds configure the points at which black becomes gray and so on. In this case, set the thresholds to the values shown above. These values will be compared with the Gross Profit amount to show whether or not we are "in the black" or "in the red" for a particular promotion.

20. Use the New Actual button to create two more actual metrics named "Total Sales" and "Gross Profit Margin." Set the data mappings in the same way as for Gross Profit above. Map the new actual metrics to the "Sales Amount" and "Gross Profit Margin" measures, respectively.

21. On the Gross Profit Margin row, click on (Default) in the Number Format column. Set the value to be displayed as a Percentage using parentheses for negative numbers and 1 decimal place (Figure 6–48).

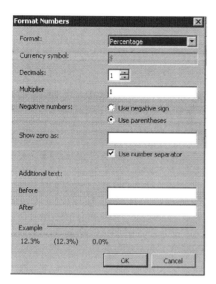

Figure 6–48. Setting the number format

22. Click on New Target to create a second target metric. In this case, instead of breaking even, our goal is to do better with a promotion than without one. Therefore, we will compare the gross profit margin obtained with a promotion to the margin obtained when the promotion is "No Discount."

23. Set the name of the new target to "GP% vs. no Discount."

24. Set the Compare to field to "Gross Profit Margin."

25. Click on the link to set the data mapping and select the Gross Profit Margin measure just as you did when setting the actual metric.

26. Instead of finishing the dialog, we will add a filter to find the value of the gross profit margin in a specific case. Start by clicking on the New Dimension Filter button under Select a dimension (Figure 6–49).

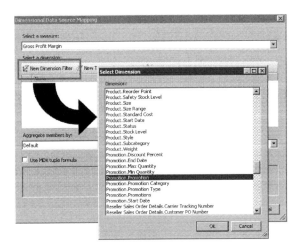

Figure 6–49. *Creating a filter*

27. The Select Dimension dialog is somewhat misnamed. The list under Dimension isn't really a list of dimensions. It is a list of dimension hierarchies that can be used to filter the selected measure. Select "Promotion.Promotion" and click OK.

28. Click on the "Default Member (All Promotions)" link (Figure 6–50).

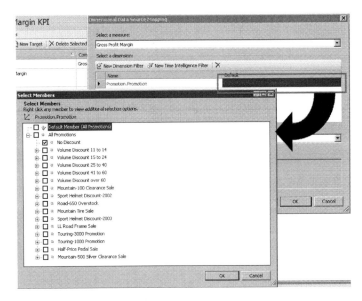

Figure 6–50. *Selecting the filter criteria*

29. In the Select Members dialog, check only the No Discount member. This will cause the target value for this metric to include only data related to the No Discount promotion. Click OK.

30. Click on the Set Scoring Pattern and Indicator... button. Review all of the default options but don't change anything. Click Cancel to close the wizard.

31. Set the thresholds as shown in Figure 6–51.

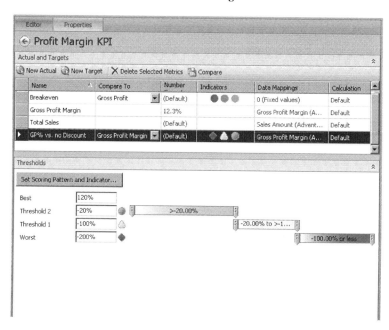

Figure 6–51. *Setting the thresholds*

32. Save the KPI and workspace file.

The thresholds used in the last target created may not seem to make sense at first. The default banding pattern used by PerformancePoint is "Band by normalized value of Actual/Target". In this mode, a calculation is performed on each actual and target value for the KPI. A percentage is assigned based on the distance the actual and target are from the "worst value" set in step 3 of the scoring pattern wizard. By default, the "worst value" is set to 0. The worst value is somewhat arbitrary since it is quite possible for actual values to be below it. The percentages calculated in that case are simply negative.

In our case, 0% indicates that the gross profit margin for the selected promotion is exactly the same as for the No Discount promotion. If it's lower, the percentage value is negative. If it's better, the value is positive. Adventure Works management has decided that our profitability goal for these promotions is to be within 20 percent of the non-discounted value (green indicator). A value worse than 100 percent below the standard indicates a serious problem, so the indicator turns red. Anywhere between -20 percent and -100 percent, the indicator will show a slight problem or a yellow indicator.

Creating a Scorecard

On our dashboard, we want to display a list of the promotions we've run and the values of our KPIs for each promotion. This is called a *scorecard* (see Figure 6–52), which we will create as a separate component in our workspace (inserted using text markup feature).

1. Open the Marketing.ddwx workspace file.

2. Right-click on the PerformancePoint Content list in the Workspace Browser and select New ➤ Scorecard.

3. Name the scorecard "Promotion Scorecard" (and add it to a display folder if you wish).

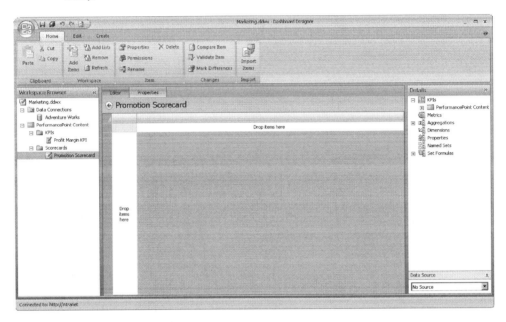

Figure 6–52. An empty scorecard

The empty scorecard shown in Figure 6–52 has two main areas. The center window is where you design the scorecard; you will be able to arrange and format items in this window. To the right are panels that provide the elements to go on the scorecard. First, we identify the KPIs to be shown, then we identify the rows and grouping to use in calculating the KPIs.

4. In the Details panel, open the KPIs branch of the tree until you reach the Profit Margin KPI (Figure 6–53).

Figure 6–53. The Profit Margin KPI

5. Drag the Profit Margin KPI from the Details panel to the header area of the scorecard (Figure 6–54).

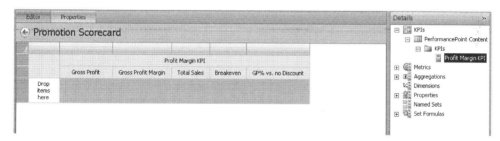

Figure 6–54. Adding the KPI to the scorecard

6. Select Adventure Works from the drop-down list under Data Source (Figure 6–55). Note that the Data Source panel is in the bottom right corner of the designer window, under the Details panel.

Figure 6–55. Choosing Adventure Works as the data source

7. Under Details, select Dimensions ➤ Promotion ➤ Promotions. This is main hierarchy of promotions that will allow us to roll up or drill down into our KPIs.

8. Drag the Promotions hierarchy onto the row area of the scorecard. This displays the Select Members dialog (Figure 6–56).

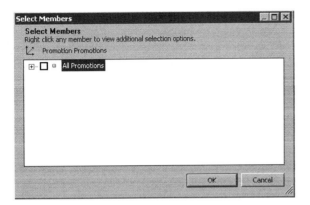

Figure 6–56. The Promotions hierarchy

9. Open the All Promotions node.

10. Right-click on the Customer node and select Autoselect Members ➤ Select All Descendants (Figure 6–57).

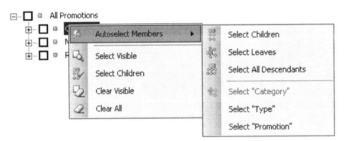

Figure 6–57. Selecting members

11. Do the same for the Reseller node.

12. Check the All Promotions, Customer, and Reseller nodes, as well as the two All descendants of nodes. Do not check No Discount (Figure 6–58).

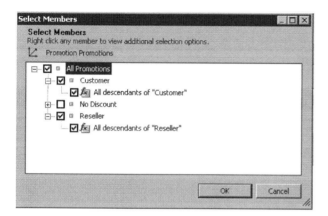

Figure 6–58. Confirming member selection

13. Click OK. The scorecard should now look like what's shown in Figure 6–59.

Figure 6–59. The scorecard with added elements

14. Right-click on the Gross Profit column header and select Delete.

15. Right-click on the Gross Profit Margin column header and select Delete.

16. Right-click on the Breakeven column header and select Metric Settings....

Figure 6–60. *Target settings for Breakeven*

17. Select "No Value" for Data Value and "Actual" for Additional Data Value (Figure 6–60).

18. Review the other settings but retain the defaults. Click OK.

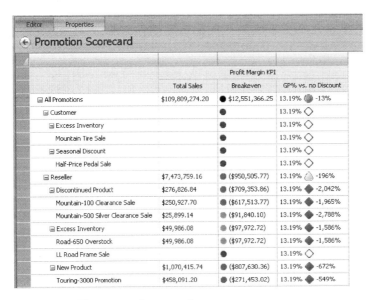

Figure 6–61. *The processed scorecard*

At this point, the scorecard will automatically be processed. It should look something like the one in Figure 6–61. The rows show the promotion hierarchy, including rolling up to parent levels. The columns show our KPIs as they are currently configured. Notice that rows are appearing for promotions even though there were no sales for those promotions.

19. Right-click on the Total Sales column header and select Filter Empty Rows. Note that the rows that should be filtered are now shown with red labels (Figure 6–62). This indicates they will be filtered at runtime.

20. Right-click on the GP% vs. no Discount column header and select Metric Settings....

21. Select Actual for Data Value and Target for Additional Data Value.

22. Click OK.

Promotion Scorecard				
All Promotions	$109,809,274.20	● $12,551,366.25	11.4%	◇ 13.19%
Customer		●		◇ 13.19%
Excess Inventory		●		◇ 13.19%
Mountain Tire Sale		●		◇ 13.19%
Seasonal Discount		●		◇ 13.19%
Half-Price Pedal Sale		●		◇ 13.19%
Reseller	$7,473,759.16	● ($950,505.77)	(12.7%)	△ 13.19%
Discontinued Product	$276,826.84	● ($709,353.86)	(256.2%)	◆ 13.19%
Mountain-100 Clearance Sale	$250,927.70	● ($617,513.77)	(246.1%)	◆ 13.19%
Mountain-500 Silver Clearance Sale	$25,899.14	● ($91,840.10)	(354.6%)	◆ 13.19%
Excess Inventory	$49,986.08	● ($97,972.72)	(196.0%)	◆ 13.19%
Road-650 Overstock	$49,986.08	● ($97,972.72)	(196.0%)	◆ 13.19%
LL Road Frame Sale		●		◇ 13.19%
New Product	$1,070,415.74	● ($807,630.36)	(75.5%)	◆ 13.19%
Touring-3000 Promotion	$458,091.20	● ($271,453.02)	(59.3%)	◆ 13.19%
Touring-1000 Promotion	$612,324.54	● ($536,177.33)	(87.6%)	◆ 13.19%
Seasonal Discount	$16,549.73	● $822.97	5.0%	◉ 13.19%
Sport Helmet Discount-2002	$7,448.83	● $620.75	8.3%	◉ 13.19%
Sport Helmet Discount-2003	$9,100.90	● $202.22	2.2%	◉ 13.19%
Volume Discount	$6,059,980.77	● $663,628.20	11.0%	◉ 13.19%

Figure 6–62. Empty rows are red, indicating they will be filtered at runtime.

23. Save the scorecard and workspace file.

Creating Filters

Our dashboard will contain two filters. The first filter will control the date range for the figures displayed. The second will allow us to select from among our sales territories.

1. Open the Marketing.ddwx file in Dashboard Designer.

2. Right-click on the PerformancePoint Content list and select New ▶ Filter.

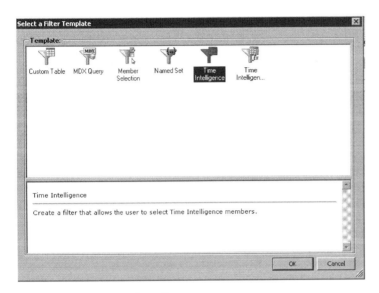

Figure 6–63. Creating a date filter

3. Select Time Intelligence from the Select a Filter Template dialog as shown in Figure 6-63. Be careful not to select "Time Intelligence with Connection Filter" by mistake.

4. Click OK.

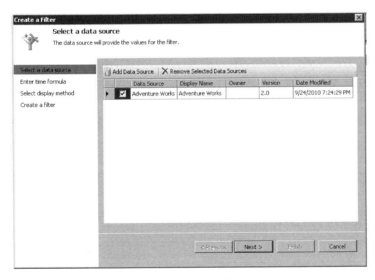

Figure 6–64. Selecting a data source for the filter

5.   Click Add Data Source and select the Adventure Works data source and click
     Next (Figure 6–64).

For the "Enter time formula" step, we will define the options the user will have for selecting time
periods. The formulas are entered on the left and the name displayed to the user is on the right. The
formulas are designed to output a list of members of the cube's time dimension as specified in the data
source. For a good overview of these formulas, go to
blogs.msdn.com/b/performancepoint/archive/2010/01/21/time-intelligence-formula-quick-
reference.aspx.

6.   Enter the formulas and display names shown in Figure 6–65 and then click
     Next.

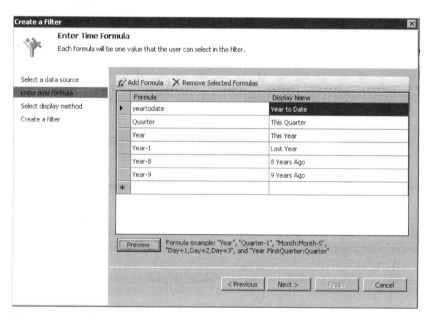

Figure 6–65. Adding date formulas

7.   Select List for the Display Method and click Finish (Figure 6–66).

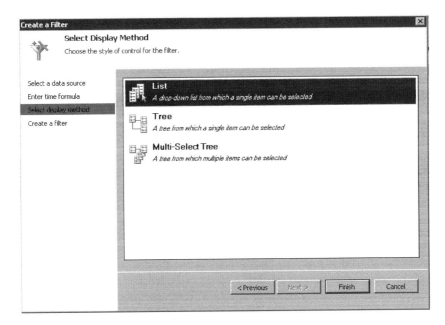

Figure 6–66. Selecting a display method for the date filter

8. Set the name of the filter to "Date."

9. Save the filter and workspace.

Now we'll create a filter for selecting from the Sales Territory dimension. This filter will display a tree for the territory hierarchy and allow us to select one territory or higher-level region.

10. Right-click on the PerformancePoint Content list and select New ➤ Filter.

11. Select the Member Selection filter template and click OK.

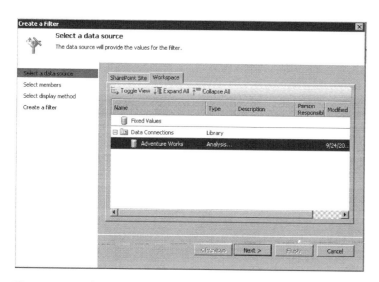

Figure 6–67. Selecting the data source for the filter

12. Select the Adventure Works data source and click Next (Figure 6–67).

13. This displays the Select Members page of the wizard where we will specify the members to show in the filter (Figure 6–68).

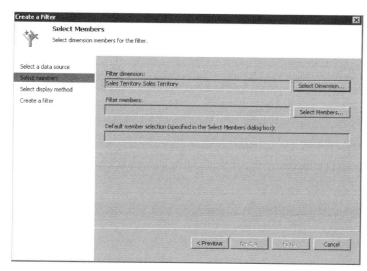

Figure 6–68. Selecting members for the filter

14. Click the Select Dimension… button.

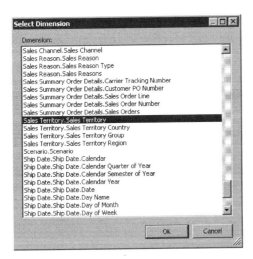

Figure 6–69. Choosing the dimension

15. Select Sales Territory.Sales Territory and click OK (Figure 6–69).

16. Click the Select Members… button.

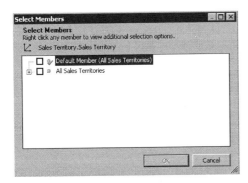

Figure 6–70. Selecting Sales Territory members

17. Right-click All Sales Territories (Figure 6–70) and select Autoselect Members ➤ Select All Descendants.

18. Check both All Sales Territories and All descendants of All Sales Territories (Figure 6–71) .

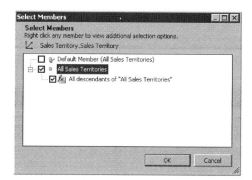

Figure 6–71. Confirming the members

19. Click OK.

20. Select Tree from the Select Display Method page and click Finish (Figure 6–72).

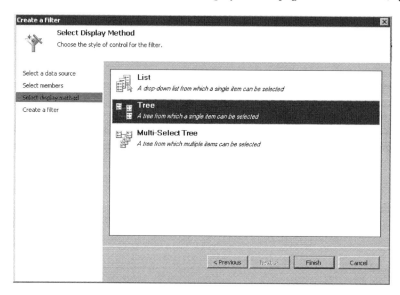

Figure 6–72. Choosing a display method for the Sales Territory filter

21. Change the name of the filter to "Sales Territory".

22. Save the filter and workspace file.

Creating Reports

KPIs and scorecards allow us to compare business data against goals. Once we have identified the problem areas in the enterprise, we need to be able to understand the conditions that are causing problems. A "report" in PerformancePoint is a generic term referring to a window of information that has been sorted out based on the filters and scorecard selections made in the dashboard.

The two most common types of reports in PerformancePoint are Analytic Charts and Analytic Grids. We will create one of each for our dashboard.

1. Open the Marketing.ddwx file in Dashboard Designer.

2. Right-click on the PerformancePoint Content list and select New ➤ Report.

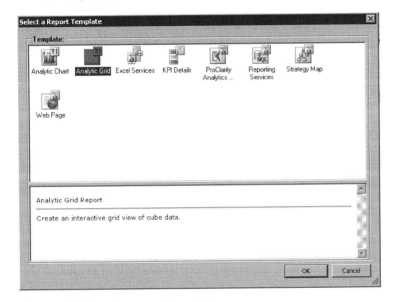

Figure 6–73. Choosing a report template

3. Select the Analytic Grid template and click OK (Figure 6–73).

4. Select the Adventure Works data source and click Finish (Figure 6–74).

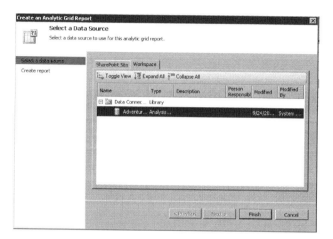

Figure 6–74. Choosing Adventure Works as the data source

5.   Set the name of the report to "Margin by Sales Channel" (Figure 6–75).

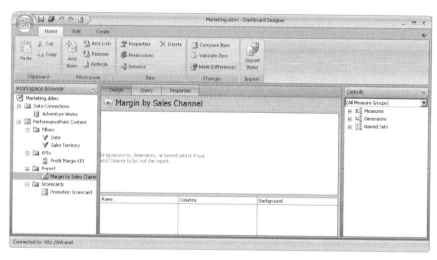

Figure 6–75. The empty Margin by Sales Channel report

The empty grid report window is divided into several areas. The draft view of the report appears in the center window. Beneath the center window are panels labeled Rows, Columns and Background that will be used to specify the contents of the report. In the report designer, "background" refers to the ways in which the data in the report can be filtered.

To the right is a Details tree from which we'll select items to add to the report by dragging them onto one of the panels at the bottom of the window.

6. From the Details panel, drag Dimensions ➤ Sales Channel and drop it on the Columns panel.

7. From the Details panel, drag Measures ➤ Sales Amount and drop it on the Columns panel.

8. Drag and drop these measures to Columns as well: Total Product Cost, Gross Profit, and Gross Profit Margin.

9. From the Details panel, drag Dimensions ➤ Product ➤ Categories and drop it on the Rows panel.

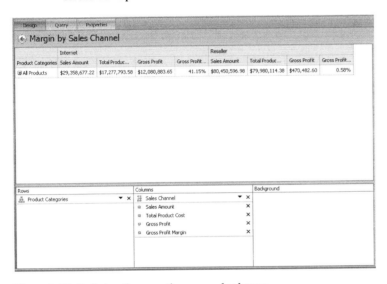

Figure 6–76. *Defining the report's rows and columns*

Now that we have defined the rows and columns for the report (Figure 6–76) it will automatically display a default view. In our dashboard, we want to see the product categories by default. We also want to be able to filter this report by date, territory, and promotion.

10. Right-click on Product Categories in the Rows panel and choose Select Members.

11. Right-click on All Products and select Autoselect Members ➤ Select Category.

12. Ensure that All Products and Category descendants of All Products are checked and click OK (Figure 6–77).

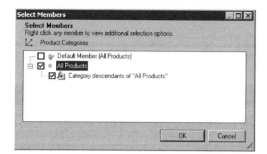

Figure 6–77. Selecting members for the report's default view

13. From Details, drag Dimensions ➤ Date ➤ Fiscal ➤ Fiscal to the Background panel (Figure 6–78).

14. From Details, drag Dimensions ➤ Promotion ➤ Promotion to the Background panel.

15. From Details, drag Dimensions ➤ Sales Territory ➤ Sales Territory to the Background panel.

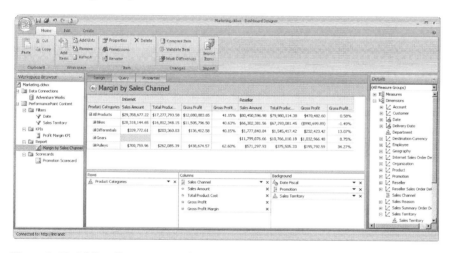

Figure 6–78. Adding dimensions to the report's default view

16. Save the report and workspace

Now let's create an Analytic Chart report. This report will compare the gross profit margin across product categories.

17. Right-click on the PerformancePoint Content list and select New ➤ Report.

18. Select the Analytic Chart template and click OK.

19. Select the Adventure Works data source and click Finish.

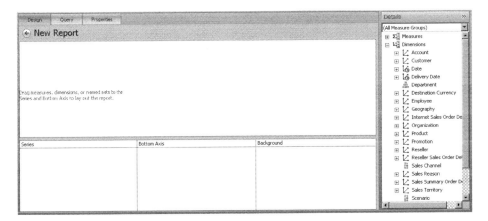

Figure 6–79. The empty analytic chart report

At this point, the chart report looks almost exactly like the grid report. The difference is that the panels across the bottom are Series, Bottom Axis, and Background (see Figure 6–79).

20. From the Details panel, drag Measures ➤ Gross Profit Margin and drop it on the Series panel.

21. From the Details panel, drag Dimensions ➤ Product ➤ Category and drop it on the Bottom Axis panel.

22. From Details, drag Dimensions ➤ Date ➤ Fiscal ➤ Fiscal to the Background panel.

23. From Details, drag Dimensions ➤ Promotion ➤ Promotion to the Background panel.

24. From Details, drag Dimensions ➤ Sales Territory ➤ Sales Territory to the Background panel (Figure 6–80).

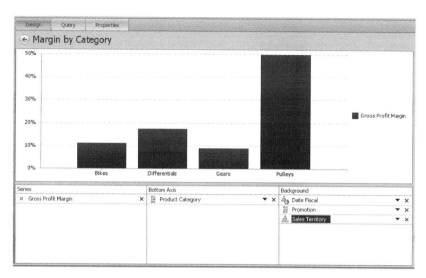

Figure 6–80. Adding dimensions to the Background panel

25. Right-click anywhere in the center window and select Format Report ➤ Don't Show.

26. Right-click anywhere in the center window and select Show Information Bar.

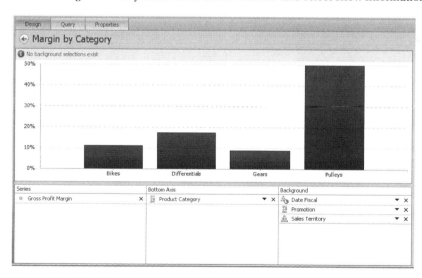

Figure 6–81. The Information Bar turned on

The Information Bar is a useful feature on reports. When this is turned on it shows the user exactly how the data in the report is being filtered. In the designer, the bar shows "No background selections exist" because there are no filters applied until the report is embedded into a dashboard (Figure 6–81).

27. Set the name of the report to "Margin by Category".

28. Save the report and workspace.

Creating a Dashboard

We have created all of the components for our dashboard. Now we'll put it all together and make it work as an integrated package.

1. Open the Marketing.ddwx file in Dashboard Designer.

2. Right-click on the PerformancePoint Content list and select New ➤ Dashboard.

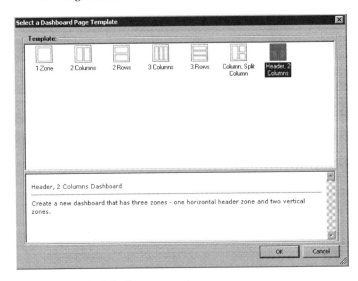

Figure 6–82. The default page template

3. Select the default page template: Header, 2 Columns, as shown in Figure 6–82.

4. Click OK.

5. Set the name of the dashboard to "Marketing Dashboard".

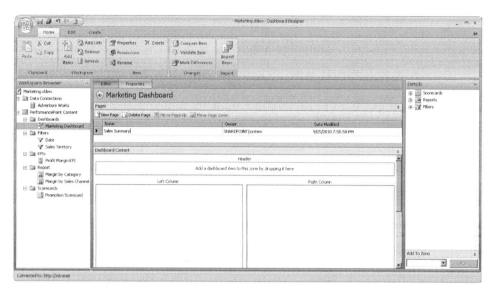

Figure 6–83. *The empty dashboard page*

This will create an empty dashboard page with three zones (Figure 6–83). At the top of the center window is a list of the pages in the dashboard. Beneath the pages is the Dashboard Content panel. This is where the selected dashboard page will be assembled from the components we've created. At the right, the Details panel contains the components that can be used.

6. Set the name of the dashboard's initial page to "Sales Summary" in the Pages panel.

7. On the Details panel, open the Filters node until you find Date and Sales Territory filters. Drag and drop both filters onto the Header zone of the page.

8. On the Details panel, open the Scorecards node until you find the Promotion Scorecard. Drag and drop it onto the Left Column zone.

9. On the Details panel, open the Reports node until you find the "Margin by Category" and "Margin by Sales Channel" reports. Drag and drop both reports onto the Right Column zone.

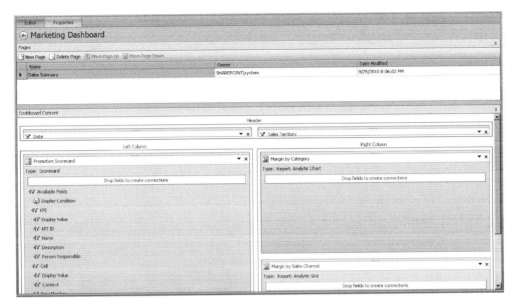

Figure 6–84. *The dashboard page with components*

The components are now on the page (Figure 6–84), but they are not integrated with one another. By dragging fields from one component to another, data is passed to synchronize or filter data throughout, or between, dashboard pages. The behavior we want is as follows:

- When a date range is selected in the filter, it should be applied to all components.

- When a Sales Territory is selected in the filter, it should be applied to all components.

- When the user clicks on a row or cell in the scorecard on the left, the reports on the right should be filtered to display data only for that promotion.

Now we will create the connections to create this behavior

10. Hover over the Date filter. A panel will drop down showing all of the fields that are available from this filter. Drag Member Unique Name and drop it onto the scorecard.

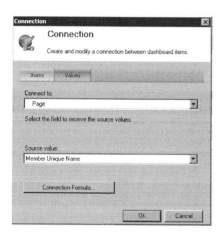

Figure 6–85. Creating connections between dashboard items

11. The default connection is to Page, which refers to the scorecard's overall filter (Figure 6–85). Click OK.

12. Drag and drop the same field from the Date filter onto the two report components. The reports will default the connection to the Date Fiscal background field that is specified in the reports.

13. From the Sales Territory filter, drag the Member Unique Name field to the scorecard. Again, Page is the connection field.

14. Drag and drop the same field from the Sales Territory filter onto the two report components. When the connection dialog appears, select Sales Territory for the "Connect to" field (Figure 6–86).

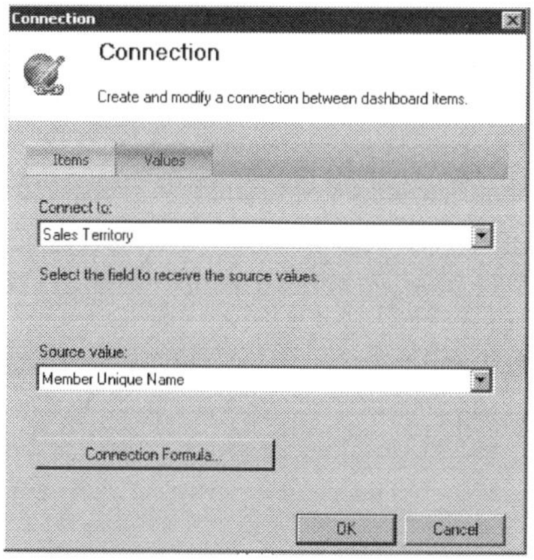

Figure 6–86. Connecting to the Sales Territory filter

15. From the Promotion Scorecard, drag Row Member ➤ Member Unique Name onto each report. Verify that the connection dialog shows that the field is connected to the Promotion field (Figure 6–87).

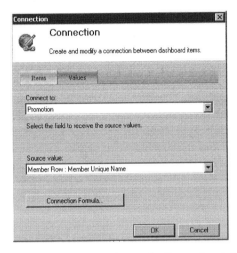

Figure 6–87. Connecting to the Promotion field

16. The dashboard is now complete (Figure 6–88). Save the dashboard and the workspace.

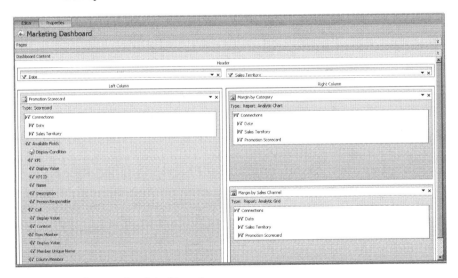

Figure 6–88. The completed dashboard

Deploying the Solution to SharePoint, and Exploring

We are now ready to deploy our dashboard and start analyzing data. Remember that the dashboard we created in the previous section is only the definition for a dashboard. That definition is stored in our PerformancePoint Content list. When we deploy the dashboard, the definition is converted into a folder of ASPX pages that implement our dashboard.

Note that PerformancePoint uses Silverlight controls to render some of the UI controls. Now would be a good time to download and install the latest version of Silverlight from www.microsoft.com/silverlight.

1. Open the Marketing.ddwx file in Dashboard Designer.

2. Right-click on the Marketing Dashboard item and select Deploy to SharePoint... as shown in Figure 6–89.

Figure 6–89. *Deploying to SharePoint*

3. Since this is the first time we've deployed the dashboard, Dashboard Designer will prompt for a destination location for the dashboard.

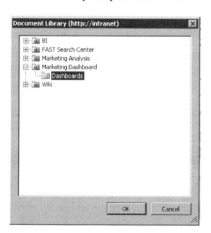

Figure 6–90. *Putting the dashboard in the Dashboards library*

4. Select the Dashboards document library in the BI Center site (Figure 6–90) and click OK.

5. After a few seconds, a web browser window will open to the Sales Summary page of the dashboard (Figure 6–91).

6. Select a time period in the Date filter that contains data. The scorecard and both reports are filtered accordingly.

Figure 6–91. The Sales Summary page

7. Select a Sales Territory. Notice the text displayed in the Information Window above the "Margin by Category" chart (Figure 6–92).

Figure 6–92. Text in the information window

8. Close the web browser and open a new window to view the dashboard. Note that the filter values selected in the previous session are remembered (Figure 6–93).

Figure 6–93. Values from the previous session are remembered.

9. Click on a row on the scorecard. Note the changes that occur on the reports to the right (Figure 6–94).

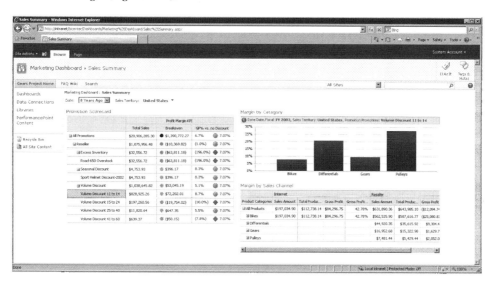

Figure 6–94. Click a row on the scorecard to modify the reports

10. Right-click on one of the cells in the Margin by Sales Channel report and select Show Details. A window is displayed containing all of the data that went into that cell. This data can also be exported to Excel for further analysis (Figure 6–95).

Sales Order	Date	Ship Date.Date	Delivery Date.Date	Product	Promotion
SO46688 Line 1	July 3, 2002	July 10, 2002	July 15, 2002	Drv Pulley -2x,OD:2,ID:0.5,P: 0.25,Teeth: 15	Volume Discount 11 to 14
SO46689 Line 1	July 3, 2002	July 10, 2002	July 15, 2002	Drv Pulley -2x,OD:2,ID:0.5,P: 0.25,Teeth: 15	Volume Discount 11 to 14
SO46692 Line 1	July 3, 2002	July 10, 2002	July 15, 2002	Drv Pulley -2x,OD:2,ID:0.5,P: 0.25,Teeth: 15	Volume Discount 11 to 14
SO46745 Line 1	July 9, 2002	July 16, 2002	July 21, 2002	Drv Pulley -2x,OD:2,ID:0.5,P: 0.25,Teeth: 15	Volume Discount 11 to 14
SO46791 Line 1	July 14, 2002	July 21, 2002	July 26, 2002	Drv Pulley -2x,OD:2,ID:0.5,P: 0.25,Teeth: 15	Volume Discount 11 to 14
SO46795 Line 1	July 14, 2002	July 21, 2002	July 26, 2002	Idler - Fin.,OD:8,ID:0.7,P: 1,Teeth: 14	Volume Discount 11 to 14
SO46811 Line 1	July 17, 2002	July 24, 2002	July 29, 2002	Drv Pulley -2x,OD:2,ID:0.5,P: 0.25,Teeth: 15	Volume Discount 11 to 14
SO46831 Line 1	July 19, 2002	July 26, 2002	July 31, 2002	Drv Pulley -2x,OD:2,ID:0.5,P: 0.25,Teeth: 15	Volume Discount 11 to 14
SO46840 Line 1	July 20, 2002	July 27, 2002	August 1, 2002	Drv Pulley -2x,OD:2,ID:0.5,P: 0.25,Teeth: 15	Volume Discount 11 to 14
SO46866 Line 1	July 23, 2002	July 30, 2002	August 4, 2002	Drv Pulley -2x,OD:2,ID:0.5,P: 0.25,Teeth: 15	Volume Discount 11 to 14
SO46868 Line 1	July 23, 2002	July 30, 2002	August 4, 2002	Drv Pulley -2x,OD:2,ID:0.5,P: 0.25,Teeth: 15	Volume Discount 11 to 14
SO46915 Line 1	July 30, 2002	August 6, 2002	August 11, 2002	Idler - Fin.,OD:8,ID:0.7,P: 1,Teeth: 14	Volume Discount 11 to 14
SO46923 Line 1	July 31, 2002	August 7, 2002	August 12, 2002	Drv Pulley -2x,OD:2,ID:0.5,P: 0.25,Teeth: 15	Volume Discount 11 to 14
SO47074 Line 1	August 1, 2002	August 8, 2002	August 13, 2002	Idler - Fin.,OD:8,ID:0.7,P: 1,Teeth: 14	Volume Discount 11 to 14
SO47088 Line 1	August 3, 2002	August 10, 2002	August 15, 2002	Drv Pulley -2x,OD:2,ID:0.5,P: 0.25,Teeth: 15	Volume Discount 11 to 14

Figure 6–95. Exporting data to Excel

11. Right-click on one of the cells in the Margin by Sales Channel report and select Decomposition Tree. A window is displayed that allows the user to decompose the results in the cell in any way needed to discern patterns (Figure 6–96).

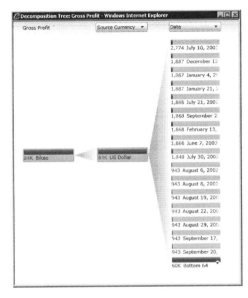

Figure 6–96. Decomposing a cell

Advanced Report Types

Now let's extend our sample dashboard to include data from two external sources: Excel and Visio. The data will be integrated using the Excel Services and Strategy Map report types, respectively.

PROBLEM CASE

Extend the marketing dashboard to allow users to analyze data by sales territory and promotion hierarchy.

Solution:

We will add two additional pages to our dashboard, one using Excel Services reports and another using a Strategy Map report.

Create an Excel Services Report

Microsoft Excel is one of the most widely used packages for doing numerical analysis. As a file-based desktop application, however, it is limited in its ability to reach a large audience and integrate with other solutions. As we saw in Chapter 5, SharePoint Server 2010 incorporates Excel Services to address these issues by creating a server environment for storing, processing, and delivering Excel content. With PerformancePoint Services, we have the opportunity to leverage Excel's analytical abilities and familiar user interface to integrate rich reports into our PPS solutions.

In this section, we will create a simple Excel Services spreadsheet and deploy it to SharePoint. Then, we will integrate the elements of that spreadsheet into our existing dashboard as a pair of new reports on a new page. The new page will allow us to view a grid and a chart with a breakdown of our sales figures by Sales Territory.

1. Launch Excel 2010 and create a new blank workbook.

2. On the ribbon menu, select Data ➤ From Other Sources ➤ From Analysis Services.

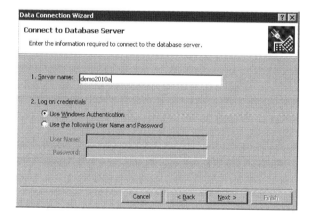

Figure 6–97. *Selecting the database server to connect to*

3. Enter the name of the SSAS server containing the Adventure Works DW database as shown in Figure 6–97.

4. Click Next.

5. Select the Adventure Works DW database.

6. Select the Adventure Works cube.

7. Click Next.

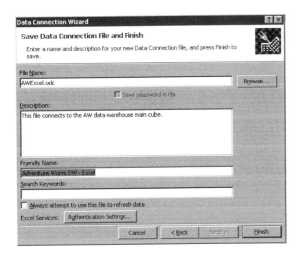

Figure 6–98. Entering a name for the data connection file

8. Enter "AWExcel.odc" for the File Name (Figure 6–98).

9. Enter "Adventure Works DW – Excel" for the Friendly Name.

10. Click Finish.

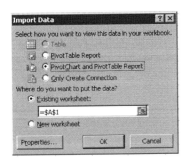

Figure 6–99. Choosing how to view data in the workbook

11. Select PivotChart and PivotTable Report (Figure 6–99) and click OK.

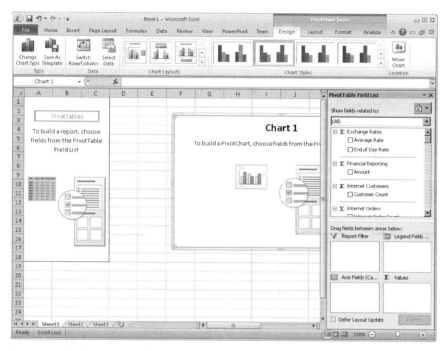

Figure 6–100. *The Pivot Table Field List*

12. From the Pivot Table Field List (Figure 6–100), drag the fields listed in Table 6–5 into the indicated panel at the lower right of the Excel window.

Table 6–5. *Pivot Table Fields*

Field	Panel
Date ➤ Fiscal ➤ Date.Fiscal	Report Filter
Promotion ➤ Promotions	Report Filter
Sales Territory ➤ Sales Territory	Axis Fields
Sales Summary ➤ Sales Amount	Values

13. The spreadsheet should now look like the image in Figure 6–101.

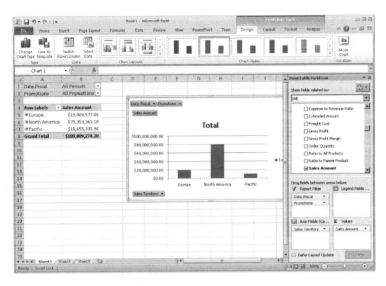

Figure 6–101. *The pivot chart*

14. Right-click on the chart and change the chart type to Pie.

15. Right-click on the chart title and select Delete.

16. From the ribbon menu, select PivotChart Tools ➤ Layout ➤ Data Labels ➤ Best Fit (Figure 6–102).

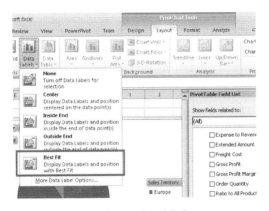

Figure 6–102. *Displaying data labels*

17. From the ribbon menu, select PivotChart Tools ➤ Layout ➤ Properties. Enter "SalesChart" into the Chart Name box (Figure 6–103).

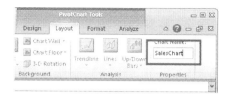

Figure 6–103. *Entering the chart name*

18. Click on one of the cells in the PivotTable.

19. From the ribbon menu, select PivotTable Tools ➤ Options ➤ PivotTable. Enter "SalesTable" into the PivotTable Name box (Figure 6–104).

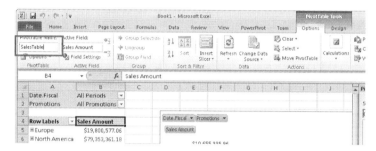

Figure 6–104. *Entering the name of the pivot table*

20. Select the "Sales Amount" column cells on the PivotTable.

21. Select Home ➤ Styles ➤ Conditional Formatting ➤ Data Bars and select one of the options shown (Figure 6–105).

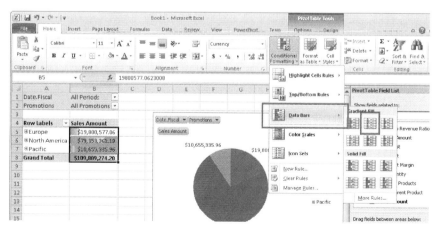

Figure 6–105. *Selecting a style for the data bars*

22. Click on cell B1. This should be the All Periods value for the Date.Fiscal filter. Be
    sure to select the value cell (B1), not the label cell (A1).

23. Type "Date" into the name box and press Enter (Figure 6–106).

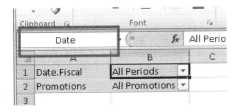

Figure 6–106. Setting up conditional formatting for the Date filter

24. Click on cell B2. This should be the All Promotions value for the Promotions
    filter. Be sure to select the value cell (B2), not the label cell (A2).

25. Type Promotions into the name box and press Enter.

The Excel spreadsheet is now ready to be published to SharePoint. For simplicity, we will store
it in the Dashboards library in our BI Center site (though it could be stored in any location trusted
by Excel Services). First, we'll create a copy of the data connection we're using.

26. From the ribbon menu, select Data ➤ Connections ➤ Properties.

27. Select the Definition tab (Figure 6–107).

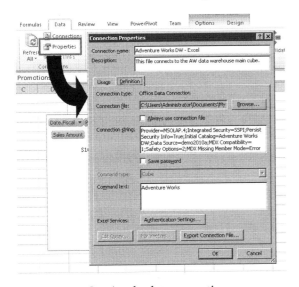

Figure 6–107. Copying the data connection

28. Click the Export Connection File... button.

29. In the File Save dialog, navigate to the Data Connections library in the BI Center site.

30. Set the file name to "AW for Excel" and click Save (Figure 6–108).

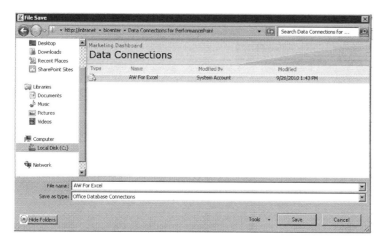

Figure 6–108. Naming the data connection file

31. Select Office Data Connection File as the Content Type and click OK (Figure 6–109).

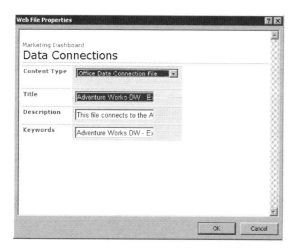

Figure 6–109. Selecting the content type of the data connection file

32. Click Cancel to dismiss the Connection Properties dialog.

Before we publish the spreadsheet to SharePoint, we need to identify the objects and parameters to expose to Excel Services. The objects we'll use are the SalesChart and SalesTable objects. We will declare the Date and Promotions cells as parameters, which PerformancePoint will use to pass in dashboard filter selections.

33. From the ribbon menu, select File ➤ Save & Send ➤ Save to SharePoint.

34. Click the Publish Options button.

35. Select Items in the Workbook from the drop-down list (Figure 6–110).

36. Check the SalesChart and SalesTable items.

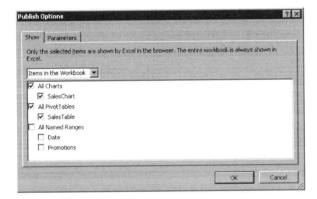

Figure 6–110. *Choosing the items that will be displayed in the browser*

37. Switch to the Parameters tab (Figure 6–111).

38. Click the Add… button.

39. Check both available parameters and click OK.

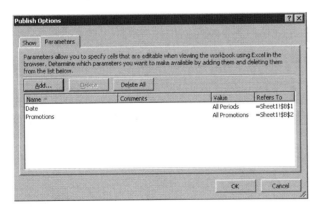

Figure 6–111. *Adding parameters*

390

40. Click OK.

41. If the Dashboards library is not shown under Locations (Figure 6–112), select Browse for a location to add it.

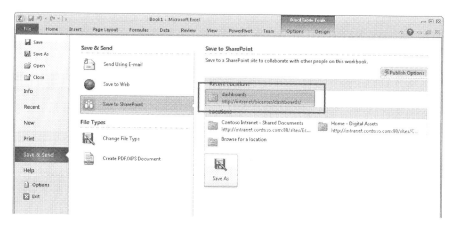

Figure 6–112. Saving to SharePoint

42. Double-click the location to publish the file to SharePoint.

43. Enter the file name "AWExcelRpt" in the Save As dialog and click Save.

44. Select Document as the content type and click OK.

45. The spreadsheet will be displayed in a new browser window.

46. Close the new browser window and Excel.

Now that we have a spreadsheet published to SharePoint, we will add the PivotTable and PivotChart as reports in a new page on our dashboard.

47. Open the Marketing.ddwx file in Dashboard Designer.

48. Right-click on the PerformancePoint Content list and select New ➤ Report.

49. Select the Excel Services template and click OK.

50. Set the name of the report to "Sales Table".

51. Enter the URL for the BI Center site in the "SharePoint site" box on the report editor (Figure 6–113).

52. Select the Dashboards library.

53. Select "AWExcelRpt.xls" file for the workbook.

54. Select "SalesTable" for the item name.

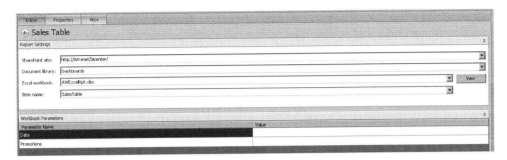

Figure 6–113. Adding a new Sales Table report

55. Note that the Dashboard Designer has already identified the Workbook Parameters: Date and Promotions.

56. Copy and paste the Sales Table report in the Workspace Browser.

57. Rename "Sales Table – Copy" to "Sales Chart."

58. Select SalesChart from the Item name drop-down on the Sales Chart report editor.

59. Save both reports and the workspace file.

60. Right-click on the PerformancePoint Content list and select New ➤ Filter.

61. Select the Member Selection filter template and click OK.

62. Select Adventure Works for the data source and click Next.

63. Press Select Dimension… and choose Promotion.Promotions.

64. Click OK.

65. Press Select Members… and select All Promotions and all of its descendants (Figure 6–114).

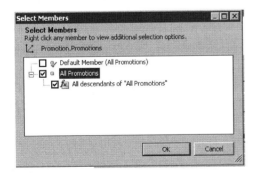

Figure 6–114. Selecting the All Promotions member

66. Click OK to move to the next screen (Figure 6–115).

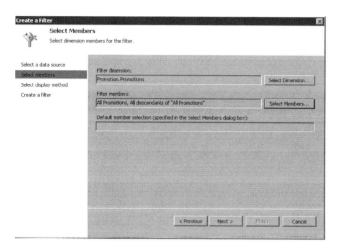

Figure 6–115. Creating a filter

67. Click Next.

68. Select Tree and click Next.

69. Name the new filter Promotion.

We now have the new filter and reports created for our new page. Next we'll create the new dashboard page and deploy the dashboard.

70. Select the Marketing Dashboard in the Workspace Browser.

71. Click New Page in the dashboard editor and select the default template.

72. Name the page "Sales by Promotion".

73. From Details, drag the Date and Promotion filters into the header of the new page.

74. From Details, drag the Sales Table report into the left column zone.

75. From Details, drag the Sales Chart report into the right column zone.

76. Add the connections shown in Table 6–6 to the page.

Table 6–6. Connections for the Dashboard

Get Values From	Send Values To	Connect To	Source Value
Date Filter	Sales Table	Date	Member Unique Name
Promotion Filter	Sales Table	Promotions	Member Unique Name
Date Filter	Sales Chart	Date	Member Unique Name
Promotion Filter	Sales Chart	Promotions	Member Unique Name

The dashboard page should now resemble the image in Figure 6–116..

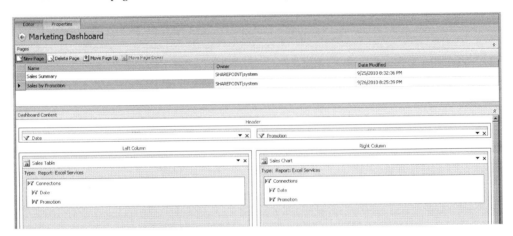

Figure 6–116. The dashboard page

77. Right-click the Marketing Dashboard and select Deploy to SharePoint....

78. When the browser window opens, click on the Sales by Promotion link.

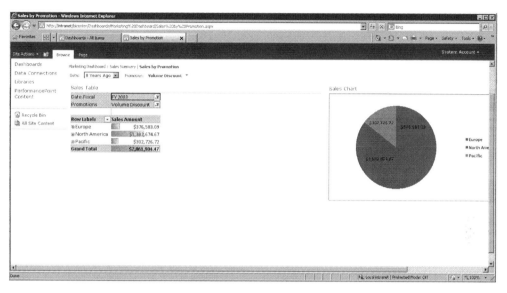

Figure 6–117. Excel reports displayed in the browser

Notice that all of the formatting from Excel is displayed on the dashboard, including the pie chart and data bars (Figure 6–117). Now any changes made to the Excel spreadsheet will automatically be reflected in the dashboard. This allows users who are more comfortable with Excel to author reports that can be integrated with the rest of a PerformancePoint solution.

Create a Strategy Map Report

Microsoft Visio is a powerful desktop visualization tool. As we saw in Chapter 2, the Visio Services component in SharePoint Server 2010 allows Visio diagrams to be brought to life with real data. With PerformancePoint Services, we can take that integration one step further. A Visio diagram can be created that visually represents the KPIs on a scorecard. Those KPIs can then be connected to the Visio diagram to create a graphical representation of the status of the enterprise. In PerformancePoint, this type of report is called a *strategy map*.

In this section, we will create a simple Visio diagram that we'll deploy to PerformancePoint as a Strategy Map report. The term "strategy map" refers to a particular type of diagram often used in conjunction with the "balanced scorecard" methodology. While this feature in PerformancePoint is ideally suited for implementing that type of map, any Visio diagram can be used as long as it contains only simple shapes that don't involve sets or groupings within Visio.

■ **Note** Readers who are not familiar with Visio or Visio Services should review Chapter 2 before proceeding with the rest of this section.

---

1. Launch Visio 2010 and create a new blank diagram using the Basic Diagram (US Units) template.

2. Create a diagram with a set of simple shapes that looks something like the image in Figure 6–118. The precise details of the diagram are not important.

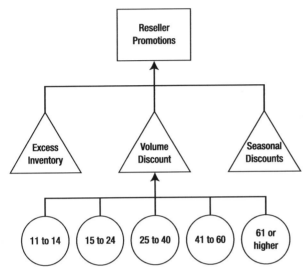

Figure 6–118. *A simple Visio diagram*

3. Save the file with the file name Promotion Tree.vsd anywhere on your local computer.

4. Close Visio.

5. Open the Marketing.ddwx file in Dashboard Designer.

6. Right-click on the PerformancePoint Content list and select New ➤ Report.

7. Select the Strategy Map template from the Select a Report Template dialog and click OK.

8. Select the Promotion Scorecard as the scorecard for the strategy map (Figure 119). The Strategy Map report uses a scorecard as a data source instead of a normal data source object.

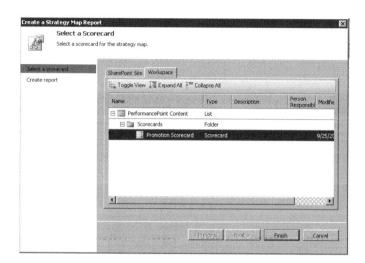

Figure 6–119. Creating a strategy map report using the Promotion Scorecard

9. Click Finish.

10. Name the new report Promotion Map.

11. From the ribbon menu, select Edit ➤ Report Editor ➤ Edit Strategy Map (Figure 6–120).

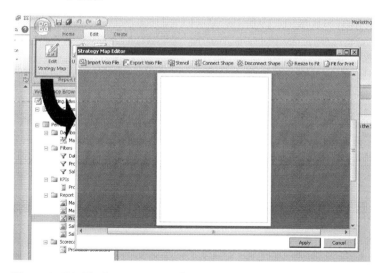

Figure 6–120. The Strategy Map Editor

12. Click the Import Visio File button.

13. To connect the Reseller Promotions shape to the scorecard, click on the shape and then on the Connect Shape button as shown in Figure 6–121.

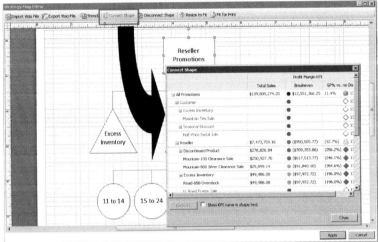

Figure 6–121. Connecting the Reseller Promotions shape to the scorecard

14. The Connect Shape dialog shows a view of the underlying scorecard. Select the cell at the intersection of the Reseller row and the GP% vs. no Discount column.

15. Ensure that the "Show KPI name in shape text" checkbox is not selected and click the Connect button.

16. Click Close and the Reseller Promotions shape will now be colored the same as the KPI.

17. Repeat steps 14 though 16 for each of the other shapes on the diagram. When complete, the diagram should look like the image in Figure 6–122. Your colors may vary depending on the filters that are active in your environment. The important thing is to connect the proper shape to the correct KPI.

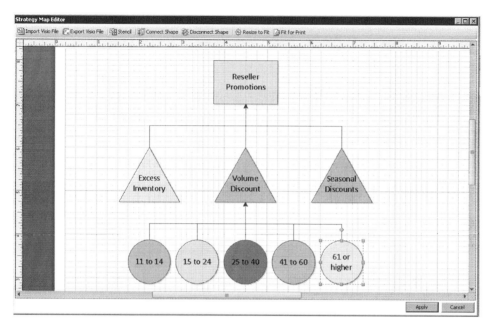

Figure 6–122. The Visio diagram with all shapes connected to the scorecard

18. Drag the cursor over the diagram to select all of the shapes.

19. Right-click one of the shapes and select Data ➤ Edit Data Graphic…

20. Click the New Item… button.

21. On the New Item dialog, select the options indicated in Table 6–7 and shown in Figure 6–123.

Table 6–7. Options for the Shapes

Field	Value
Display ➤ Data Field	Status
Display ➤ Displayed as	Text
Position ➤ Use default position	unchecked
Position ➤ Horizontal	Center
Position ➤ Vertical	Below Shape
Details ➤ Label Position	Not Shown
Details ➤ Border Type	None

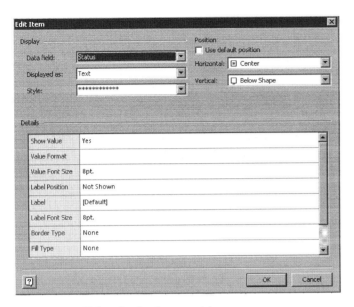

Figure 6–123. Values for the data graphic

22. Click OK to create the Data Graphic.

23. Click OK to save Data Graphics.

24. Answer "Yes" to "Do you want to apply this data graphic to the selected shapes?"

25. Now the map should look something like Figure 6–124.

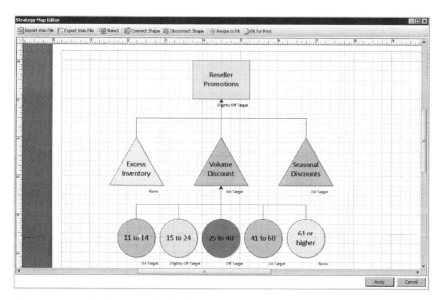

Figure 6–124. The shapes with the data graphic applied

26. Click Apply.

27. Save the Promotion Map report and the workspace.

28. Select the Marketing Dashboard in the Workspace Browser.

29. Add a new page to the dashboard with the default template.

30. Name the page "Promotion Map."

31. Add the components in Table 6–8 to the zones of the new page.

Table 6–8. Components for the New Page

Component	Zone
Date Filter	Header
Sales Territory Filter	Header
Promotion Scorecard	Left Column
Promotion Map Report	Right Column

32. Create the connections shown in Table 6–9.

Table 6–9. *Connections for the New Page*

Get Values From	Send Values To	Connect To	Source Value
Date Filter	Promotion Scorecard	Page	Member Unique Name
Sales Territory Filter	Promotion Scorecard	Page	Member Unique Name
Date Filter	Promotion Map Report	Page	Member Unique Name
Sales Territory Filter	Promotion Map Report	Page	Member Unique Name

33. The dashboard should now look like Figure 6–125.

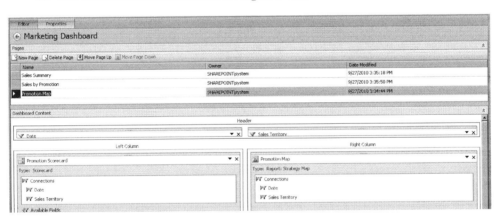

Figure 6–125. *The Marketing Dashboard*

34. Save the dashboard and workspace.

35. Deploy the dashboard to SharePoint.

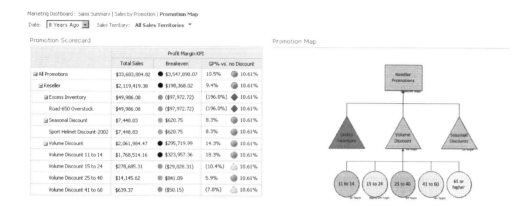

Marketing Dashboard : Sales Summary | Sales by Promotion | **Promotion Map**

Date: 8 Years Ago ▾   Sales Territory: **All Sales Territories** ▾

Promotion: Scorecard

		Profit Margin KPI			
	Total Sales	Breakeven	GP% vs. no Discount		
⊟ All Promotions	$33,683,804.82	● $3,547,898.07	10.5%	◕ 10.61%
⊟ Reseller	$2,119,419.38	● $198,368.02	9.4%	◕ 10.61%
⊟ Excess Inventory	$49,986.08	◕ ($97,972.72)	(196.0%)	◆ 10.61%
Road-650 Overstock	$49,986.08	◕ ($97,972.72)	(196.0%)	◆ 10.61%
⊟ Seasonal Discount	$7,448.83	◕ $620.75	8.3%	◕ 10.61%
Sport Helmet Discount-2002	$7,448.83	◕ $620.75	8.3%	◕ 10.61%
⊟ Volume Discount	$2,061,984.47	● $295,719.99	14.3%	◕ 10.61%
Volume Discount 11 to 14	$1,768,514.16	● $323,957.36	18.3%	◕ 10.61%
Volume Discount 15 to 24	$278,685.31	◕ ($29,028.31)	(10.4%)	◔ 10.61%
Volume Discount 25 to 40	$14,145.62	◕ $841.09	5.9%	◕ 10.61%
Volume Discount 41 to 60	$639.37	◕ ($50.15)	(7.8%)	◔ 10.61%

Promotion Map

Figure 6 126. *Trying out the strategy map*

Try selecting different values for the Date and Sales Territory filters (Figure 6–126). Both the scorecard and the map are updated simultaneously. There are several features of the map to note:

- The end user can zoom in and out as desired by right-clicking on the map.

- By holding Ctrl and clicking on a shape, users can select that shape. Right-clicking a selected shape provides the option to view a detailed list of KPI properties.

- While it is common to display the scorecard associated with a strategy map on the same page, it's not required. The scorecard is still an active part of the dashboard even when it's not visible on the current page. Therefore, you could remove the scorecard from this page and the only effect would to be to hide it. The strategy map would still function correctly.

There is an important limitation when using strategy maps that can be handled with a little additional planning. In our example, if we select a different date range and sales territory, we may see rows on the scorecard that don't appear on the map, or we may see rows on the scorecard disappear due to a lack of data. These shapes still appear on the map, but they don't show a color. When we connect shapes to the scorecard, that connection is static. We can't change that association as needed to fit how the scorecard is filtered. We also can't add shapes as new rows appear in the scorecard.

There are different strategies for handling such situations. One way is to include every possible shape on the map. You could also limit the filtering of the page to prevent unwanted rows from appearing in the scorecard. Regardless, the shapes on the map and how they are associated are fixed at runtime.

Strategy maps are a versatile way to add visualization to your solution. They can be used to provide a user-friendly means of interpreting your key performance indicators.

Summary

In this chapter, we have explored PerformancePoint Service as outlined in Figure 6–127, including:

- The components of the PerformancePoint Services architecture.

- How to configure PerformancePoint Services using both Central Administration and PowerShell commands.

- How to enable the features of PerformancePoint Services within a SharePoint site and deploy the Business Intelligence Center.

- How to use Dashboard Designer to author and deploy a dashboard and its supporting components to SharePoint 2010.

- How to integrate PerformancePoint Dashboards with diagrams using Visio Services and spreadsheets using Excel Services.

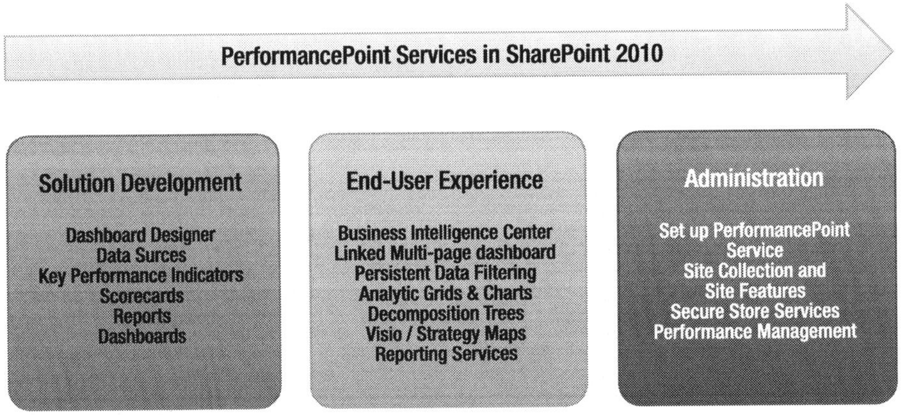

Figure 6–127. PerformancePoint Services Road Map

Index

■ ■ ■

413

Made in the USA
Lexington, KY
11 October 2011